The Short Oxford History of France

Renaissance and Reformation France

The Short Oxford History of France

General Editor: William Doyle

The Short Oxford History of France

General Editor: William Doyle

Renaissance and Reformation France

1500–1648

Edited by Mack P. Holt

OXFORD

UNIVERSITY PRESS

OXFORD

UNIVERSITY PRESS

Great Clarendon Street, Oxford OX2 6DP

Oxford University Press is a department of the University of Oxford.
It furthers the University's objective of excellence in research, scholarship,
and education by publishing worldwide in

Oxford New York

Auckland Cape Town Dar es Salaam Hong Kong Karachi Kuala Lumpur
Madrid Melbourne Mexico City Nairobi New Delhi Shanghai Taipei Toronto

With offices in

Argentina Austria Brazil Chile Czech Republic France Greece
Guatemala Hungary Italy Japan South Korea Poland Portugal
Singapore Switzerland Thailand Turkey Ukraine Vietnam

Oxford is a registered trade mark of Oxford University Press
in the UK and in certain other countries

Published in the United States
by Oxford University Press Inc., New York

British Library Cataloguing in Publication Data

Data available

Library of Congress Cataloging in Publication Data

Data available

ISBN 0-19-873166-3 (hbk)
ISBN 0-19-873165-5 (pbk); 978-0-19-873165-8

Typeset in Minion
by RefineCatch Limited, Bungay, Suffolk
Printed in Great Britain by
Biddles Ltd., King's Lynn, Norfolk

General Editor's Preface

During the twentieth century, French historians revolutionized the study of history itself, opening up countless new subjects, problems, and approaches to the past. Much of this imaginative energy was focused on the history of their own country—its economy, its society, its culture, its memories. In the country's later years this exciting atmosphere inspired increasing numbers of outsiders to work on French themes, so that, more than for any other country, writing the history of France has become an international enterprise.

This series seeks to reflect these developments. Each volume is coordinated by an editor widely recognized as a historian of France. Each editor in turn has brought together a group of contributors to present particular aspects of French history, identifying the major themes and features in the light of the most recent scholarship. All the teams are international, reflecting the fact that there are now probably more university historians of France outside the country than in it. Nor is the outside world neglected in the content of each volume, where French activity abroad receives special coverage. Apart from this, however, the team responsible for each volume has chosen its own priorities, presenting what it sees as the salient characteristics of its own period. Some have chosen to offer stimulating reinterpretations of established themes; others have preferred to explore long-neglected or entirely new topics which they believe now deserve emphasis. All the volumes have an introduction and conclusion by their editor, and include an outline chronology, plentiful maps, and a succinct guide to further reading in English.

Running from Clovis to Chirac, the seven volumes in the series offer a lively, concise, and authoritative guide to the history of a country and a culture which have been central to the whole development of Europe, and often widely influential in the world beyond.

William Doyle

University of Bristol

Contents

List of contributors

PHILIP BENEDICT is the William Prescott and Annie McClelland Smith Professor of History and Religion at Brown University. His publications include *Rouen during the Wars of Religion* (1981), *The Faith and Fortune of France's Huguenots, 1600–1685* (2001), *Christ's Churches Purely Reformed: A Social History of Calvinism* (2002), and as editor, *Cities and Social Change in Early Modern France* (1989), and *Reformation, Revolt and Civil War in France and the Netherlands, 1555–1585* (1999).

JONATHAN DEWALD is Professor of History at the State University of New York at Buffalo. His most recent books include *Aristocratic Experience and the Origins of Modern Culture, France 1570–1715* (1993) and *The European Nobility, 1400–1800* (1996). He is currently finishing a study of European historical thought during the nineteenth and early twentieth centuries.

BARBARA B. DIEFENDORF is Professor of History at Boston University. Her publications include *Paris City Councilors in the Sixteenth Century: The Politics of Patrimony* (1983), *Beneath the Cross: Catholics and Huguenots in Sixteenth-Century Paris* (1991), and as editor, *Culture and Identity in Early Modern Europe, 1500–1800* (1993). She is currently writing two books: on Catholic reform in seventeenth-century France and on religious practices and experiences among women during the sixteenth and seventeenth centuries.

PHILIP T. HOFFMAN is Professor of History and Social Science at the California Institute of Technology. His publications include *Church and Community in the Diocese of Lyon, 1500–1789* (1984), *Growth in a Traditional Society: The French Countryside, 1450–1815* (1996), *Priceless Markets: The Political Economy of Credit in Paris, 1660–1870* (2000), and as editor, *Fiscal Crises, Liberty, and Representative Government, 1450–1789* (1994).

MACK P. HOLT is Professor of History at George Mason University. His publications include *The Duke of Anjou and the Politique Struggle during the Wars of Religion* (1986), *The French Wars of Religion, 1562–1629* (1995), and as editor, *Society and Institutions in Early Modern*

France (1991). He is finishing a study of the Reformation and religious wars in Burgundy, *c.*1477–1630.

VIRGINIA REINBURG is Associate Professor of History at Boston College. She is the author of articles on religious life and practice in late medieval and early modern France, and co-editor of two exhibition catalogues of medieval religious art.

Introduction

Mack P. Holt

This volume aims to provide a general overview of French history in the century and a half between 1500 and 1648. Neither its title nor its terminal dates are meant to suggest that this is a period without significant continuities with both what came before as well as what followed. Moreover, the adjectives Renaissance and Reformation in the volume's title should also be understood in other than purely traditional ways. It is certainly true that in 1500 many contemporaries saw France as the state most likely to dominate Europe in the coming century. Except for the nominal port city of Calais, English troops had been forced out of France altogether by 1453 at the end of the Hundred Years War, and Louis XI had restored royal authority shortly thereafter. France had the largest—and still growing—population of any state in Western Europe, whose people, even the peasants, were enjoying a higher standard of living than at any time in the previous two hundred years. France's economy had recovered from the vast disruption caused by warfare in the fourteenth and fifteenth centuries, and the artistic and cultural Renaissance had already made its way across the Alps from Italy to the French court and into French intellectual circles. The chancellor of France asserted in 1484 that 'the beauty of the country, the fertility of the soil and the healthiness of the air outdo all the other countries of the world'. Another contemporary claimed that 'France is the jewel of the earth'. While a third insisted that France was 'the best of the ninety kingdoms that God made in this world'.[1] This was hardly just French chauvinism, however, as even an early sixteenth-century Spanish ambassador in Paris admitted that France was the most beautiful kingdom in

---

[1] All quoted in Colette Beaune, *The Birth of an Ideology: Myths and Symbols of Nation in Late Medieval France*, trans. Susan Ross Huston (Berkeley, 1991), p. 296.

Christendom. In the first half of the sixteenth century French kings led armies into Italy, fought with their Habsburg and Tudor rivals for hegemony of Europe, and even launched overseas expeditions to Brazil and Florida. Every indicator seemed to point to France as the state most likely to dominate the continent of Europe by 1600. Yet by the beginning of the seventeenth century, Spain had become the most dominant power in Europe with a vast overseas empire that stretched from the East Indies to Mexico to the Mediterranean. And two other smaller Protestant states—England and the Dutch Republic—were quickly establishing empires of their own as well as opening new markets in trade and commerce. What went wrong?

This volume will explain why the cultural, political, and economic renewal by 1500 was soon shattered by a violent struggle over religious reformation that sparked the most extended crisis of the French monarchy prior to the French Revolution. France alone of all the Western European states suffered the experience of extended civil war in the sixteenth century as a result of the Reformation. And it is this series of civil wars that really forms the fulcrum and focus of this volume. Its violence and its legacy left a profound mark on French men and women of every religious confession. This book is also about France's difficult and groping recovery from the civil wars that by 1648 was still not quite complete—the country after all stood on the verge of another civil war in the Fronde and was already in the midst of a series of popular uprisings—but that nonetheless had placed the monarchy on the threshold of a new period of splendour under Louis XIV, when France could finally live up to the claim of being 'the jewel of the earth'.

Another justification for an extended look at France in the century and a half between 1500 and 1648 is that during this period the beginnings of the transformation of France from a late medieval royal state (*état royal*) into a *nation* first took root. I do not mean to suggest that France became a modern nation-state in this period, with all the trappings of nationalism that such a state would imply. But after 1500 one can begin to recognize a number of ideas that would allow the diverse subjects of a dynastic state like France to perceive a national identity and feelings of national consciousness. Thus, this volume will be concerned with the evolution from a medieval royal state centred on sacral monarchy to a more modern dynastic state based on a sense of nation. And one of the principal goals of this volume is to explain why that transformation took so long, which in the end is another explanation about why French polity broke down in extended civil war unlike anywhere else in Western Europe. Questions of governance and authority in the first half of the seventeenth century are thus connected to the problems of recuperation from the Wars of Religion (1562–98) and restoring the authority of the crown that was so badly damaged during that long conflict. In this sense, the policies of Henry IV (1589–1610), Louis XIII (1610–43), and Cardinal Richelieu should be seen more as the legacy of the civil wars rather than as an inevitable prelude to the absolutism of Louis XIV (1643–1715). This perspective emphasizes that France's rise to power among the other European monarchies could not really begin until the authority of the state could be restored both at home and abroad. And the most explicit markers of this watershed are France's role in the ultimate defeat of the Spanish and Austrian Habsburgs in 1648, as well as Louis XIV's declaration of majority in 1651 that brought about the end of the Fronde. Hence, the focus of this volume is more about the oscillating shift from growth and recovery in 1500 to the crisis of civil war from 1562 to 1598, then back to recovery and stability from 1598 to 1648, than it is about a modern, forward-looking Renaissance state replacing an outmoded medieval state.

The volume addresses a number of specific questions: How did a decentralized collection of provinces manage to become a nation by the mid-seventeenth century? How did the Reformation and religious wars challenge the ruling elites at the top of French society, and which traditional cultural practices of all social groups were transformed as a result? What role did economic change play in this narrative, and how did France cope nevertheless with significant periods of economic stagnation? Why did the advent of Protestantism in France produce a thirty-five year long civil war, unlike any other state in Western Europe? How did Catholic reform manage to transform much of traditional spiritual life? How did the experience of religious change affect the roles of women in the family and in society at large? How did Protestantism manage to survive such a fierce battle against the Church, the state, and a majority of its people? And finally, how did France manage to recover from two generations of civil war to reach the point where Louis XIV could challenge other European monarchs for supremacy in Europe and the world? The answers to these questions tell us a great deal about why France's transition from a kingdom based on sacral monarchy to a state based on a shared sense of nation took such a long and winding path.

In late 1561 Jean de Montluc, bishop of Valence, wrote a remonstrance to Pope Pius IV, urging him to come to France to observe first-hand how the advent of Protestantism had seriously weakened the French kingdom. If His Holiness should make such a visit, Montluc noted, he would be shocked by what he encountered:

He would on the one hand see in France a great many lost souls for want of knowing the true path they should take for their salvation and would be so distressed at such a miserable situation that he would, if necessary, risk his own life to remedy it. On the other hand, he could understand that a quarter of his kingdom has left the communion of the church, which quarter is made up of gentlemen, men of letters, the chief bourgeois of the cities and the lesser people, all of whom know the world and are trained in arms. Thus these separated people have no lack of military resources, including in their number a great many gentlemen and some old soldiers experienced in war. They have no lack of good counsel, having with them more than three-quarters of the men of letters; they lack no money to support their affairs, for they have among them a good proportion of the great cities and powerful families, both of the nobility and of the third estate. Furthermore, there is such unity among them and such resolve to support each other, that there is no hope of dividing them and still less of bringing them back by force without putting this kingdom in danger of becoming prey to foreign conquest, or so weakening it that it would not return to its former state for fifty years.[2]

Although Montluc exaggerated Huguenot strength in a variety of ways in 1561, his long-term prognostication proved all too accurate. The history of France from 1500 to 1648 can thus be seen as a narrative of growth, crisis, war, and recovery.

[2] David Potter (ed. and trans.), *The French Wars of Religion: Selected Documents* (New York, 1997), pp. 29–30.

1

The Kingdom of France in the sixteenth century

Mack P. Holt

How do we define the French nation at the beginning of the sixteenth century? Is it even possible to think in such terms when the nation-state, not to mention nationalism, are still nearly three centuries away? Moreover, in the year 1500 nearly one-fourth of the kingdom's roughly 450,000 km^2 had only been recently acquired in the previous fifty years. Five principal languages were spoken—French, Occitan, Basque, Breton, and Flemish—not to mention scores of local and regional dialects all across the kingdom. So, just what can the term 'nation' mean in the sixteenth century, when the state was based much more on the king's sovereignty over his subjects rather than on a defined territory with fixed boundaries? If the nation of France in 1500 was simply all those people who declared Louis XII to be their sovereign king—that is, a community of people rather than a defined segment of real estate—what ties, if any, united these diverse people together into a community? For many scholars a nation can only be built upon a shared culture and common social organization, because the latter are universal and perennial while states and nations are not. This still begs the question, however, of how such a culture gets constructed, and how it ends up being shared. One way to get around this dilemma is to consider the nation as an 'imagined community'. This definition gets us beyond the narrow limitations of simply describing the French nation, and forces us to investigate how the nation was actually imagined or constructed and by whom. Since this process is both historical and contingent, it is necessary to ask how, why, and by whom the French nation was imagined, rather than simply describe such a nation as if its evolution from a feudal to an absolute monarchy was historically inevitable. Moreover, it will be necessary to enquire how such things as the Reformation, the religious wars of the second half of the sixteenth century, economic changes, and exploration and expansion overseas impacted this historical process of imagining a nation.

To begin, although France was not wholly defined by fixed geographical boundaries in 1500, it is still necessary to look at how the map of the kingdom grew and evolved from about 1450 (see Map 1). A significant portion of France in 1500 was new and only recently incorporated into the kingdom via marriage alliance, conquest, or inheritance. Foremost, the end of the Hundred Years' War in 1453 restored much of the territory of the realm that had been temporarily occupied by English and Burgundian forces during the war, including much of the northern half of the kingdom. The entire south-western regions of Guyenne and Gascony had been legally under English authority since the marriage of Elinor of Aquitaine to the English King Henry II in the twelfth century. This region was thus re-incorporated into the French realm for the first time in three hundred years when the English were finally driven out of Bordeaux in 1453. Other parts of the south-west, such as the domains of the Armagnacs, were confiscated upon the killing of Jean V d'Armagnac in 1473. In eastern France, the duchy of Burgundy was repossessed by Louis XI when the last Valois Duke of Burgundy, Charles the Bold, was killed in 1477 without a male heir. (The county of Burgundy—the Franche-Comté—was retained by the Habsburgs when Charles the Bold's daughter Mary married the Habsburg heir Maximilian and would only become part of France as a result of the territorial acquisitions of Louis XIV in the seventeenth century.) The region of Picardy on France's northernmost border was also seized from the Burgundian territories at the same time. In the south-east, the county of Provence was incorporated into the French crown in 1481, along with the duchy of Anjou and the county of Maine, at the death of the childless Charles IV of Anjou, who left these territories to Louis XI in his will. The western region of Brittany only became administered by the French crown in 1491 with the marriage of Anne of Brittany to

Charles VIII, though legal attachment to the French state took another forty years. And these are just the largest and most significant of the new lands acquired by the French monarchy in the fifty years following the end of the Hundred Years War. Scores of other smaller territories, apanages, and fiefs were incorporated into the French state during this period that transferred this real estate from the control of powerful individuals to the French crown, or at least to members of the royal family.

But should we view this transfer as inevitable, and was it a historical process we can refer to as centralization or even state-building? And however we view it, what relationship did the state have to the nation? It is undeniably true that the French monarchs in the Renaissance period—Louis XI (1461–83), Charles VIII (1483–98), Louis XII (1498–1515), and Francis I (1515–47)—made explicit efforts to strengthen the power of the crown, as well as extend its authority to these newly incorporated territories and provinces. The creation of new sovereign courts called *parlements* in Dijon, Aix, Bordeaux, Rennes, and Rouen, for example, as well as the royal officers to staff them, are but the most visible examples of this process at work. But the extension of royal power, even with the beginnings of a royal bureaucracy, did not automatically translate into a nation-state. For one thing, the process was dialectic and depended as much on the acceptance of the authority of the king by his subjects as it did on his own will or even his ability to articulate his will through propaganda, political theory, and ritual, if not by force. Second, the process was historically contingent on factors far beyond the control of any one monarch. Thus, the history of the polity in France from the late fifteenth to the early seventeenth century can hardly be the simple story of the rise of a weak, feudal, and dynastic state which evolved inevitably into a bureaucratic nation-state ruled by an absolute monarch, though this is the way too many historians of France have depicted it. The reality is a good deal more complicated and much more interesting.

The central locomotive that drives the 'rise of the state' model of French history is almost always the monarchy. Indeed, most historians have written about little else in their efforts to explain how an occupied and divided state in the first half of the fifteenth century could develop into one of the most powerful nations in the world by the late seventeenth century. Whether as an institution or simply as the collection of personnel attached to the French crown at one time, the monarchy is usually credited with strengthening the authority of the crown and ultimately forging a nation out of the diverse provinces of ancient Gaul. The heroes in this narrative of the 'rise of France' are invariably Louis XI, Francis I, then after the religious wars Henry IV (1589–1610), Cardinal Richelieu, and ultimately Louis XIV (1643–1715). But to return to the polity in 1500, how did French monarchs actually extend their authority and eventually build a nation-state? Several means that historians often point to, though others could be cited, are through ritual and ceremony, language, law, war, and religion. Not all of these were equally successful, and monarchs often encountered outright opposition. An examination of how French kings sought to construct a nation through each of these means in the sixteenth century not only reveals some of the limitations of royal power, but also shows how dependent kings were on their subjects.

Ritual and ceremony

One means of forging a nation as well as trying to influence public perceptions of the French nation-state in the early sixteenth century was through royal ritual and ceremony. Historians in the last forty years have made great strides in showing how attempts to manipulate and recast various royal rituals—royal entries, royal funerals, coronations, and the like—tell us much about the political aspirations of individual monarchs, and how over time the monarchy used these inventions of tradition as a means of royal propaganda to carry out its particular political agenda. Great strides have been made in attempting to tease out the various political meanings from the way various kings used and shaped royal ceremonial over the course of the early modern period. One of the many striking metaphors used by these historians is how French kings used ceremonial as theatre: they were actors staging an often well-rehearsed royal drama designed to influence their subjects' perceptions of kings and the monarchy. In short, ritual was just another expression of royal power.

A good case in point is the royal coronation ceremony: a double ritual emphasizing the sacred aspect of monarchy—depicted in the anointing of the king with holy oil before he could receive any of his new symbols of office—and the constitutional aspect, as contained in the two oaths each new king was required to swear. Although the ritual of the coronation had ancient origins, by the sixteenth century the sacred aspect of it had become the centrepiece of the ceremony, which was manifest in several specific innovations by 1500. That kings of France were already called by the title of *Rex christianissimus*—the Most Christian King—was a sign of their particular elevation above all other secular monarchs in Europe. But by 1500 they considered themselves to be much more than just uniquely Christian kings: they could function as priests and even gods. The former was visibly manifested in the new king's receiving the Eucharist in both kinds—the bread as well as the wine—at the conclusion of his coronation. This was a privilege reserved only for ordained clergy until the Reformation and singled out French monarchs as having sacerdotal as well as secular power. And immediately after receiving the Eucharist, the newly anointed and crowned king demonstrated that he was much more than even a priest, as he healed victims of scrofula by his royal touch. The power to heal—or thaumaturgical power—was used periodically throughout a king's reign in this period to underscore even further to his subjects how sacred the king's own body actually was. Of course, it is unclear how many of those who were touched were actually healed, or even how many believed they were healed. Given the nature of scrofula, it is likely that many of those who suffered from it were likely to recover anyway, though that was not entirely appreciated at the time. The main point here is that large numbers of the king's subjects believed he had the power to heal and turned out to be touched by him as a result, which only increased his authority among them.

The royal funeral ceremony demonstrates some of the same themes. Various elements were added to it by individual monarchs to further buttress the sacred nature of the monarchy. Perhaps the best example is the elaborate funeral of Francis I in 1547. One of the most significant innovations was a magnificent even though sombre procession of the royal corpse from Saint-Cloud just west of the capital to Notre-Dame in Paris, and from there to the basilica at St-Denis north of the city, the royal burial place of French kings. This procession bore more than a passing resemblance to Corpus Christi Day processions when Christ's own consecrated body was paraded throughout the streets of the capital. Moreover, the burial itself at St-Denis encapsulated the idea of the 'king's two bodies': although the mortal body of a king might die, his sacred body lived on in continuity of the dynasty. It was thus only in the early sixteenth century that the famous dictum 'The king is dead; long live the king!' became a regular part of the funeral ritual. And Francis's own tomb in St-Denis further underscored the idea of 'the king's two bodies'. Lying on top of the marble casket was a carved image of the king's dead body. Up above on top of a triumphal arch was the sculpted image of the living king, kneeling in prayer for the soul of the dead body below. These images were intended to reinforce the 'royal religion' surrounding the monarchy in the sixteenth century, further buttressing the impression in the royal coronation that the nation-state of France revolved around the monarch, and that only he was capable of forging a nation out of the diversity of traditions, cultures, and languages in the kingdom.

A principal weakness in this approach, however, is that too often the historians studying royal rituals tend to take their efficacy at face value. They often accept uncritically the royal propagandists who describe all these ceremonies, without asking whether the propaganda was actually understood, believed, and accepted by the very subjects whose minds it was designed to influence. The metaphor of ritual as theatre is a very telling one, since the audience in the theatre is just as significant to the drama as the actors on stage. If the audience does not find the action on the stage very compelling, the show usually closes down. So, while the rich studies of royal ceremonial have much to tell us about the intentions of kings and their efforts to sway public opinion about the monarchy, they really cannot be so easily accepted as examples of royal power without at least asking whether the king's subjects were willing accomplices in the drama. Indeed, the central question is not just what kind of monarchy the various ceremonies were designed to construct, but what kind of monarchy did the king's subjects construct out of such rituals? Again, royal intentions and popular perceptions were usually symbiotic in shaping each other. The king alone was unable to forge a nation by himself.

A good example to illustrate this point is the king's healing for scrofula after his coronation ceremony. Although its origins as part of the royal coronation are somewhat hazy and unclear—the ritual appeared sometime in the early Middle Ages—its demise in the eighteenth century tells us much about the relationship between king and his subjects. The first king to stop touching for scrofula was Louis XV (1715–74). It seems very clear that Louis XV stopped touching for scrofula, not because he was uninterested whether his people saw him as a kind of god, but only because the French people stopped believing in the ritual altogether. Though there were always victims of the disease who were willing to be touched, public derision of the ritual is what led to its demise. When Charles X attempted to revive it in 1825, for example, he was soundly ridiculed by nearly everyone in the kingdom. What this ought to tell us about the ritual in the sixteenth century is clear enough: its ability to boost the power and authority of the king depended on the acceptance by the people of the ritual's efficacy. Kings did not touch for scrofula just as a form of royal propaganda to buttress their authority; they did so because they realized their subjects believed that touching for scrofula was a sign of the sacred power of kingship. When their subjects came to question this thaumaturgical power, kings stopped touching. Thus, both the king and his subjects were protagonists in the evolution of political ritual.

Language

Another means of forging the French nation that historians have often cited is the use of language. One of the most popular myths that still seems to surface among historians, in fact, is that French kings attempted to unify and construct a nation by forcing all their subjects to use French instead of their local dialects and regional languages (spoken by up to two-thirds of the king's subjects). The various guises of this myth generally culminate in Francis I's Ordinance of Villers-Cotterêt issued in 1539. Although its principal function was to reform the judicial system, Article 111 decreed that all legal documents in the kingdom—including parish records of baptisms, marriages, and deaths, which the ordinance required all parish priests to maintain—were to be written in 'the French mother tongue and no other'. The assumption too often made is that the crown used the ordinance to unify a linguistically diverse kingdom, thus setting the realm on the teleological road of Francophone nationhood. While

French had certainly replaced Latin in most legal documents by 1500 in law courts all over France, local dialects and vernaculars continued to be widely spoken throughout the kingdom. And if the elites in southern France abandoned Occitan for French as their principal spoken dialect by the seventeenth century, this was hardly true of the mass of the population, whose local and regional dialects remained unchanged until the late nineteenth century.

But the myth is without foundation even concerning royal intentions in 1539. Recent scholarship has shown convincingly that Francis's intentions—or those of his chancellor, Guillaume Poyet—had nothing to do with unifying a polyglot kingdom under the French tongue. The real target was not linguistic diversity, but Latin. The legal minds of the day understood 'mother tongue' to mean any spoken vernacular in France, not just the official *langue d'ouil* of the court in Paris. Thus, the ordinance of Villers-Cotterêt was intended to eliminate the use of Latin in legal documents so that all witnesses and other participants could understand the proceedings, not to homogenize the written (much less spoken) usage of the king's subjects. When a law court in Toulouse actually applied the ordinance to its own procedures and operations, for example, it ordered that 'all the ordinary notaries of this court must transcribe their rulings and acts in French or in the vernacular tongue'. This interpretation of the ordinance is also supported by the legal scholar Pierre Rebuffi, who noted in his legal commentary on the ordinance that 'this law says *Mother French*, not simply *French*, in order to signify that it is not ordering whomever to make use of the French language, but that of the country's people'.[1] The myth of the Ordinance of Villers-Cotterêt doubtless arose during the nineteenth century when concepts of nation-building meant something very different than in 1500. In fact, there is no evidence to suggest that any French king before the Revolution ever pursued a systematic national language policy. Though Louis XIII and Louis XIV did make efforts in the seventeenth-century to implement the use of French in recently conquered territories where French was not the native language (Béarn, Alsace, and

[1] Both quoted in Paul Cohen, 'Linguistic Politics on the Periphery: Louis XIII, Béarn, and the Making of French as an Official Language in Early Modern France', in *When Languages Collide: Perspectives on Language Conflict, Language Competition, and Language Coexistence* (Columbus, Ohio, forthcoming).

Flanders, for example), they tolerated publications in the local languages even there. Moreover, when French kings made their royal entries into cities and towns throughout the kingdom in the sixteenth and seventeenth centuries, they routinely received oral as well as published greetings in French, Latin, and local dialects as well. The monarchy was hardly trying to project itself as a form of language police, and it is doubtful in any case whether the crown could have succeeded even if it had tried.

It is certainly true that there was a general trend away from local dialects toward a greater use of French by many educated elites in the sixteenth century. Long before 1539, in fact, French had been making inroads against Occitan in the Midi, and in town halls and law courts throughout the kingdom as well as at court, intellectuals argued for as well as wrote in French on an ever-increasing basis. In Metz, for example, local dignitaries spontaneously encouraged a greater use of French in order to create a modest sense of linguistic community as well as to combat its overtly German surroundings. As has already been mentioned, law clerks, notaries, lawyers, and judges were already in the process of adopting French as the language of the law long before 1539. This had less to do with the Ordinance of Villers-Cotterêt than the fact that jurists and judges sought to make inroads against a complex and confusing system of local customs and legal procedures (see below).

Finally, the greatest literary writers connected with the court made an explicit and concerted attempt to promote the use of the French language over Latin and Italian. Perhaps the most visible defender of French was Joachim Du Bellay, whose *Defense and Illustration of the French Language* was first published in 1549. Like many humanist writers before him, Du Bellay found himself forced to reflect on the tensions between the beauty and elegance of classical Latin and his desire to promote his own native vernacular. He ultimately came to conclude that fame and immortality could only occur by writing in French. Writing in Latin might initially make his name more well-known in more places, but it could also result in spreading his reputation very thinly and unevenly. If he wanted his writings to survive, he argued, he must write in his own tongue. By building his reputation upon a linguistic space, the kingdom of France, and by linking his career to the Valois court, Du Bellay and his contemporaries sought to construct a national community for the intelligentsia by means of the French language. But this promotion of the French language by Du Bellay and his contemporaries was never meant as an assault on local dialects. On the contrary, they believed local dialects served a national purpose too in helping to sustain French. Pierre de Ronsard, in a preface to his unfinished epic, the *Franciade*, aimed to define French nationhood through his epic poem the way Virgil's *Aeneid* had done for Rome. He noted that French was spoken in many different forms in many different regions of the kingdom. Poets as well as kings, he argued, should take advantage of all of them. To be sure, the French vernacular of the court was the most beautiful, but it could not exist on its own: 'It [the French vernacular] cannot be perfect without the help of the others: for each garden has its own flower and all nations have dealings with each other. . . . All provinces, however barren, support the more fertile ones, just as the smallest members of the body support the more noble ones.'[2] Thus, Ronsard may have constructed a clear hierarchy of competing vernaculars with French at the apex, but he certainly did not intend to see French supplant the local and regional dialects throughout the kingdom. Other writers echoed this view, suggesting that the various spoken vernaculars throughout the kingdom were like the king's own subjects, 'the languages which the most Christian King of France commands . . . which are subject to the Crown . . . all are French since all are from the King's regions.'[3] The principal point here is that the promotion of the French language that did occur in the sixteenth century as a means of forging a sense of nation in France was not the work of the French monarchy. It was a process of spontaneous effort by various individuals and groups which were working largely outside royal channels. The crown certainly played a role, but it was hardly the engine of state-building through language that it has often been portrayed to be. The state has never been very effective in dictating language use and enforcing a national language upon a recalcitrant population without some form of negotiation and consent from the people who were actually supposed to speak the language. As Abel Matthieu wrote in his treatise on language in 1560, 'Truly Kings and Princes . . . cannot impose a particular language on their peoples, nor

[2] Quoted in Timothy Hampton, *Literature and Nation in the Sixteenth Century: Inventing the French Renaissance* (Ithaca, NY, 2001), p. 194.
[3] Quoted in Cohen, 'Linguistic Politics on the Periphery'.

prevent them from shaping or changing language according to their inclination or desires, so stubborn is the liberty of language.'[4]

War and finances

When Charles VIII invaded Italy in 1494, his goals were to extend French territory generally, to limit the extension of Habsburg power in Italy, as well as to effect a more advantageous relationship with the papacy in the process. If all went especially well, Charles even hoped to be able to make good on his rather tenuous claims to the vacant duchy of Milan as well as the kingdoms of Jerusalem, Naples, and Sicily, adding further territories under his authority. Neither he nor his successor Louis XII managed to achieve significant success toward these goals, and the Habsburg-Valois Wars (1494–1559) only encouraged rather than discouraged Habsburg involvement in Italy. So why did these kings as well as a majority of their nobles risk so much on a foreign policy based on a lengthy war in Italy? It probably was not economic motives. Even though Genoa, Pisa, and Livorno would doubtless be valuable strategic sites, and the kingdom of Naples a worthy economic prize, all these places would cost more to defend than they would yield in revenue. The fact is that a Renaissance state like France was led socially by a class of nobles whose principal function was to fight. It was next to impossible for any ruler to go for protracted periods without waging war when both the geo-political and dynastic pressures were focused so acutely on the Italian peninsula, as they were around 1500. With Charles VIII's claims to the kingdom of Naples as heir to the house of Anjou, combined with Louis XII's claims to the duchy of Milan as a descendant of the Visconti dukes of Milan, it did not require any additional economic motives for France to become involved in a rivalry with the Habsburgs for control of Italy.

The earliest confrontations were decidedly mixed. Charles VIII did lead a French army into Naples in 1494, but on his return he barely avoided a heavy defeat at Fornovo in August 1495. Louis XII likewise managed to conquer Milan in 1499, but French troops were chased

[4] Quoted in Cohen, 'Linguistic Politics on the Periphery'.

out of Naples altogether in 1503 by Ferdinand of Aragon, ally of the
Habsburg Emperor Maximilian I. Ferdinand's daughter Juana was
married to Maximilian's son Philip of Burgundy, which was to bring
Spain into the Habsburg orbit for the next two centuries. Indeed, by
1507 Louis was opposed by a coalition of Pope Julius II, Emperor
Maximilian I, Ferdinand of Aragon, Henry VIII of England, as well as
the Swiss, who were allies of the Pope. Louis's French army suffered a
heavy defeat at Novarra in June 1513, and the Swiss also laid siege to
Dijon a few months later in September. This Habsburg-Papal alliance
quickly drove French forces out of Lombardy and most of northern
Italy altogether, as well as exposed some of France's northern ports to
attack by England.

It is Francis I who is usually credited with turning things around
and advancing the cause of the French nation in the process. To be
sure, Francis parlayed his military and diplomatic missions in Italy
into some real gains. In the very first year of his reign, in fact, he
won a decisive victory over a Habsburg-backed Swiss army at
Marignano and marched victorious into Milan and occupied much
of Lombardy. The next year he followed this victory up by brokering
a deal with Pope Leo X, who had backed the wrong side at Marignano and was anxious to come to terms with the young French king.
The Concordat of Bologna signed in 1516 was designed to reshape
the relationship between the French Church and Rome. This relationship had depended on a much older arrangement, the Pragmatic
Sanction of Bourges (1438), that guaranteed the independence of
French cathedral chapters by allowing them to elect their own
bishops and abbots. The Concordat of 1516 replaced the Pragmatic
Sanction and gave the French king the legal right to nominate
bishops himself when vacancies occurred, though the Pope still
retained the right to refuse any nominees who were unqualified for
office. In short, it certainly seems as if Francis's purpose in signing
the Concordat was to gain royal control over the French Church,
and after his victory at Marignano, that he had imposed this on
Pope Leo X. Nearly thirty years ago, however, historians called this
view into question. First, French kings already had *de facto* power to
influence the appointments of bishops and abbots even under the
Pragmatic Sanction and had been doing so regularly. So, the Concordat changed little. Moreover, the parlement of Paris, which
delayed for two years before registering the Concordat, as well as the

University of Paris and many French churchmen, vigorously opposed it. Francis had to use up a lot of political capital to gain its begrudging registration in the parlement of Paris, whose judges saw themselves as the defenders of the independence of the French Church—the so-called Gallican liberties safeguarded by the Pragmatic Sanction.

While there is no question that the Concordat did ultimately strengthen royal control of the French Church despite the widespread opposition to it, Francis's political gains in Italy quickly dissipated. If the Italian wars appeared to be a means of extending royal power by the French king in 1515 after Marignano, this changed radically just a decade later. On the battlefield at Pavia in northern Italy in February 1525, Francis led a French army against the Imperial troops of the young Habsburg Emperor Charles V (who, as grandson of Ferdinand and Isabella, was also Charles I, King of Spain). Not only did the French suffer a humiliating defeat, with the worst slaughter of French noblemen since the Battle of Agincourt (1415) in the Hundred Years War, but Francis himself was captured and taken prisoner. Thousands died on the battlefield, thousands more drowned in the Ticino River, and maybe 10,000 more Frenchmen were taken prisoner as result of this battle. Worst of all was the imprisonment of the king. He eventually was pirated away to Spain, where he spent more than a year as a prisoner and nearly died.

The relevance of this sequence of events to the French nation is in the reaction of Francis's subjects, specifically those in the newly incorporated territories of the realm, like Burgundy, which had not been part of the French nation for very long. As the Habsburg emperor already controlled Franche-Comté—the free county of Burgundy—he demanded the surrender of the duchy of Burgundy, acquired by France in 1477, in return for Francis's release. The French king reluctantly agreed to the alienation of this part of his domain, over the objections of all his advisors and ambassadors, and duly signed Burgundy away to Charles V in the Treaty of Madrid (January 1526). Although he denounced the treaty immediately upon his release, claiming he had no intention of ever following through with the transfer of Burgundy to Charles V, Francis's authority as king in Burgundy was surely challenged. And while some among the popular classes in Burgundian towns may have chanted 'Long live the Emperor', the elites in the province responded very differently, which was critical to understanding how integrated into the French nation Burgundy had become.

When the provincial estates of Burgundy—representatives from the clergy, the nobility, and the principal towns of the province—met in Dijon in June 1526, the deputies made their will very clear to the king's representative. Finding the Treaty of Madrid to be 'contrary to all reason and equity', they pledged their loyalty to Francis as their sovereign, because 'the said duchy [of Burgundy] is one of the principal jewels in the French crown and is united and incorporated into it inseparably.' Although the Habsburgs had many times attempted to stir up rebellion in the duchy against the French king, 'the said inhabitants of Burgundy have always resisted their schemes and defended this duchy as true, good, and loyal subjects of the French crown.'[5] And the deputies pledged their loyalty to the king of France forever. While it is very true that Francis had already made up his mind to renounce the treaty before the provincial estates had ever met and had no intention of abandoning the duchy of Burgundy whatever the loyalties of its inhabitants, the response of the Burgundian deputies nevertheless makes it very clear that the elites of the province already saw themselves as Frenchmen and Burgundy as part of the French nation only fifty years after its re-incorporation into the kingdom. Moreover, the popular response of the Burgundians made renouncing the treaty that much easier for the king, who would have had a much more difficult time holding on to the province if there had been any serious overtures to the Habsburg emperor. In short, what Francis I's military ventures demonstrate is that war alone was insufficient either to generate a national spirit or to bind together disparate populations into a common cause. Although a war to fend off a foreign invasion might be more successful at this, a foreign campaign to incorporate distant territory into the French state could not, at least without widespread support from the king's subjects. In the end, a war was not just the result of royal policy; it necessarily implicated the subjects who financed it as well as those who were affected by it.

Curiously, however, the fiscal impact of the Habsburg-Valois Wars was not fully realized until the 1550s. Whatever gains had been

---

[5] Quoted in Henri Hauser, 'Le Traité de Madrid et la cessation de la Bourgogne à Charles-Quint', *Revue bourguignonne*, 22 (1912), pp. 163–4.

achieved under Francis I were soon jeopardized in the reign of his son Henry II by the crown's inability to meet the financial commitments necessary to protect and safeguard French claims in Italy. Whereas in the reigns of Charles VIII, Louis XII, and Francis I, crown revenues managed more or less to cover whatever fiscal demands the wars put on the royal treasury, this was not the case after 1550. For a start, fighting and maintaining a military presence on the northern and eastern borders of the kingdom as well as in northern Italy dramatically escalated costs. In addition, there was no uniform system for assessing and levying taxes throughout France, as revenues were assessed and collected differently and by different officials in various parts of the kingdom. By 1550 crown revenues were simply unable to keep up with the necessary funds to cover the costs of war.

So what did the king do? Mostly he tried to borrow what he could not raise through direct taxation. This occurred initially in the form of *rentes*, or public loans guaranteed by local cities and towns (which will be discussed in more detail in Chapter 2). Ultimately, however, Henry II was forced to seek credit on the international market, paying upwards of 16 per cent interest, simply to keep his troops in the field. Finally, special war levies were needed, which only further increased popular opposition to royal taxes. With the royal treasury going deeper and deeper in debt—by 1559 the total royal debt was in the neighbourhood of 43 million *livres*, which was three times the annual budget, with interest of about 8 million *livres* per year—there can be no surprise that French military success began to wane. In the last phase of the wars France was fighting on almost the whole of the northern and eastern frontiers as well as in Italy. The capture of the city of Metz in 1552 was one of the few French victories in this phase, but it was soon offset by other losses elsewhere. François, duke of Guise, was dispatched to Italy in late 1556 to aid Pope Paul IV, a Neapolitan who was an enemy of the Habsburgs, and who was besieged by the Spanish viceroy in Naples. No sooner had Guise arrived, however, than Emmanuel-Philibert of Savoy invaded France with an army of his own in the spring of 1557. With Guise and the bulk of French troops in Italy, the duke of Savoy laid siege to the French town of Saint-Quentin on the north-eastern border. The patchwork forces under the command of the Constable Montmorency that were sent to relieve the siege were no match for the army of the duke of Savoy. The French army was smashed and Montmorency himself was captured in August 1557. Although Guise beat a hasty retreat back to France, leaving the bulk of his army behind in Rome, it was too late. The French crown was bankrupt and could no longer fight. The resulting peace treaty signed at Cateau-Cambrésis in 1559 made manifest the seriousness of the French fiscal and crisis. For the six and a half decades of fighting for claims in Italy, France ended up with only the towns of Metz, Toul, and Verdun in the north-east. All territorial claims in Milan and Naples were abandoned.

The Habsburg-Valois Wars also exposed how fragile the king's hold on his nobles was, with the explicit enmity and rivalry between the Guise and Montmorency families in the last phase of the wars an obvious example. Ever since the advent of feudalism in the early Middle Ages, nobles had always been taught that their principal duty and function was as warriors, and military service for the crown had always been considered their highest ideal. The Habsburg-Valois Wars opened up plenty of opportunities, and all the surviving evidence indicates that many, in fact, took part. The memoirs of one nobleman, the seigneur de Vielleville, indicates that Henry II intended in 1552 to put an army in the field against the Emperor consisting of 4,500 men of arms (heavy cavalry), 6,000 light horse, 8,000 to 10,000 men from the feudal levy, and some 8,000 gentleman volunteers. Had he actually raised this entire number, it would have amounted to virtually the entire adult male nobility.[6] Nevertheless, a great many nobles did do military service during the course of the wars, and it had repercussions for the crown on two levels.

At the top, the competition and rivalry among the greatest aristocrats for royal patronage from the crown inevitably led to tensions among them, as the stormy relationship between the Anne, constable of Montmorency, and Francis, duke of Guise, made clear. Montmorency certainly had a considerable fortune from his own estates in the Île-de-France. But his royal offices of marshal, constable, first gentleman of the king's bedchamber, grand master of France, governor of Languedoc, and governor of Nantes not only added considerably to his wealth, but gave him greater leverage in increasing the income from his own estates. All told, by the end of the Habsburg-Valois Wars Montmorency was probably earning a combined income from

---

[6] David Potter, *A History of France, 1460–1560: The Emergence of a Nation State* (London, 1995), p. 205.

all sources of about 180,000 *livres* per year, which was easily the largest lay aristocratic income outside the royal family. That Guise and the other great nobles at court should be jealous of both him and his family is hardly surprising. This aristocratic rivalry at court required even strong kings such as Henry II to keep an eye on and occasionally discipline his greatest nobles. When weaker kings came to the throne, as was the case when Henry's sons succeeded him after 1559, the rivalry proved disastrous for the crown and helped to provoke a political crisis.

It was the lower end of the patronage-clientage network, however, that ultimately proved to be the more significant problem. All of the king's great nobles had clients of their own, many of whom were lesser nobles, who sought access to the prestige and wealth of the crown through their aristocratic patrons. The Habsburg-Valois Wars openly exacerbated the weakness of the system, as the great nobles who were given command of *gendarmerie* companies in the royal army had to hire 40 men of arms (heavy cavalry) and 60 archers for each company. These posts were commanded by the aristocracy, but paid for by the crown. Thus, there was considerable competition for these posts, especially for the officer positions. The result was that most of the great aristocrats had large cohorts of their own armed clients, paid for by the crown, but whose first loyalty was to their aristocratic patron. Although there were very few cases of nobles turning their clients against each other or against the crown in the first half of the sixteenth century, the potential was clearly there. Both the Wars of Religion in the second half of the sixteenth century (see Chapter 6) as well as the Thirty Years War in the seventeenth century (see Chapter 8) fully exposed the tensions that were already inherent in the system in 1559.

Law

French kings and their royal propagandists had traditionally claimed that the king was the living law and all law was embodied in his person. They thus perpetuated the notion that France was united through 'one king, one faith, one law'. In 1500, however, the 'one law' was the weakest link in this chain of royal propaganda, because it was explicitly clear that the kingdom of France enjoyed as diverse a legal system as existed anywhere in Europe. It is certainly true that there was a traditional division between the north and south of the kingdom, with the northern territories largely following legal traditions based on customary law, while the south of the kingdom was still strongly influenced by the precepts of Roman law that had been introduced there more than a thousand years earlier. This did not mean, however, that in northern France the law was always changing with each new precedent, while in the south courts followed an absolute written law that could be traced back to Justinian. For a start, in the north customs in each province of the kingdom had been written down and many were published in many editions in the sixteenth century. The law seemed to change no more quickly there than in the south, where even Roman law had always evolved to reflect local need as much as any absolute legal tradition. The main point here is that in nearly every province there was a separate written legal code and set of legal procedures which the crown had long sought to centralize without much success.

A good example is the way the law limited inheritance of property. Roman law traditionally favoured the eldest son in property inheritance, chiefly because of the responsibilities given to the *paterfamilias* in the ancient world. Thus, in southern France most, though not all, property could be given to the eldest surviving son, though even there this was certainly not required. In parts of northern France—such as Brittany, Normandy, the Île-de-France, Orléannais, and Champagne—legal customs required equal division among heirs. In other provinces, however, such as in Artois and Burgundy, legal customs allowed for unequal division of property (for more on inheritance laws, see Chapter 4). There was thus a great variety of legal customs and traditions all over the kingdom which a claim of 'one law' had a difficult time reconciling. Even the sovereign courts of the king—the parlements—which were largely courts of appeal, were spread out all over the kingdom and run independently of one another. While the parlement of Paris administered to most of northern France and was easily the oldest and most prestigious of the sovereign courts, it did not control the other provincial parlements. A royal decree that the king registered in Paris was not necessarily as well received in Dijon or in Bordeaux. In short, while the kings of France certainly attempted to unite their kingdom through 'one law', this was perhaps the least efficacious means of doing so. Indeed, the legal codes of France would not become unified until the French Revolution.

Religion

The tenuous and constructed community that was founded on 'one king, one faith, one law' was most seriously threatened by the religious divisions of the kingdom already apparent by the end of the Habsburg-Valois Wars. The advent of Protestantism in the 1540s not only shattered the unity of religion, but it led to the contesting of the monarchy itself, as each side drew from and legitimated its actions upon two different strands of legal tradition. As civil war raged intermittently from 1562 to 1598 (see Chapter 6), two very different and competing notions of the nation emerged, each departing in significant ways from the original formula of 'one king, one faith, one law', even as both claimed to be defending it. And the French Wars of Religion, fought out over two generations, not only wreaked havoc on the French people and the agrarian economy on which most of them depended for their survival, they also proved to be the single most dangerous threat to the French state and monarchy before the Revolution of 1789. The nation did ultimately survive the civil wars, though not before being challenged by extremists on both sides of the confessional divide. The nation that emerged after 1598 was forever changed, however, even though the resulting peace still claimed the legacy of 'one king, one faith, one law'. Thus, how religious division transformed the polity of the early sixteenth century into something very different by 1600 is a significant part of the history of the Old Regime.

The advent of Calvinism in France, whether born from humanist circles at Meaux and elsewhere in the 1530s or exported directly from Calvin's Geneva in the 1540s and 1550s, threatened the perception of nation forged by both king and subjects, because the king's own coronation oath required him to protect and defend his realm and subjects from heresy. Indeed, much of the symbolism and ritual of the coronation itself served to imbricate the monarchy and the Catholic Church together, making Protestantism or any other form of heresy a threat to royal authority. Thus, for the king—and indeed for many and maybe even most French Catholics—the dissolution of the unity of the Church was much more than just an intellectual struggle over doctrines and beliefs. Protestantism brought with it the perceived danger of dissolving the nation itself as well as the secular and religious authority on which that sense of nation was based. This was first brought to light with Francis I's swift reaction to suppress those who posted placards denouncing the Catholic mass in cities throughout the kingdom in 1534. His son Henry II (1547–59) made even more explicit efforts to suppress the growing Protestant movement in France in the 1550s, as he urged the royal law courts to prosecute heresy, even creating a special chamber for this purpose in the parlement of Paris. But Henry's efforts to emulate his father in extirpating heresy proved no more successful than his efforts to carry on Francis's legacy in the wars against the Habsburgs.

When Henry II was accidentally killed in a jousting tournament celebrating the marriage of his daughter in the summer of 1559, the French nation was plunged into a crisis that developed into a civil war within three years. He left four young sons to the care of his widow Catherine de Medici. And while the eldest—Francis II (1559–60)—was legally able to rule in his own right, he was dominated by the Guise family (his mother-in-law was Mary of Guise, sister of both the duke of Guise and the cardinal of Lorraine). The aristocratic Guise, Bourbon, and Montmorency families had all been rivals at the court of Henry II, and now the latter two saw to their horror that the Guises dominated the court. Because several well-placed members of the Bourbon and Montmorency families had either already converted to Calvinism, or were on the brink of doing so, politics at court came to colour the entire confessional struggle of the Reformation in France. That the duke of Guise favoured a continuation of the repression of heresy begun under Francis I and Henry II only widened the gulf separating the two sides. Even with the sudden death of the young Francis II in December 1560, the crisis continued, because at 9 years old his younger brother Charles IX (1560–74) was too young to govern in his own right. A regency government was required to govern until Charles reached his thirteenth birthday, and the Queen Mother, Catherine de Medici, took charge as regent, removing the Guises from their positions of influence at court.

Because Protestant growth was so sudden in the late 1550s,

Catherine sought a different solution to the religious problem, recognizing that the stark persecution of French Protestants of the past decade was not slowing the conversion to the new religion. By 1560, in fact, maybe up to one-tenth of the entire population of France had joined the Calvinist faith, and these new converts, who came to be called Huguenots, were simply too numerous to suppress. Thus, Catherine sought a means of reuniting the two faiths at the Colloquy of Poissy in 1561, a hope which even the cardinal of Lorraine entertained for a time. Although there was some support for such a plan, it became clear to both sides that the differences were simply too great for the two confessions to reunite. Thus, hoping to avoid the outbreak of violence on a large scale, Catherine was forced to make do with some kind of settlement based on limited religious co-existence. The result was the Edict of January issued in January 1562, granting the Huguenots limited rights to practise their religion in private in a few designated places (and the new religion was explicitly forbidden in all the major cities and towns where most of them lived). Instead of de-escalating religious tensions, however, the new edict only exacerbated them, as Catholics all over France refused to accept it. Above all, they wondered, how could the regent, wife, and mother of a king of France advocate the Huguenots' legal right to exist within the kingdom, when the king's own coronation oath required their suppression? It did not take long for the very violence the Queen Mother sought to avoid pushed the nation into civil war. In March 1562 the killing of several Protestants worshipping inside the town of Vassy by some troops of the duke of Guise led the Bourbon Prince of Condé to issue a call for Huguenot troops to defend the new religion. With the mustering of armies on both sides, accompanied by a number of attempts by French Protestants to take over several towns and cities (some peacefully and some by force), the French nation was on the brink of disintegration. Only after four decades of civil war would the nation re-emerge with any semblance of community, imagined or otherwise.

Although historians have been very quick to credit the monarchy with successfully forging the sense of French nation by 1500, the monarchy itself undermined the idea of a united nation during the religious wars. Catherine's own vacillating policies as well as those of her sons Charles IX and his successor Henry III forced Protestants and Catholics alike to rethink their ties to the crown and to the king, and even re-imagine them at various points. For the Huguenots, they certainly considered themselves to be part of the French nation, and they naturally disagreed with Catholic claims that the king was bound by a sacred oath either to bring them back into the fold of orthodoxy, or else drive them from the kingdom altogether. This is what nearly all French Catholics expected their king to do, however, and was the policy followed more or less consistently by Francis I, Henry II, and Francis II. So, if the sense of nation in the sixteenth century was based on the king's ties to his subjects, then the difficulties for French Calvinists were fairly obvious. But if the crown overlooked its responsibility to eradicate heresy and legally recognized the Protestants' right to exist within the nation—which is what the Edict of January, in fact, recognized—then the tables were reversed. It then was very easy for the Huguenots to remain loyal to a king who recognized their legal rights and protected them, while French Catholics' links to the crown were thus jeopardized by the monarch's own straying from his constitutional and sacred duty to defend the Catholic religion of his subjects.

To be sure, Catherine and her sons all hoped for a solution that would restore the normal order of pre-Reformation France, where all French subjects shared a common sacred bond to the monarchy. The rapid growth of Protestantism in France, however, prevented such an outcome, since that very bond was itself so tightly shrouded in Catholic ritual and culture. Thus, events rapidly overtook the principal leaders at court. The older policy of suppression was now ineffectual, and the alternative of limited co-existence was counter-productive. Two attempts to resolve the disputes via a convocation of the Estates-General—in Orléans in 1560 and again in Pontoise in 1561—failed completely. These meetings of selected representatives from the traditional three estates of the kingdom—clergy, nobility, and commoners—were rarely convoked and usually only in times of emergency, such as royal minorities or bankruptcies. The last meeting of the Estates-General prior to 1560, for example, had been in 1484 during the minority of Charles VIII. So, when civil war broke out in 1562, the monarchy's inability to forge a nation on its own was both obvious and explicit, and three different kings would struggle to find a religious policy that was acceptable to their subjects over the next thirty-six years.

2

Social groups and cultural practices

Jonathan Dewald

'One faith, one king, one law': the lawyers' proverb circulated widely in sixteenth-century France and expressed important aspirations. Men and women wanted to see their society as a community, bound together by a common history and shared loyalty to their kings. They understood themselves to differ from other Europeans, to whom they attached clichéd ideas of national character. Yet they knew also that they spent only part of their lives in a national culture. Much more of their time passed within smaller groupings, which they defined according to a series of overlapping criteria, distinguishing urbanite from peasant, noble from commoner, learned from ignorant, rich from poor, male from female. Within each of these categories, geography created further divisions. Residents of each region of France saw themselves as profoundly different from outsiders, whatever their apparent similarities of social position. They might even speak different languages.

This chapter attempts to understand French society during the sixteenth and early seventeenth centuries by looking closely at these constituent groups. After briefly examining the ideologies and life experiences that most French men and women shared, it considers in turn the society's most significant categories: first the villagers who made up about 90 per cent of the population, then city dwellers, civil servants and magistrates, scholars and intellectuals, and the military nobility. (Two equally important groups, the clergy and women, are discussed elsewhere in this book.) Each of these groups changed dramatically over the sixteenth and early seventeenth centuries, and one task of this chapter is to make sense of the changes. Late medieval France was a relatively open, even egalitarian society— paradoxically, in that medieval ideologies stressed the value and naturalness of inequality. In the countryside, land was plentiful and wages were high, while the cities offered a variety of new opportunities. By the early seventeenth century, society had become far more rigid, and the distance between its haves and have-nots had widened. To some extent, these changes resulted from basic conditions of early modern life; backward technology, rising population, warfare, and other material circumstances all contributed. But (as historians have increasingly recognized in recent years) cultural changes contributed just as much to the shifting character of sixteenth- and early seventeenth-century life. New cultural ideals and institutions created new barriers between some groups and new connections between others. Understanding the social groups of the sixteenth and early seventeenth centuries requires understanding their ideas and assumptions, as well as the material constraints on them.

Social categories

In the early sixteenth century, official ideology coped with the diversity of French society by emphasizing the fundamental divisions within it. The most important were the three great orders of medieval tradition: the clerics who prayed, the nobles who fought and governed, the commoners who worked. Together, so people were told, the three orders constituted a social whole founded on interlocking functions. Each group contributed its share to the others' well-being, despite differences in numbers and ways of life. Social harmony, so ran the theory, could co-exist with inequality, indeed required it: if one group interfered with another's duties or rights, the result as in any family could only be confusion, anger, and dysfunction. Hence the enthusiasm of governments for having this vision of difference and mutuality acted out in public events, as a living lesson in the benefits of cooperation. At moments of national crisis, political gatherings divided according to order, with clerics, nobles, and commoners meeting separately to work out their views and present them to the king. When kings or other great persons visited cities, the population marched to greet them according to these divisions. Such events illustrated as well the finer divisions within society, for each order was made up of many smaller corporations, based on professions or other working units. The doctrine of the three orders appealed to lived experience as well as to hope.

Already in the early sixteenth century, though, there was available a different kind of social theory, and over the next century its influence expanded. This was an image of society that questioned cooperation between groups and stressed instead their differences of property and opportunity. It spoke not of functions and contributions, but of possessions and abilities. To some extent this vision derived from social criticisms that had developed in the late Middle Ages, years especially fertile in attacks on clerics and nobles. By 1500 savage anti-clericalism marked even the highest social levels: in the 1540s, Marguerite de Navarre, the sister of one king and the grandmother of another, satirized the clergy as not merely corrupt and unhelpful, but actually dangerous to society. The nobility's image had dimmed because of its humiliating military failures during the Hundred Years War. When villagers rebelled against their lords in the mid-fourteenth century, a contemporary explained, it was because they had lost faith in the nobles' readiness to protect them: 'one of them got up,' so it was reported, 'and said that the nobility of France ... were disgracing and betraying the realm, and that it would be a good thing if they were all destroyed.'[1] Such critics rejected as fraudulent claims that clerics and nobles contributed to everyone else's welfare. Only money and power distinguished the first two orders from the rest.

But this rethinking of social categories was not the work of angry commoners only. Renaissance revivals of ancient thought also encouraged educated men and women to think about their society in new ways, by broadening ideas of what social leadership meant and by suggesting more fluid visions of how society functioned. Claude de Seyssel, an early sixteenth-century cleric and noble, divided society into three classes that had nothing to do with the three orders of feudalism. Instead, he proposed a division according to wealth, and he encouraged the ambitious to think of moving up this social

---

[1] Jean Froissart, *Chronicles*, ed. and trans. Geoffrey Brereton (Middlesex, 1968), p. 151.

hierarchy. Families might need more than one generation to accomplish such advancement, but he saw it as normal and desirable. Other writers contributed to this current of thought by stressing the breadth of accomplishments that true gentlemen and ladies ought to command. For these writers warfare was only one of several activities suited to a nobleman, and individuals had to equip themselves for these other roles. Such stress on self-cultivation implied that ultimately noble birth might matter less than individual achievement, and that in some cases an educated commoner might count for more than a boorish nobleman.

By the seventeenth century, ideas like these circulated very widely through French society. They appeared not only in the works of isolated individuals, but also in mass-market publications. The political crises of the era—the League, the regency of Marie de Medici, and the Fronde-—gave them particular relevance, as pamphleteers sought to sway the urban public. Even some villagers produced manifestos that stressed the inadequacies of nobles' behaviour and suggested their essentially parasitic role in society.

Disasters

In 1500 French society was just emerging from the terrible experiences of the fourteenth and fifteenth centuries. Like the rest of Europe, it had suffered from the plague, which arrived in 1348. The next three years, those of the Black Death, brought population losses of about one-third, and visitations of plague recurred thereafter. But France also experienced other disasters in these years, which set it apart from other countries. The Hundred Years War brought significant destruction from its beginning in 1337; after 1415, when English invasion opened a new and more destructive phase of fighting, the losses became much more dramatic. In Normandy, population in 1460 was at 30 per cent of its thirteenth-century level, and one-half of what it had been in 1413.

Well into the eighteenth century, French men and women continued to suffer tragedies of this kind. Plague remained endemic, striking every generation or so through the 1660s; its last great appearance came at Marseilles in 1719–1720. There were other diseases, less terrifying but very dangerous, especially for children; infant mortality remained well above 20 per cent, and childhood mortality was about the same. Warfare too continued to threaten ordinary people, mainly because it disrupted a delicately balanced, technologically backward economic system. Soldiers took food and livestock for themselves, and destroyed crops to prevent the enemy from supplying himself. During the Fronde, the manoeuvrings of even small armies around Paris sufficiently disrupted farms and markets that widespread starvation ensued; village death rates increased at least threefold in 1652, the worst year of the fighting. In frontier regions such as Picardy and Burgundy, the sites of repeated confrontation between French and Habsburg troops, war could have still worse effects. Even in peacetime French armies were a menace to ordinary people, since there were no barracks to house them; they lodged in villagers' homes, a demanding, occasionally violent presence. Such experiences gave a distinctive imprint to all social life in the sixteenth and seventeenth centuries. Most people had witnessed first-hand the effects of war and disease, and had also witnessed periods of food shortage, some of which brought starvation. They had seen the deaths of loved ones and knew that their own deaths might come with little warning. Insecurity and fear were the normal backdrop to sixteenth- and seventeenth-century life, affecting relations with neighbours, spouses, and children, and shaping economic decisions as well.

However destructive and frightening, none of these later experiences matched the scale and intensity of France's late medieval disasters, nor were their sociological effects comparable. Because of them, for about a century after the Hundred Years War ended, in 1453, French society remained unusually open, affording numerous chances for social and economic advancement. In the countryside, land was cheap to own or rent, since so much of it had fallen out of cultivation during the war years. Agricultural labourers earned good wages, and food was cheap. As throughout Europe, after 1500 commerce revived in the cities, and they experienced also a spectacular growth in the legal professions. Even the army offered opportunities, as successive French kings led their troops over the Alps, to enforce claims on the wealthy regions around Naples and Milan. Early sixteenth-century France had the feel of a society in reconstruction, led by kings with grand ambitions and a willingness to innovate and spend. The able and fortunate profited, at every social level, in both city and country.

By 1550, however, conditions had already changed, and thereafter social mobility became more difficult and less common. Population rose throughout the sixteenth century, and very quickly competition for places intensified. Farms left vacant by the Hundred Years War were now occupied, and numerous peasants competed for any new land that came on the market; rural wages also fell as population rose. Other changes had their origins in political and institutional developments. The civil wars of the later sixteenth century damaged commerce; and the creation of government offices slowed as well. Some expansion continued through 1600, but already by mid-century the principal new institutions of state power had been established and staffed. Ambitious individuals could hope eventually to replace those already in place, but the age of dramatic growth was over. The century after 1550 would be one of dynasties rather than newcomers, according inheritance a larger role in social organization than it had ever played during the Middle Ages.

Rural life

In 1650 as in 1500, France remained a rural society; only about one French subject in twenty lived in a city of at least 10,000, and probably 90 per cent lived in communities of a few hundred. These villages varied widely in the ways they organized space and activity. They tended to be most elaborately structured near the Mediterranean, where houses grouped near one another in large, well-regulated villages. In western France, in the provinces of Brittany and lower Normandy, villages tended to divide into a series of isolated hamlets and individual farms, and often spread over very large territories. Upper Normandy and the Paris basin offered yet a third model, villages whose houses straggled for two or three kilometers along their principal streets, with farmland spreading behind them. However different their geography, though, French villages shared a relatively loose political organization. In contrast to other regions of Europe, no formal rules limited residence within them or rights to village resources. Anyone with a house in the village counted as an inhabitant and could participate in the local assembly that ran village affairs. In fact most inhabitants seem not to have bothered with these gatherings, leaving decisions to a minority of leading residents.

Most villages were very old, some dating to the Gallo-Roman era, others to the great wave of land clearance and new settlement of the twelfth and thirteenth centuries. Common village names like La Neuville, Villeneuve, and Villefranche (New Town, Free Town) testified to these recent origins and to the attractive terms that medieval lords had used to lure peasant settlers. Like so much else in French society, this ancient village structure underwent severe strains in the fourteenth and fifteenth centuries. Some villages disappeared altogether, others had only a few inhabitants by the time peace returned. But complete abandonment was very rare, and nearly all were resettled during the years of reconstruction. Villagers' determination to re-establish their communities expressed the strength of their ties to familiar territories and modes of life; in this regard, the process of reconstruction after 1453 was a deeply conservative one.

Such local attachments were among the several forces that made the village community a powerful reality in sixteenth-century life. Religious ritual also contributed, for the Catholic parish defined the village's boundaries, and the parish church was its main public space; every year many parish priests led their parishioners around these boundaries, re-enacting the superposition of communal feeling and religious practice. Other facts of daily life had the same effect. The village's small scale required some forms of cooperation among its residents, and also allowed little space for privacy. Living so near, neighbours followed all the intimate details of one another's lives. The limited space and darkness of most village houses ensured that many daily acts would take place outdoors, in contact with others. Economic arrangements also contributed to the strength of communal attachments. Especially in the south, many villages had public lands, whose use all residents shared and which they had a strong interest in defending against outsiders. In most regions residents had collective rights also over private lands that had been harvested; they could glean grain that had fallen during harvesting and then pasture animals on the stubble that remained. Agriculture continued to be carried on in pursuit of individual and familial gain, but personal and communal interests meshed tightly.

The social conditions of the early sixteenth century shaped the functioning of these communal bonds in complex ways. The abundant opportunities that the age presented—to take up abandoned farms, to earn higher wages in another village—encouraged movement and probably loosened traditional feelings about home and territory. Villages were never entirely static places, and turnover was especially apparent in the late fifteenth and early sixteenth century. In the villages of lower Normandy, near Caen, about half of village surnames disappeared between 1431 and 1500, with new family names taking the place of those that disappeared. Possibly this mobility diminished over the sixteenth century, as rural opportunities narrowed, but in early seventeenth-century Brittany about 5 per cent of the population still left their villages every year. If early sixteenth-century opportunities weakened village bonds by encouraging movement, however, they also favoured solidarity by reducing social differences. With land cheap and large landowners eager for tenants, a substantial middle class of farmers dominated most villages. These families had the livestock and other capital needed to manage substantial farms. Most villages also had significant numbers of day labourers, who owned little more than their homes and survived by working for others, but in the early sixteenth century their numbers were limited. In upper Normandy, nearly half the villagers owned at least 6 hectares of land, close to the minimum needed for self-sufficiency. In any case the high wages that labourers enjoyed reduced tensions with their employers, the village farmers.

During the century after 1550, this relative social equilibrium broke down, and in its place there developed an entirely different class dynamic, which would continue to shape French rural society through 1789. The change was most dramatic in northern France, the richest part of the country and the region most exposed to economic changes, but in lesser degrees it was visible everywhere. The middling class of farmers shrank fast after 1550, the victim of multiple pressures. Regional law codes mainly favoured equality of inheritance, so that in this period of population growth families tended to have fewer resources with each generation. Rising taxation hit farmers harder than any other social group and made them more vulnerable to short-term economic shocks; however bad the harvest, taxes had to be paid. Urban and rural elites were both buying up land in these years, making it much more difficult for villagers to establish themselves as independent landowners. Marketing systems across Europe were slowly improving, so that farmers faced more competition in selling their produce. All of these pressures encouraged the creation by around 1600 of a new kind of village elite, a small group of very wealthy farmers. They dominated local economic life far more completely than the mid-century farmers had done, and during the harvest season the majority of village residents worked for them. Increasingly, their attachments were regional rather than merely local. Having few equals within their own villages, they intermarried with similar families elsewhere; and they marketed their produce over considerable distances. Their daily experiences also set them farther apart from their neighbours than their early sixteenth-century ancestors had been. Wealth allowed them to marry younger, and they had more and healthier children; infant mortality rates were lower in farmers' families than in those of typical villagers. Their houses began to acquire new forms of comfort, more elaborate furniture and utensils, books. Able outsiders had little hope of rising into this group, since leasing a large farm required heavy investment long before any return could be hoped for. Few families had the reserves and connections that could see them through the unstable economic conditions of the seventeenth century; and even within this village elite farms tended to fall into fewer hands as the century progressed.

The mass of village day labourers grew accordingly, and by the mid-seventeenth century it included about nine-tenths of the population in most villages. Usually these men and women owned their houses and small amounts of land. They rented additional plots, both from their neighbours and from large landowners; because individuals plots were often scattered throughout the village, labourers were typically both landlords and tenants, since this allowed them to group parcels together for maximum efficiency. Yet ultimately they depended on wage labour for the bulk of their incomes, and for most finding enough work represented a difficult challenge. The large farmers usually employed two or three farm servants throughout the year. During the harvest months of July and August their labour needs expanded, allowing everyone to find work; but most villagers survived the rest of the year in a condition of under-employment, making ends meet from any work that presented itself. By 1600 a number of urban entrepreneurs had recognized the potential profits that these circumstances offered. They could confide some manufacturing processes to village labourers, since villagers would work for lower wages than urban artisans. The textile trades suited this situation especially well, and in the years around 1600 numerous villagers began spinning thread and weaving cloth. Urban merchants provided the commercial substructure for this activity, selling raw materials to the villagers, buying back the finished products to sell in distant markets. By 1650, many villages were as dependent on these manufacturing activities as on agriculture itself.

All of this meant significant degrees of change, instability, and tension in the villages of the later sixteenth and early seventeenth centuries. For both rich and poor, monetary relations and calculations had become unavoidable facts of life. The large farmers paid high taxes and rents, with little long-term security; their leases usually lasted only nine years. They could scarcely avoid seeking maximum profits if they were to meet their obligations, and their colleagues' occasional bankruptcies demonstrated the dire consequences of lax management. Village labourers found themselves almost as tightly bound to the marketplace, since they needed to buy much of their food and work for wages. Neither group could afford to allow tradition to dictate economic choices, nor could they place the community's interests ahead of their families'. Though villagers relied on one another in some circumstances, they lived in a competitive and unforgiving environment, and they faced one another as much more than neighbours. They were also one another's landlords, employers, and food suppliers, playing each of these roles under economic circumstances that allowed small margin for error.

Yet communal attachments held firm in the seventeenth century, and in some respects actually became stronger. The arrival of manufacturing employment in the village played an important role in this regard, for it helped villagers manage their transition to a highly concentrated, market-oriented organization of agricultural production. They could maintain traditional modes of life even as property and employment patterns radically changed. As important, villages acquired new structures of communal organization in these years. Village taverns became more numerous, and villagers spent a good deal of time in them. They became centres of village talk, conversations that were in some ways the essence of village life. Parish churches also became more important centres of village life, another point at which villagers encountered one another. In theory they had always performed this function, but through the sixteenth century they rarely did so. Priests were poorly trained and little interested by their functions; many stayed away from their parishes for long periods, and church attendance was low. After 1600, though, the parish became a more effective framework of village life. Priests insisted that their flocks attend mass regularly, and supplied more content to that experience. Preaching became a normal priestly duty, and priests increasingly occupied themselves with other forms of local improvement: many worked hard to educate their parishioners, and they monitored village morals.

In these efforts, many of the most conscientious parish priests saw themselves as engaged in something of a cultural war with their parishioners. Frightened of storms, harvest failures, human and animal diseases, so many priests claimed to discover, villagers turned to a variety of magical, impious remedies. They called on village healers and sorcerers, and they held strange ideas about the protective powers of rituals and sacred objects. Often they sought these protections because they assumed human agency behind many of the natural disasters that they suffered. They often believed that neighbours had caused the deaths of livestock or persons, and more intimate troubles as well: by a simple ritual (it was thought) any ill-wisher could render a newly-wed husband impotent, and only counter-magic could cure him. To many reforming priests, the villagers' vision of the world was at once excessively and insufficiently spiritual: excessively, in that villagers attached so many occurrences to invisible forces, and in that they turned so readily to magic to defend against practical troubles; insufficiently, in that they resisted interpreting their troubles in specifically Christian terms, and in that they treated prayer and ritual as mere tools for material protection in an insecure world.

To some extent the events of village life confirmed the priests' vision of it, and demonstrated how very tense relations among villagers might be. Sorcery complaints, in which they accused one another of using supernatural means to do harm, expressed these tensions in the clearest terms; and the greatest number of sorcery accusations came between 1580 and 1630, just as rural social relations were changing fastest. In these years of land sales and diminishing economic independence, villagers had excellent reasons for viewing their communities as tensely balanced, competitive places, in which neighbours might use all possible means against one another. At the same time, village fear was not a purely local phenomenon. Much of it came from outside, the product not of local antipathies but of larger cultural forces. Reforming priests often believed that their flocks lacked sufficient moral sensitivity, and that they had to be made more aware of evil's presence in the world and of their own failings. For these purposes, their sermons stressed the devil's power and the fearsomeness of divine judgement, which might come at any moment. Royal judges seconded these preachings, giving some of them the force of law. Under the joint guidance of priests and judges, sorcery accusations tended to acquire a new seriousness in the later sixteenth century. Villagers had viewed the practice as mere malice against a neighbour, different from other malice only in its supernatural means. Learned theorists in the sixteenth century redefined it as a deliberate renunciation of God and alliance with the devil, a form of treason that was far more serious than the mere infliction of harm. As such it called for the deployment of the full apparatus of state power. Accused witches were now tortured by royal judges to confess their own doings and the involvement of others. By the mid-seventeenth century leading Parisian judges had begun to question these procedures, and some had even relinquished belief in sorcery altogether; but to the end of the century their provincial colleagues sternly resisted any suggestions that punishments be lightened or investigations abandoned. If the seventeenth-century village was an anxious place, this to some extent reflected the authorities' efforts to make it so.

Even with those efforts, moreover, most villagers had rather limited experience of sorcery investigations and the anxieties that accompanied them. For the entire period 1565–1640, there were about 1,100 such accusations in the immense jurisdiction of the Parlement of Paris, which covered nearly half the country—fifteen cases in an average year, in a region that counted several million inhabitants and well over 10,000 villages. Furthermore, the clerics and lawyers brought important sources of confidence to the village, along with pressures and fears. Parish priests wanted an educated laity, who could understand the essentials of their faith, and their efforts substantially improved rural literacy, at least in the northern half of the country. There, by the end of the seventeenth century about one-third of all men and well over 10 per cent of all women could read; the prosperous elite of farmers were mainly literate and had begun buying books, now widely available in the countryside thanks to an increasingly active publishing industry. Rural lawyers might have a similar cultural impact, connecting villagers to a wider world and giving them greater confidence in dealing with it. Legal representation at this level was cheap in the seventeenth century, and villagers were very ready to make use of it. In doing so, they could hear their own circumstances redescribed in the language of legal rights, and they could find support for their position beyond the realm of the village itself; appeals to higher jurisdictions became easier and more common.

Urban life

Despite villagers' growing familiarity with the world beyond their communities, the divide between city and country remained in the sixteenth century as sharp as at any point in French history. The contrast was immediately apparent to any traveller, for cities had carefully guarded walls, many of them recently strengthened to withstand new technologies of siege warfare. This had not always been the case. In the relative peace of the high Middle Ages, many cities had been left unfortified, one reason for the ease of English conquest after 1337. Sixteenth-century walls, on the other hand, both symbolized the potential violence of early modern society and marked out the city as an island within it of relative security. They also marked the city as a domain of special political rights. City-dwellers paid relatively low taxes, an important privilege in an era of rising fiscal pressure. Government authorities oversaw urban food supplies, motivated by a well-founded belief that urban shortages might lead to rioting, and in some of the largest cities they established effective systems of poor relief. Not all comparisons favoured the cities. Disease spread more quickly and occasioned more fear in sixteenth-century cities than in the countryside: Lyon suffered five epidemics of plague between 1564 and 1586. Rich and poor alike found these experiences terrifying, leaving their cities when the could and lashing out at scapegoats. In the middle years of the century the well-educated city fathers of Geneva (outside the French state, but definitely within the French

cultural orbit) executed about eighty men and women for delib-
erately spreading the plague, demonstrating that waves of panic were
no rustic monopoly. But overall the cities enjoyed protections and
governmental attentions lacking elsewhere.

Contemporaries recognized about 200 places in France as cities,
most of them small, their urban status defined more by their privileges and the administrative powers exercised within them than by
population. At the start of the sixteenth century, only thirty-two had
populations of at least 10,000, a number that rose slowly to forty-
three in 1650. The larger cities grew more dramatically. In 1500 only a
dozen had at least 20,000 inhabitants, and only three had 40,000; by
1650 there were twenty cities in the former group, seven in the latter.
Like the pattern of French villages, this array of cities had ancient
origins. Most had flourished in Gallo-Roman times, and had grown
up as centres of church administration; only one new city was
founded in the sixteenth century, the Norman port of Le Havre. Yet
the French urban network had changed significantly since the Middle
Ages, probably more than the system of villages. Cities in 1550 were
more evenly distributed geographically than in 1300, when they had
been concentrated either in the north or along the Mediterranean.
More even spatial distribution reflected their expanding administrative and cultural functions. They were the focal points of sixteenth-
century government, from which the crown's agents controlled the
surrounding countryside, and they grew as government became
stronger, even in regions whose economic activity might not seem to
justify much urban life. This was one reason that sixteenth-century
cities had more impact on French society than population numbers
alone would suggest. Villagers needed to visit them for administrative
and judicial matters, as well as for marketing their produce. Another
reality of urban life had the same effect: early modern cities needed
immigration to sustain stable levels of population, since urban birth
rates were lower than those in the countryside and death rates higher.
In 1597 at least 59 per cent of Lyon's population had been born elsewhere. A stream of migrants flowed through the cities, maintaining
some contact with their rural families and in some cases returning to
them; cities had substantial rates of out-migration as well. Urban
influences continually reached the countryside.

Among the growing cities of the sixteenth century, of course, was
Paris itself. Already in 1500 it was the largest city of northern Europe,

with about 100,000 people; by 1650 it had more than quadrupled in population, and was now the largest city anywhere in Europe. As the first European city of modern dimensions, Paris concentrated enormous wealth and influence within its walls, and it required vast economic networks to assure its daily needs. Political change played the central role in this explosive growth. The city had been a site of rebellion during the fourteenth and fifteenth centuries, and monarchs tended to stay away long after the peace of 1453. Charles VII settled with his followers at Bourges, Louis XI at Tours, Louis XII at Blois. Francis I, however, spent more time in the capital, and in 1527 he formally announced his intention of making it his principal residence. His successors continued this pattern, making Paris the nearly exclusive centre of national life; even Louis XIV's move to Versailles after 1670 can be seen as part of this process, since it permanently established the court near the city, much closer than the palaces of the Loire valley. The kings' residence in the city meant that leading nobles also spent more time there; French nobles had seldom resided in the cities during the Middle Ages, but in the sixteenth century anyone who hoped for government office or favour had at least to visit the city frequently. The expansion of government brought other elites to the city as well. Sixteenth-century Paris swarmed with judges, lawyers, and lesser legal practitioners.

This presence of national elites changed the city's character and even its geography. Kings wanted comfort and grandeur, and in pursuit of these they undertook important building projects, starting with their own residence in the city, the Louvre. The royal family, great nobles, and leading administrators imitated these projects on a smaller scale; from the mid-sixteenth century on, a series of great palaces appeared in the city, offering nobles suitably visible accommodation and giving an aristocratic imprint to city life. Somewhat less assertive were the new neighbourhoods that appeared around 1600, under the monarchy's direct encouragement. Henry IV sponsored two such developments, both designed for aristocratic residents but both marked by restrained, geometrical architecture. They consisted not of palaces but of elegant townhouses, on a scale that a broad elite might aspire to. Later seventeenth-century developments—such as the Île Saint Louis and the Place des Victoires—followed a similar model. Even the city's streets were marked by this aristocratic presence, for in the late sixteenth century carriages became a common symbol of status. So large that they required six horses, forcing pedestrians out of their path, carriages made clear to everyone that aristocrats dominated city life.

Most lesser French cities replicated the essentials of Parisian urbanization, without Paris's dynamism. They were regional capitals, housing growing numbers of administrators, more dependent on these functions than on commerce. There were of course a few great exceptions. Lyon had only a small administrative class, but it became the most vigorous provincial city of the sixteenth century, by 1550 the country's most populous city after Paris. Its vitality rested on trade, manufacturing, and banking, and these derived from its geographical setting: Lyon came to serve as the intermediary between northern Europe and Italy, and in the sixteenth century numerous Italian mercantile families established branches there. The great Mediterranean port of Marseilles also exercised few administrative functions, but its population more than doubled between 1550 and 1650, also because of trade; despite the development of the Atlantic, the Mediterranean remained an important focus of seventeenth-century commerce. But the Atlantic's growing importance also affected French urban patterns: the Atlantic port city of Nantes tripled in population between 1500 and 1650, largely on the basis of this trade. More characteristic were regional capitals like Bordeaux and Rouen, which combined several urban functions. Both were active ports and commercial centres, but both also had large numbers of officials and clerics. Thus equipped, they grew quickly over the period, though more slowly than their rivals. Cities that lacked commercial functions had more difficulty maintaining their rank. Dijon and Toulouse, for instance, were both administrative centres but stood farther from the commercial currents of the century, and suffered as a result: between 1500 and 1650, Toulouse grew by only 20 per cent, Dijon by 50 per cent.

Numerous influences encouraged cohesion in sixteenth-century cities. Even modest citizens had some rights to participate in civic affairs. At Dijon most male residents could vote for municipal officers, though actual participation was more sporadic, and everywhere large numbers performed militia service, guarding their cities against assault from outside and crime from within. Militia service assembled diverse classes, and it defined municipal identity in terms of vigilance against the outside world. City governments did their best to reinforce these messages with ritual and propaganda. They encouraged writing and speech about their cities' history and excellence, and sponsored elaborate parades at moments of public importance. Local patriotism permeated urban rhetoric, encouraging a vision of the city as an autonomous community, in which all residents had a significant stake.

These institutional efforts worked partly because they fitted with basic realities of urban experience. Sixteenth-century urbanites, like villagers, lived close to one another, and could scarcely avoid frequent interchange with their neighbours. Urban geography ensured that this propinquity brought together members of different social classes. Crowded within their protective walls, numbering only a few thousand inhabitants, most cities scarcely had room for residential segregation. Instead, rich and poor tended to live together in the same neighbourhoods, sometimes in the same houses: about 10 per cent of the population in most cities consisted of domestic servants (in some cities, such as early seventeenth-century Lyon, the percentage was even higher); others were apprentices and journeymen workers, who at least shared their meals with their employers. Ritual moments displayed the real closeness that might develop from such patterns. Rich and poor might serve as god-parents of one another's children, a relationship that was taken very seriously in the early modern period: in mid-seventeenth-century Toulouse, as many as one-fourth of artisans' children had god-parents drawn from the city's elite of officials, lawyers, and merchants. Partly because of such contacts, city dwellers absorbed one another's fashions, knowledge, and values.

All of these systems of urban integration functioned less well after 1550, partly because the demands on them increased so dramatically. The demands had always been high, even in the early sixteenth century. Masters and servants had notoriously touchy relations, and servants changed jobs often. With large numbers of immigrants, many of them young men without local attachments, cities always had high rates of violent crime. About half the young men in fifteenth-century Dijon had participated in a gang rape, so natural did this kind of violence seem.[2] Bloodshed, on the other hand, was unusual in these

<hr/>

[2] This is the estimate of Jacques Rossiaud, 'Prostitution, Youth and Society in the Towns of Southwestern France in the Fifteenth Century', in Robert Forster and Orest Ranum (eds.), *Deviants and the Abandoned in French Society: Selections from the Annales, Economies, Sociétés, Civilisations* (Baltimore, 1978), pp. 1–46, esp. pp. 6–7.

years; only about one case of homicide a year was reported in seventeenth-century Lyon. The authorities thus worried more about collective than individual violence, and they had steadily more reason to do so over the century. Food prices rose, in response to rising population, and occasionally led to violent urban protests. Already in 1529 there was the Grande Rebeyne of Lyon, several days of rioting during which crowds seized grain from the houses of leading citizens and from convents. Taxes and forced loans rose, even in the privileged cities, and manufacturing jobs were beginning to migrate to the countryside, in response to the growing differential between urban and rural wages. Changing residential relations contributed as well to making the city more atomized than it had been in the past, because the new, more elegant neighbourhoods of the early seventeenth century allowed less contact between rich and poor. A new civic rhetoric showed the effects of these changes. After 1550, urban authorities increasingly expressed their fear of the very poor and spoke of the need to regulate them as closely as possible; many sought to expel the poor altogether. The city fathers of Lyon typified upper-class attitudes throughout France when they sought in 1614 'to lock up the poor of this city, as has been done in Paris, to protect the city's inhabitants from the immense importunity that they suffer from the excessive number of beggars'.[3]

This combination of circumstances made the cities rather explosive places after 1550. Religious divisions encouraged urban violence, producing massacres of Protestants in 1572 and militancy in the 1590s, when numerous cities withstood sieges in order to prevent the accession of a Protestant king. But the cities remained just as explosive in the early seventeenth century, when religious exaltation had ebbed. Every year from the 1580s on witnessed some form of urban disturbance, and from the 1620s through the 1640s there were large-scale uprisings in many of the most important cities, typically directed against tax collectors. Such violence could not be dismissed as the work of only the poorest segments within the community. Respectable men and women participated in vandalizing tax offices and threatening their occupants, in some instances killing them.

[3] Jean-Pierre Gutton, *La Société et les pauvres: L'Exemple de la généralité de Lyon, 1534–1789* (Paris, 1970), p. 300.

Lawyers, officials, judges

Sustaining a unified urban community became more complicated in these years for an additional reason: in the sixteenth century ruling elites in most cities underwent a fundamental change, which set them at a greater distance from ordinary residents. Merchants and artisans had dominated medieval cities, but in the sixteenth century leadership passed to royal officials and lawyers—with whom it would remain until the end of the old regime. The change directly translated changes in royal government itself. Kings had few civil servants in the fourteenth and early fifteenth centuries, and many of them were clerics. A very small group supervised royal finances, partly because taxation was low before the fifteenth century. A single appellate court, the Parlement of Paris, heard cases from throughout the country, assisted only by the delegation of magistrates to Toulouse, in the south-western corner of the kingdom, and more occasional visits elsewhere. All of this began to change in the mid-fifteenth century. In 1443 Toulouse received its own parlement, and six others followed by 1553, in Grenoble, Bordeaux, Dijon, Rouen, Aix-en-Provence, Rennes. Their placement indicated the political functions these institutions were to fill. The crown established them in outlying provinces that had recently come under direct royal control, because it wanted the newly installed judges to ensure closer relations with potentially rebellious regions. Territorial expansion in the early seventeenth century had similar results, with new parlements in Pau, Metz, and Nancy; later in the century, Louis XIV's conquests led to parlements for Besançon and Tournai, and to similar institutions, the *conseils souverains*, for Perpignan, Alsace, and Arras. Lesser courts, tax collection boards, and fiscal courts all expanded as well. By the mid-sixteenth century about ninety-seven cities had bailliage courts, each with a growing number of judges and lawyers, and nearly as many had elections, the primary tax boards for most of the country.

This institutional activity produced an essentially new social class, which quickly acquired a dominant position in most cities. In 1515, so one historian has estimated, France had one royal official for every 4,700 inhabitants; by 1665, there was one for every 380 inhabitants. In the cities, where courts and administrative offices clustered, their importance was even more obvious. Dijon in 1600 included about 600 royal officials, within a population of about 25,000. Together with their families, they represented about one-eighth of the city's population, and around them worked an even larger group of collaborators, the lawyers, clerks, bailiffs, and other practitioners who staffed the courts. Social customs added to their visibility within their cities. Judges were expected to wear their robes throughout the day, whenever they appeared in public, and they stressed their corporate identity in other ways. They heard almost all cases as large panels, and they often appeared as a group in other public settings, at religious events and civic processions. They played an increasingly important role in local governance as well, because they represented the king and held some portion of his powers. Especially in the parlementary cities, they tended to make decisions in moments of crisis, infringing on the powers of elected city councils.

The upper levels of this legal world became conspicuously richer over the sixteenth century. Contemporaries agreed that judicial work should be profitable, though they might disagree about the extent of legitimate profits, and judges charged fees at each step in the cases they heard. Their rising power also encouraged wealthy families to seek them out for marriage alliances, bringing them powerful connections and large dowries. Lesser judges, established in smaller cities and hearing less important cases, could not hope to match the wealth of the parlementary magistrates, but they too tended to establish solid fortunes. Financial offices had less social status than judgeships, but they brought higher profits, since many officials received a share of all the monies that they collected. All of this new wealth, deriving ultimately from the exercise of public power, provided the basis for an increasingly aristocratic mode of living—and eventually for claims to formal nobility as well. Over the sixteenth century, the officials had more servants, larger houses in the cities where they practised, and more properties in the countryside nearby. During the same years, the most important judges and some other royal officials came also to enjoy the tax exemptions and other advantages of noble birth. After 1600, this informal consensus received increasingly clear legal confirmation. For some officials, this meant immediate ennoblement on assuming office; more commonly, families could claim noble status when they held an office for three generations. The highest levels of royal officialdom now constituted a 'nobility of the robe', distinct from the traditional nobility in its manners and functions, but similar in its enjoyment of privilege and esteem.

Most European countries underwent a comparable expansion of officialdom during the sixteenth century. Ordinary people everywhere appreciated the security that stronger legal systems offered, and they turned eagerly to the law courts to settle their disputes; kings wanted greater resources to finance their international ambitions, and they wanted greater control over their societies. Yet the French experience of sixteenth-century government was nearly unique in one respect. Only in France and the Papal States did a public, systematic—and extremely vigorous—commerce in offices develop. Bribery and corruption existed everywhere, of course, and they may have been at the origins of the French practices, though French kings appear also to have been influenced by the already functioning papal system. Francis I regularized these hidden practices in 1522, when he established a bureau to sell positions publicly, continuing piously to deplore such sales even as he did so. Individuals quickly followed the royal example, selling positions they held and bequeathing them to sons and nephews, with additional payments to the king to ensure his consent. Offices remained public positions, exercised in the king's name and at his formal nomination, but with few exceptions they also acquired characteristics of private property. Increasingly expensive property: judgeships in the Parlement of Rouen, for instance, remained relatively inexpensive through 1575, but then doubled in price by 1588 and doubled again by 1604. In that year an additional royal measure, known as the Paulette, made the transmission of offices even easier by removing the delays that kings had previously required; in exchange for a small annual tax paid by the officials, sale or gift could now take place at any time. With this additional security, office prices quadrupled in the next thirty years. By this point an office of any significance cost as much as a large country estate.

The rise of venal office-holding cemented the dynastic and monied aspect of the new urban elite. Families needed to have large resources to place their sons in official careers, either their own cash or access to loans from relatives and friends. Few newcomers from even middle-class backgrounds could meet these requirements, as many had managed to do in the early sixteenth century, and families that already held offices enjoyed enormous advantages over even wealthy outsiders. These only increased as office prices rose. At Rouen, the per centage of parlementary judges whose fathers had held comparable positions doubled between 1598 and 1638, to 60 per cent of the total. With such large sums at stake, the officials tended to become even touchier about defending their corporate interests.

In significant ways the early seventeenth-century city had thus been hollowed out. It was losing manufacturing to the countryside, where wages were lower and workers' organizations weaker, and the commitment of its leading citizens to the urban community was weakening. Judges and royal officials could scarcely avoid looking beyond the city walls, to the monarchy that founded their power and determined their status. Increasingly over the sixteenth century, they also thought of themselves as part of a landed elite, with significant interests in the village properties they had purchased. The essayist Michel de Montaigne in some ways exemplified this new urban elite. Montaigne had served as a councillor in the Parlement of Bordeaux and (briefly) as the city's mayor. Yet his extensive and personal writings described only his retired life as a country gentleman, viewing the world from the detachment of a tower on his estate, with scant reference to urban experiences of any kind. Those who led urban society now understood that they moved in national settings.

Educational systems

The officials' prominence within sixteenth- and early seventeenth-century urban life gave new importance to the handful of cultural institutions with which they were especially involved. This meant above all educational institutions, for, though they bought or inherited their positions, the officials nonetheless needed extensive formal education before they could begin exercising them. They spent several years acquiring the preliminary arts degrees needed for advanced study, then three years in the law faculties for the baccalaureat and licence degrees in the law, required for legal practice and admission to judicial office. Their passage through these studies made the urban elites of sixteenth- and seventeenth-century France an unusually coherent group. They had attended many of the same institutions as their colleagues, studied the same texts, and absorbed the same ideals. Almost omnipresent within officialdom, this cultural background was scarcely known outside it, at least during the sixteenth century. Their educations separated the officials from all but a few nobles and a very few urban merchants. The dividing line ran through even their own homes: women had no access to universities and very few learned Latin.

There were fourteen universities in sixteenth-century France, divided evenly between medieval foundations (five dated from the twelfth and thirteenth centuries, one from the fourteenth) and those from the recent past; six were founded in the years 1432–1464 alone. The frequency of university creations during the dark years of the mid-fifteenth century, when recovery from the Hundred Years War had just begun, suggests the political role that these institutions were to fill: great aristocrats wanted them as a propaganda tool in their efforts to preserve regional autonomy against royal encroachments. Regional pride continued to count in the universities' lives after the defeat of these princely hopes. Cities now sustained their universities, and, in hopes of attracting both attention and free-spending students, they sought to hire the academic stars of the era. The professors responded predictably, quarrelling with one another and moving about in response to enticing offers. Andreas Alciato taught four years at Avignon, returned there after two years of travelling, taught four years at Bourges, then returned to his native Italy, where he changed jobs four times in the next fourteen years; Jacques Cujas held positions at Toulouse, Cahors, Bourges, Valence, and Paris over the course of his career; François Hotman taught at Valence, Bourges, and Orléans during the decade after 1561. Students matched this professorial mobility. Their parents expected them to wander from one university to another, in search of famous professors and interesting experiences. With this geographical variety went a mixing of age groups and social classes, for most universities supplied several levels of training. Very young men, of thirteen and fourteen, acquired the rudiments of humanistic study there, notably competence in reading Latin texts. These teenagers studied alongside future professionals in law, medicine, and theology, who were often already in their twenties. Fees were burdensome, but not so high as to preclude ordinary people from sending their sons, and many students made it through their university years living in deep poverty. For encouragement they had the example of Erasmus, illegitimate son of a Dutch priest, who nonetheless managed to put together enough resources for lengthy studies at Paris, and succeeded in making himself the leading scholar of his age.

As one consequence of this loose structuring of student careers, universities varied widely in size and quality. Some were mere degree mills, whose attraction lay in low fees and minimal requirements: candidates arrived days or hours before their examinations, paid off the local professors, and left with their degrees the next morning. Tales of such academic corruption and incompetence circulated widely in the sixteenth century and suited numerous interests. Educational reformers, humanists, novelists, Protestants—all found the universities irresistible targets of complaint, because they seemed to exemplify a rigidly medieval culture. Critics complained about the bad Latin style that they taught, the squalor in which students lived, the obscurity of the issues that interested many professors and their reliance on Aristotle as an intellectual authority. Michel de Montaigne exemplified this current of opinion: 'I have heard men of understanding maintain,' he wrote, 'that it is the colleges to which young men are sent—of which there is such an abundance—that makes them into such brutes.'[4] Yet the principal universities remained large and vigorous, and their students showed considerable seriousness. The University of Paris may have had as many as 11,000 students around 1500, one-fifth of the city's male population, the more visible because they clustered in one district south of the Seine. Montpellier, as a great centre of medical education, and Toulouse, as the greatest arts faculty in the south, displayed similar vitality. University instruction was entirely in Latin, and even the law students— usually described as the least serious of the universities' clientele— had to make their way through the texts and commentaries of Roman law. At the highest levels, likewise, the sixteenth-century universities produced a string of great intellectuals.

Hence the most serious criticisms of the universities concerned not intellectual but moral slackness. Critics worried that universities exercised too little control over their students, and that students' wanderings undermined their moral development. Such warnings could already be heard in the fifteenth century, but only in the later sixteenth century did they receive a persuasive solution, with the first

---

[4] Michel de Montaigne, *Essays*, trans. J. M. Cohen (Baltimore, 1958), p. 71.

appearance of Jesuit education in France. The order had originally intended its schools mainly to train new members, but popular demand almost immediately dictated otherwise: leading families wanted the benefits of this education for their sons, however unlikely they were to take religious vows, and cities begged the order to take over failing local schools. The order founded the Collège de Clermont in Paris within a decade of establishing its first college in Rome in 1551, and it immediately attracted enough students to anger the rival university. Expelled from most of France in 1594, on the grounds that its members preached regicide, the order returned in 1603 at Henry IV's invitation, and entered on its phase of greatest importance. Its Parisian college became still more popular, attracting sons of the magistracy, the Parisian bourgeoisie, and the high nobility; in the late seventeenth century, 3,500 young men studied there, 500 of them boarders, the rest mainly Parisians. In 1607 Henry IV established a second great centre at La Flèche, near the heavily Protestant region of Poitou, and it too attracted students from the highest social classes. Just as important, by 1650 several dozen smaller colleges dotted the country, attracting students of all social classes, but especially drawing the sons of officials. The colleges appealed to such men for multiple reasons. Jesuit education was free, in contrast to the universities, but above all it was carefully structured. The fathers divided students by age group, establishing for this purpose a system of classes, and they encouraged students to deepen their command of Latin culture, for instance by producing student dramas in Latin. At the same time, Jesuit teachers seemed more receptive to modern ideas than their university competition. As science became more important in the mid-seventeenth century, it too acquired a place in the Jesuits' curriculum, and they produced French-language as well as Latin dramas; to encourage elegant manners, some colleges hired dancing masters and taught other forms of physical activity. But they also watched closely over students' behaviour outside the classroom. Parents needed no longer worry about the wanderings and promiscuity of student life. To the irritation of the universities, the Jesuit colleges dominated upper-class education in seventeenth-century France, leaving to their rivals mainly control over some forms of degree certification, still university monopolies, and advanced instruction in law, theology, and medicine.

The shift of academic leadership from the universities to the colleges almost certainly deepened the typical official's knowledge of Latin culture. Not all of them, of course, took this culture very seriously. Complaints about judicial ignorance and laziness already circulated in the early sixteenth century, and the developing commerce in offices added to the problem; young men who expected to inherit or buy a position had little need to study carefully. On average, though, the mid-seventeenth-century magistracy were an impressively cultivated group. Studies of book ownership demonstrate the vast superiority of their libraries to those of any other social group, even the wealthiest nobles, and they increasingly dominated the humanist discussion groups and academies that had formed in most seventeenth-century cities. The leading French writers on history and ancient literature came from this milieu, and the evidence of book dedications suggests that the officials were the principal financial supporters of humanist writing as well.

This did not mean complete cultural isolation from their less educated fellow-citizens. The magistrates' world overlapped with that of lesser legal figures, the clerks, copyists, bailiffs, lesser lawyers, and attorneys. Many of them were poor, but most possessed some formal education. In most legal centres they had their own organization, the *basoche*, which defended its members' professional interests and provided them a social anchor within the city. In seventeenth-century Paris, this combination of social club and professional association counted 6,000 members, a huge group, another indication of how much its legal functions meant for the city's economic life. Many had themselves been to the Jesuit schools and knew the Latin classics; government officials regularly complained that too many sons of the lower classes were being educated, and it was from these men that the lower levels of the legal profession were recruited. Given their background and limited prospects (excluded as they were by the system of venal office-holding from any chance of distinguished careers), they made ideal cultural mediators. They shared the high officials' humanist education, yet they also had good reason to examine it critically. The *basoches* gave them public platforms for criticism, sponsoring satirical plays about urban society, and doubtless encouraging more informal discussions.

Literary life

Latin culture thus possessed great vitality in the sixteenth century, anchored as it was in the rising class of officials and in the larger, more heterogeneous milieu of the *basoche*. Yet by this point it had already begun to come under criticism, and thereafter it steadily lost ground to a different model of culture. Against the Latinity of the officials, there developed a growing interest in the French language and in the culture that might be based on its specific qualities. Such interest had many sources. French writers had before them the example of Italian vernacular literature, which had already produced a string of recognized classics and with which they acquired considerable familiarity in the years around 1500: Frenchmen visited Italy in large numbers, as both cultural tourists and soldiers, and significant numbers of Italians were settling in France, some seeking business opportunities, others in the entourages of kings and queens. Writers also knew that national feeling was rising around them, enhancing the desirability of a specifically French culture. Even the Latinists might speak in these terms, stressing the need for scholars to study specifically French institutions and laws and advocating what they called a 'French way' of understanding ancient texts, which would give more attention to the study of social and institutional contexts. The judges and officials in fact occupied a divided cultural terrain. Brought up on the Latin language and the study of Roman law (only in 1679 did the universities first offer instruction in French law), they also felt a deep professional commitment to advancing the French monarchy and nation.

Advancing the French language seemed an obvious element of that project. Hence the officials themselves were responsible for a critical move in the development of French-language culture: in 1539 the royal ordinance of Villers-Cotterêts required that all legal business be conducted in French dialects rather than Latin. A decade later the poet Joachim Du Bellay published his *Defense and Illustration of the French Language*, an extended argument for the vernacular's literary value, and for the possibility that French-language works could equal those of antiquity. This was also the first French text to use the term *patrie* (fatherland), indicating clearly the link between literary debate and patriotic sentiment. Du Bellay was no lone voice, but rather a leading member of a group of court poets, the Pléiade, committed to realizing this programme, both in lyric poems that imitated the Italians and in more grandiose projects, modelled on Latin epics. The following century witnessed conscious efforts to diminish this dependence on outside models, and to construct a French poetry that would reflect the specific nature of the language. Early in the seventeenth century François de Malherbe, another nobleman and courtier, argued for a simplified poetic language and an end to the complicated allusions of the Pléiade poets; French poetry did not need to model itself on Latin elaboration. Prose styles inspired similar discussion and underwent comparable changes, and in this domain also writers saw their principal task as that of linguistic pruning and disciplining. To seventeenth-century readers, earlier writings seemed over-complicated in language, confusing in argument, and muddled in subject matter, bringing together incompatible materials and views, and falling often into indelicacy. Hoping to control this chaos, in the late 1620s a group of well-connected writers established themselves as a regular discussion group, a forum for debating literary tastes and French usage. In 1635 Cardinal Richelieu, the king's powerful minister, effectively absorbed the Academy into the French state by offering its members financial and political support. French writing had become an important facet of national identity, and in consequence it attracted state regulation. Partly because of this alliance with state power, the Academy succeeded in its aims to an extraordinary degree. French prose style acquired more regularity and clarity, and writers sought to follow its pronouncements about acceptable word choices.

The rise of French produced a new relationship between culture and social structure, for access to French was far wider than to Latin. Lack of university training posed no barrier to full participation in this culture, nor did gender; at least in the north, a majority of urban men could read, and after 1550 so could a majority of upper-class women. At the highest social levels, literary learning became something of a fashion, and it was now assumed that elegant women would write letters and memoirs, if not for print, at least for wide circulation. By the mid-seventeenth century, a handful of women had become professional writers. Madeleine de Scudéry established herself as the pre-eminent novelist of her era, turning out a series of multi-volume romances that described, thinly-veiled, doings of the great aristocracy. They were enormously popular and allowed de Scudéry, who was from the poor nobility, to live by her writing. Yet she viewed this as a humiliating position, not really compatible with high social status, and most women of her circle limited themselves to amateur efforts. For them, the seventeenth century offered a new cultural institution, the salons, regular gatherings in private homes to discuss literature and ideas. Women held an ambiguous place in these, facilitating men's talk as much as offering their own, yet a number of seventeenth-century women were noted for their sharp opinions and readiness to express them. Probably more than their eighteenth-century successors (in which professional intellectuals played a more domineering role), seventeenth-century salons permitted women a central place.

At the same time, French-language cultural products increasingly drew the interest of ordinary people, most clearly in the city, to a lesser extent in the countryside, and publishers oriented some of their wares to them. At the start of the seventeenth century, publishers in Troyes began producing brochures retelling medieval romances and offering practical wisdom; by 1611, forty-five authorized pedlars circulated through the country selling them, and competitors had begun publishing similar books in other provincial cities. News represented another cultural product with a mass market. From the opening phases of the Wars of Religion, in the 1560s, political crises stimulated pamphlet literature, and the quantities increased steadily in the seventeenth century. During the four years of the Fronde, Parisian presses turned out about 5,200 separate pamphlets, nearly all in print runs of at least 1,000 copies. By this point Parisians were also attending the theatre in large numbers. In 1629 there were two Paris theatres, with resident companies putting on regular performances. In that year Pierre Corneille arrived in Paris, to write for one of these rival troupes, and he brought a new seriousness to dramatic poetry, making the theatre a matter of central cultural concern. The public discussion of his play *The Cid*, performed in 1636, involved even Richelieu himself, because it was seen to raise important issues about the nature of political morality. French-language culture had become both a big business and an aspect of the nation's political life.

Corneille exemplified a new social type produced by this business, the professional writer trying to earn fame, high social status, and a

living by producing for public consumption. Like many of his colleagues and rivals, he came from the provinces—in his case Rouen,
where his father was a middling official and he himself a lawyer, and
where his first plays were performed. By his time, the move to Paris
had become essential to careers such as this, for only the capital
offered the audiences and powerful patrons that a writer now needed.
Even in the mid-seventeenth century, the great commercial centre
Lyon had no permanent theatre and made do with occasional visits
from itinerant troupes of actors. This centralization was new in the
seventeenth century, reflecting the widening disparities between Paris
and the provincial cities in population and in the wealth of its leading
citizens. Numerous mid-sixteenth-century writers had pursued their
careers mainly in the provinces. Étienne Dolet, Clément Marot, and
François Rabelais had spent much of their time in Lyon itself, where a
vigorous printing industry and wealthy church allowed them to piece
together a living. Such careers made less sense in the seventeenth
century. Like anyone else with high ambitions, writers now had to
come to Paris.

When they did so, they encountered a world that awkwardly combined elements of a market economy with patronage and power.
Publishers paid small fees for authors' work, or simply printed it
without permission. Rather than royalties, writers depended on
courtship of the great, and this included giving wealthy patrons direct
or indirect control over their work. Great nobles employed stables of
writers to glorify and justify their political choices; they offered their
aesthetic opinions in informal discussion; and they took pleasure in
seeing glamorous versions of themselves and their lives in published
novels—one reason that so many of the most striking characters in
seventeenth-century plays, novels, and poetry were aristocratic warriors. Yet would-be professional writers were not entirely bound by
these feudal conventions. However dependent their material circumstances, mid-seventeenth-century writers already enjoyed a degree of
prestige associated with the power of their words. Printing and the
theatre had given a new importance to their function, and writers had
begun to speak of their professional standards and autonomy, which
justified freedom from the opinions of even the most aristocratic
outsider. Contemporaries had a strong sense that French writing in
their day surpassed that of their predecessors, and they believed that
debate about literature was a serious matter, deserving both public

attention and freedom of opinion. In keeping with these values, the founders of the French Academy decreed that their institution would have no regard for the social standing of its members. The critical evaluation of literature was to go on unencumbered by concerns for the participants' social background.

Nobles

Though mitigated by these ideas of literary independence, aristocratic influence on early seventeenth-century culture remained very powerful. That the nobles held so central a position within the cultural life of the later sixteenth and seventeenth centuries was in some respects surprising, for they confronted a difficult situation in the years around 1500, and some of their difficulties only worsened thereafter. Numerous early sixteenth-century observers thought them interested only in military exploits and indifferent to all forms of learning. Their failures in the Hundred Years War had occasioned widespread criticism, and humanist writers like Erasmus mocked their ignorance and questioned even the value of their military successes. The rising prominence of the royal officials raised other questions about the nobles' position atop the social order. They were wealthier than many nobles, and every lawsuit demonstrated their power to affect the nobles' lives and properties. Probably most important, the nobles faced serious economic difficulties. The very circumstances that made the early sixteenth century a golden age for labourers and middling farmers meant difficulties for large landowners. If they managed their lands directly, they had to deal with low prices for agricultural products and high wages; if they leased out their lands, they had to offer advantageous terms in order to attract tenant farmers. Royal currency manipulations and a rising money supply added a further danger, inflation. Low by modern standards, it nonetheless represented a serious problem for landowning nobles, since much of their income came from permanently fixed rents. For even the richest nobles, the sixteenth century was a period of difficult adjustments.

Such problems were the more acute in that most nobles had few resources to deal with them. The large majority were relatively poor, with incomes that scarcely distinguished them from the villagers they lived among. Most in fact had peasant ancestors, who had risen to higher status by some form of military action, usually in the service of some better-established neighbour. Regarded by their neighbours as 'living nobly', in the contemporary phrase, such men simply assumed noble status, with no further legal steps. Their descendants returned to social obscurity with as little formality. After three or four generations, it appears, most families of the lesser nobility either failed to produce male heirs or lacked sufficient resources to live as nobles—to live, that is, without manual labour, regarded as incompatible with life as a nobleman. This steady movement into and out of the nobility was yet another aspect of the social mobility that characterized the early sixteenth century.

From the later sixteenth century on, though, monarchs sought to control social mobility more closely. Legislation prohibited claiming noble status without official titles, and the crown began enforcing these prohibitions—at first sporadically, more effectively after 1660. Kings had practical interests in limiting ennoblement, because nobles enjoyed exemption from the most important royal taxes, a privilege that became more valuable as taxation rose over the sixteenth century. But this was also an effort to establish their own control over the basic configuration of French society. They sought in other ways as well to shape the structure of the nobility. Already in 1469 Louis XI had created the order of St Michael the Archangel, the first great chivalric order in France. Its purpose was to bring together the country's most distinguished nobles into a single group, oriented to royal service. As this group expanded, new forms of distinction appeared. A second order—the more restrictive Order of the Holy Spirit—was founded in 1578, and kings began to grant favoured families the lofty status of 'duke and peer'; eleven families had received the honour by 1588, in addition to members of the royal family itself and some ecclesiastics, thirty-eight by 1661.

Such efforts produced important changes in the nobility's structure. As the wealthiest nobles enjoyed more attention and more honorific distinctions, the poorest were subjected to increasing controls from the state and had increasing difficulty maintaining themselves within the order. Another of the state's efforts accentuated this change. Over the sixteenth century, the royal court became an increasingly important institution. Kings had always lived surrounded by followers, officials, and servants, and some prestige had always attached to these roles. But after 1515, when the glamorous Francis I became king, the court took on a new importance in national life, becoming the point where new styles originated and social contacts were made. Francis and his successors added to its appeal with their building projects and by sponsoring increasingly elaborate entertainments. More important than its amusements, though, were the practical realities of court life. As royal taxation increased and kings had greater resources at their disposal, any family that wanted a share of this wealth had to spend some time near the king. Those who did so could hope for both direct and indirect benefits. Kings gave their close followers appointments and pensions; tax farmers needed their assistance in securing contracts, and offered in exchange a share of their profits; and everyone needed their assistance in pursuing litigation. For noble families of any importance, this mix of fashion, money, and influence was irresistible. Through about 1550 many noble families had come to court reluctantly and had avoided staying very long; by 1600 prolonged residence had become normal.

The court's development thus constituted an important element in the higher nobility's economic recovery after 1550, but it was only one cause among several. The high nobility were also the leading beneficiaries of the reversal of economic circumstances that France underwent after 1550. Their farm revenues had suffered from the low agricultural prices and high wages of the early sixteenth century; a century later, they enjoyed the corresponding benefits of a now-overpopulated society, characterized by low wages, competition for farm rentals, and very high agricultural prices. A few nobles dabbled as well in urban real estate development, profitable for the same reasons, and many had forest properties that had become enormously valuable by 1600, in a society that desperately needed wood for fuel and construction.

As a result, the wealthier nobles dominated early seventeenth-century France to a striking degree. Their renewed economic vitality helps to account for their cultural role in these years, in that it gave them the financial means to educate themselves and to exercise cultural patronage. That they used their money in these particular ways, though, reflected other aspects of their situation. By the early seventeenth century, for instance, warfare was widely believed to require careful study of mathematics to make proper use of artillery and fortifications, and of ancient military writers such as Julius Caesar, since Roman infantry tactics were seen to have ongoing relevance to contemporary practice. Theorists likewise stressed the need for education on the part of those who advised the king. Nobles who wanted to play a role in public affairs, it was increasingly agreed, should have some acquaintance with history and some command of rhetorical technique. In their social encounters as well, nobles were expected to display verbal agility and some command of contemporary culture.

Under these mixed pressures, some highly practical, others reflecting the changing demands of life in high society, later sixteenth-century nobles turned to the task of educating themselves. Very few of them sought educations that would match those of the officials. Most ended their studies in their teens, and few acquired real competence in Latin. Even in the mid-seventeenth century few owned substantial libraries. Noblemen began their military careers very young, and they did not want to delay these for the sake of an advanced education. But after 1550 a growing number of institutions met their specific needs. In Paris a few academies opened to teach the techniques needed at court and in the army—riding, fencing, some mathematics. The growing number of Jesuit colleges offered the nobles an especially attractive educational package, given the Jesuits' concern to teach their students social graces as well as academic subjects, and their sensitivity to students' specific needs, including the needs of high social status. Those who remained through the full programme could count on receiving an excellent humanist training, but those who left early—as most noblemen did—received a much better education than the universities provided.

The Jesuit schools embodied some of the larger paradoxes of French culture in the mid-seventeenth century, in that they were at once aristocratic and open. They charged no fees, and many ordinary families sent their sons to them. In class, these students mixed with nobles, and some lasting connections resulted. Yet the Jesuit fathers had no doubt that one of their principal tasks was to prepare the French governing elite for its role in society. They sought to attract students from the highest social levels, and to train them in the specific skills they would need. This concern led to a second tension, between the Jesuits' orientation to Latin humanism and the seriousness with which they took the French language. The schools became the training ground for both the closed Latin culture of future magistrates and an increasingly open French-language culture. French society as a whole could be described in similar terms. Gaps between rich and poor, noble and commoner, were much wider in 1650 than in 1500, yet the foundations of a national culture were already visible. This was a written culture that was increasingly accessible to previously excluded groups, and it permitted a degree of unity across class divisions. In the years after 1650, it would begin, hesitantly, to mitigate those divisions.

3

Rural, urban, and global economies

Philip T. Hoffman

What was life like in early modern France? Were men and women rich or poor? How did they support themselves? Did the economy produce enough for them to eat or did they go to bed hungry? Did their material circumstances improve or worsen over time? Could they expect to survive to a ripe and healthy old age or did they often die young?

Economic historians ask questions such as these. They might pose others as well: why reputations played a peculiarly important role in early modern markets, or why the French monarchy sold government offices in the sixteenth and seventeenth centuries. At bottom, though, all of their questions have something to say about economic growth, the key issue of economic history. It lies at the heart of economic history, and for obvious reasons. In the past, when much of the planet was mired in poverty, growth meant salvation from hunger, disease, and an early death. That is still the case in developing countries today, and it was true in early modern France as well.

Despite the dazzling wealth of nobles, of officers, and of ministers like Richelieu and Mazarin, average French men and women remained poor throughout the early modern period. They never managed to boost their earnings or their consumption in the sixteenth and seventeenth centuries—or at least that is what the meagre records suggest—and without the fruits of economic growth, they were repeatedly threatened by sickness and want. One might of course regard economic growth as inconceivable so long before the Industrial Revolution. But other parts of Europe managed to enjoy the benefits of economic growth in the sixteenth and seventeenth centuries, or even before: parts of the Low Countries, for example, and England too. (Here, the term 'Low Countries' will mean the principalities ruled by the Habsburgs in the early sixteenth century—roughly modern Belgium, Luxembourg, the Netherlands, and bits of northern France; to refer to the territories that eventually became the Dutch Republic, we will simply say the Netherlands.) Furthermore, there were sections of France itself that witnessed growth, particularly in the first half of the sixteenth century. The problem was that the growth could not be sustained, and when it collapsed, the economy regressed. The failure to maintain economic growth left France an underdeveloped country, like much of the rest of Europe.

Underdevelopment did not mean, however, that the French economy was uniform and immobile. Economic outcomes varied greatly from century to century and region to region. After a vibrant recovery from the devastation of the Hundred Years War (1337–1453), France experienced inflation and then a commercial slump in the late sixteenth and seventeenth centuries, as economic leadership in Europe passed from Italians along the Mediterranean to the Dutch and English along the Atlantic. Meanwhile, the French monarchy was boosting taxes and borrowing, including the borrowing that it did by selling offices, and wealth started to flow into cities, at the expense of the countryside. Some places thrived—the city of Lyon in the early sixteenth century is a prime example—while others faltered, and some social groups did worse than others. Even peasants were buffeted by the economic change, for they too were involved in markets.

Still, output and incomes as a whole did not rise. Why then did the French economy fail to grow? The question is all the more puzzling given the promise the French economy displayed in the late fifteenth and early sixteenth centuries, during the recovery after the Hundred Years War. This was a time of prosperity in cities like Lyon and of rising productivity on farms outside Paris. Why was France unable to build on such promising beginnings?

Over the years, historians have advanced a number of possible explanations for France's failure to achieve long-run growth. Because France, like most underdeveloped countries, was largely agricultural, much of the blame for its economic stagnation has fallen on the peasantry. Population growth, it has been argued, left French peasants tilling small, inefficient farms. Worse yet, their mentality made them hostile to new crops and techniques of production. Their only concern was producing enough to eat, and once that goal of self-sufficiency was met, they would neither innovate nor invest in the sort of rudimentary capital goods (livestock, farm buildings, and better seed) that could have boosted production. And even if individual peasants had tried to do something new, they would have run afoul of property rights and village customs, which forced everyone (so it is claimed) to plant the same crops and follow the same time-worn routines.

France's merchants have not escaped blame either. Lured away by government offices and the prospect of entering the nobility, they abandoned commerce—a 'treason of the bourgeoisie' that some historians believe retarded French economic growth. At the same time (so it is argued), the triumph of Catholicism in France wiped out the 'capitalist spirit' that Calvinism supposedly encouraged, at least according to the famed sociologist, Max Weber. Conceivably, these failings might have been compounded by yet another shortcoming: France's failure to develop the sort of colonies and commercial empire that eventually helped enrich England and the Netherlands.

As we shall see, however, the true causes of France's economic torpor actually lie elsewhere. To understand them, we first must examine the evidence for economic stagnation in early modern France and look more closely at its consequences. We must also get a better sense of how the French economy operated. We have to learn a bit more about early modern demography, agriculture, and trade, and about the changes that buffeted the sixteenth and seventeenth-century economy, including the opening of exchange with the new worlds across the Atlantic. Only then can we understand what really held France's economy back.

Economic stagnation

Historians generally agree that France did not experience lasting economic growth in the early modern period, despite the promising beginnings in the late fifteenth and early sixteenth centuries. But what evidence do they have? And if the evidence is persuasive, what were the consequences of France's economic stagnation?

Whatever the evidence for stagnation is, it has to come from clever historical detective work, for there were as yet no bureaucrats collecting economic statistics, as modern governments do. Fortunately, historical sleuths have shed a great deal of light on the early modern French economy, particularly on agriculture, which was far and away its largest sector. In early modern France, some 80 to 90 per cent of the population lived in the countryside, and 60 to 80 per cent of French adults toiled in agriculture. That many people had to till the soil simply to feed the others. In the summer, when grain was painstakingly harvested with sickles for the bread that was the staple of the early modern diet, farmers put women, children, and migrant workers to work. Near Paris they hired day labourers from the city to help bring in the crops.

Because agriculture dominated the economy, what happened on farms and fields by and large dictated the rate of overall economic growth. Yet the French farms could barely produce enough to feed the growing population. We know as much from a variety of ingenious historical investigations which have examined agriculture from a variety of different sources—prices, tithe returns, and population and income estimates. Each method is open to criticism, but for France as a whole, they all point to relatively modest growth in agricultural output. On the eve of the French Revolution, the typical French farmer was producing perhaps only a quarter more than his counterpart in 1500. In England, output per farmer nearly doubled over the same period, by one estimate, and much of the jump in agricultural productivity took place in the seventeenth century. The story in the Netherlands is much the same, with great increases in farm production and output per farmer before 1700.

England and the Netherlands demonstrate that farmers could produce more in the sixteenth and seventeenth centuries. They failed to do so in France, and their failure left France vulnerable to subsistence crises which struck the country repeatedly in the sixteenth and seventeenth centuries. The crisis might begin when an army passed through, seizing grain and driving up the demand for food. Or it might be triggered by bad weather, which could cut grain yields by a half or more even on the best of soils. Near Valenciennes, for example, wheat yields could soar to 30 bushels an acre when everything worked out—a figure well above average for early modern farmers. But the same fields might produce only a third that much grain if the weather turned savage or if armies disrupted the work of preparing the fields and bringing in the crops.

Whatever the cause of the subsistence crises, the price of bread skyrocketed and the poor went hungry. A day labourer might have to work two or three days just to earn enough to feed himself for a week, and he would still have nothing for his family. Death rates inevitably shot upward, less because of actual starvation than because people wandered far from their homes in search of food, exposing themselves to new strains of disease. With their immune systems weakened by hunger, scores then fell victim to disease. Many fled to cities to beg or seek a handout at a cathedral or an urban monastery. They even flocked to small cities like Le Puy, which in 1580 found itself inundated with some 4,000 refugees from the countryside—men, women, and children, all clamouring for food.

Town governments reacted to the subsistence crises in two ways. First of all, they sought to block the influx of paupers from the countryside, but from the 1520s onward, they also created municipal charities to stave off hunger, particularly among poorer city dwellers. Meanwhile, magistrates and royal officials commandeered grain supplies and sometimes imported food to prevent rioting within the city walls. In the end, those who suffered included not just the poor but anyone without the resources to tide them over: peasants with meagre scraps of land in the countryside, and day labourers and even journeymen in cities.

England managed to escape such crises by the seventeenth century, but they continued to afflict France until the early 1700s, in large part because French agriculture lagged behind. Back in 1500, it took three farm workers to feed one city dweller in France and in England too. By 1700, French farmers had improved their productivity slightly: it now took only two of them to nourish the city dweller. Their English counterparts, though, were by now far ahead: in 1700, two English farm workers could grow enough for three city dwellers.

Not that it was impossible for French farmers to eke out more from the soil. There were in fact a number of them in sixteenth and seventeenth-century France who managed to coax more from every acre of land and every day of labour. In the first half of the sixteenth century, for instance, tenant farmers outside Paris cleared land, dug ditches, and reoriented their crops for the Parisian market, thereby boosting the productivity of their farms. Agricultural productivity rose in Normandy too. Grain farmers there achieved high yields by 1600, and stock raisers then converted arable fields to pasture in order to specialize in livestock production. And in the south of France farmers responding to market forces achieved similar gains by planting more vines or by introducing artificial meadows and expanding their livestock herds.

The problem, though, was that these successes could not be extended throughout the entire kingdom. Nor could they be sustained across two centuries, as in England and the Netherlands. Outside Paris, the Wars of Religion wiped out the farmers' gains, and productivity growth eventually halted in Normandy and the Midi too.

It was not just agriculture that failed to achieve sustained growth in France. Again, long-run economic growth was a possibility in other sectors of the economy, if we judge from the examples of the Netherlands or England. In the seventeenth century, for instance, the Netherlands thrived as a centre for commerce, finance, ship building, and textile production, the biggest industry in early modern Europe. In an era when most clothing was woven from wool yarn, the Dutch became the first to dominate the huge market for inexpensive woollen fabric, and their country grew so prosperous that it drew immigrants from France and other countries, immigrants who were attracted by living standards higher than anywhere else in Europe. Later in the century the English then managed to supplant the Dutch in the textile market, and they could boast of a standard of living that was nearly as high.

As in agriculture, France could certainly point to some successes in commerce and manufacturing. Lyon, for instance, flourished in the sixteenth century, when it was a focal point for European finance and trade with Italy. It too attracted immigrants from abroad: in the middle of the 1500s, roughly one in five young men in the city hailed from abroad. A century later, Lyon was still important economically as the leading producer of silk on the continent. In between, however, the city suffered greatly as business with Italy slackened, foreign merchants fled the violence and fiscal exactions of the Wars of Religion, and finance shifted to Paris and to new markets like Amsterdam.

As the history of Lyon demonstrates, French advances in commerce and manufacturing were often interrupted or upset, just as in agriculture. And Lyon is not the only example. Paris, for instance, was a great centre of book production throughout much of the sixteenth century. By the end of the century, however, printers in other countries could turn out books at much lower cost and book production in Paris had lost its vitality. Similarly, in the second quarter of the seventeenth century, the textile industry in Amiens, Beauvais, Lille, and Reims fell victim to a European wide trade slump, and when the slump was finally over, cloth makers in these northern cities found it difficult to compete against their English counterparts.

Even when French industry and trade did thrive for a long period, they did not grow large enough to lift incomes throughout the monarchy. France did have merchants engaged in the growing trade in the Atlantic, a trade that reached beyond Europe to the Americas. In the sixteenth and seventeenth centuries, merchants were engaged in this trade in Rouen, Nantes, Bordeaux, La Rochelle, and other ports. But they could not hold a candle to their counterparts in Lisbon, Seville, Antwerp, and Amsterdam, and none of them generated enough business to increase average incomes throughout the entire kingdom. The same limitations muffled the impact of the commerce in luxury goods such as silk, where France was no doubt the low-cost producer in Europe. Specialization in items such as silk set France down the path to becoming perhaps Europe's premier manufacturer of high-quality products, but as yet the luxury trade was too small to generate noticeable economic growth. In contrast to cheap textiles woven in England and the Netherlands, there was no mass market for luxuries and the inexpensive products that were turned out in France (canvas from Brittany, for example) did not have the volume to take up the slack. One clear sign of France's failure was the gap that began to open up in the seventeenth century between real wages in France and real wages in England and the Low Countries. (Here real wages are simply a way of correcting a worker's wages for the local cost of living; they do so by measuring earnings in terms of the goods they will buy.) Already noticeable in the last half of the sixteenth century, the gap grew even wider thereafter. And while the English, the Dutch, and the Flemish boosted productivity enough to keep pace with population growth and the cost of living, the French did not.

The economy of early modern France thus failed to grow as fast as in England or the Low Countries. French agriculture lagged behind, and so did French commerce and manufacturing. France did lead in the production of luxury goods such as silk, but its leadership did not boost average incomes. France therefore remained relatively poor—relative, that is, to the Low Countries and England. This poverty may have been shared with many other countries in early modern Europe, but, as we shall see, it unfortunately stamped France with all the features of an underdeveloped country.

Demography

Among these features were the grim demographic traits that we today associate with underdevelopment. Poverty simply accentuated them. We have already mentioned the subsistence crises, but they were hardly the only unfortunate consequence of poverty. Mortality as a whole was in fact high, particularly for children. Epidemics raged even when harvests were good, spread by armies, by lice or infected drinking water, or by new diseases (typhus, syphilis) that overwhelmed immune systems. Childhood was especially risky, with only one child in two reaching his tenth birthday. The youngest infants died whether their families were rich or poor, victims of illnesses that struck without regard for social class. But after the age of 1, their deaths correlated with poverty, if we judge from evidence from the eighteenth century. In the countryside, children of day labourers were more likely to succumb to disease than the offspring of wealthier peasants. In cities, merchants lost more boys and girls than nobles and bourgeois. Contemporaries acknowledged the connection between poverty and mortality. 'Death turned upon the poor,' said the attorney Nicolas Versoris of the 1522 epidemic in Paris that killed disproportionate numbers of miserable porters, day labourers, and their families. The Jesuit Jean Grillot noticed a similar pattern when the plague struck Lyon in 1628: 'Few of the well off died relative to the large numbers of the populace who were carried off by the sickness.'[1]

Despite the crises and epidemics, the average person still had the prospect of living to a reasonable age if he (or she) managed to make it through childhood. Death continued to lurk everywhere—it

---

[1] Jean-Pierre Babillon, *Nouvelle histoire de Paris: Paris au XVIᵉ siècle* (Paris, 1986), p. 174; Richard Gascon, 'La France du mouvement: Les Commerces et les villes', in Fernand Braudel and Ernest Labrousse (eds.), *Histoire économique et sociale de la France*, i, *De 1450 à 1660* (Paris, 1977), p. 443.

interrupted many marriages, as husbands succumbed prematurely and wives died in childbirth—but 25-year-old men and women might expect to live another 30 years, particularly if they were rich. Wealth, after all, meant a better diet and cleaner living quarters. It also made it possible to escape the most indiscriminate killers, such as the plague. The rich could move with relative ease to a region untouched by disease or abandon an infected city for estates they owned in the countryside.

Mortality rates were in fact highest in cities. Garbage piled up on city streets, and sewage contaminated water supplies. Neighbours then drank from the same contaminated well or spread disease to one another in close urban quarters. Meanwhile, city dwelling parents could not raise enough surviving children to offset the huge number of deaths. Cities therefore had to draw newcomers from the countryside in order to replenish their populations.

In the long run, though, the crises and epidemics actually had surprisingly little effect on the size of the population. The reason was simple. Once a crisis was past, widows and widowers remarried, quickly had more children, and soon the population was back to normal. Because nearly everyone wed—apart from the clergy—it was the decision to marry that by and large dictated the size of the population. One might assume that without birth control the population would simply explode, but couples delayed marriage until they had the means to live as an independent household, thereby keeping the number of new children under control. At bottom, marriage was primarily a decision about property and future careers, one reached by the bride's and groom's families. They found appropriate partners for their children, and if they were wealthy enough, they gave the young couple the assets they needed to make their way in the world. Prosperous peasants, for example, bestowed the capital needed to start farming: livestock, seed grain, and the financial backing needed to lease a farm. Artisans and merchants might give the newlyweds a share of a business, while nobles endowed them with estates. The children would not marry, though, until the families had assembled the necessary marital capital.

In the sixteenth century, that typically came when the newlyweds were young—in their late teens for a bride and groom marrying for the first time. With men and women marrying young, the population of France grew rapidly by early modern standards, from perhaps a bit over 13 million souls in 1500 to over 18 million by the middle of the sixteenth century, if we count people using France's current frontiers. Population growth then slowed, as the typical bride's and groom's age climbed into the early or mid-twenties by the early seventeenth century. During the Wars of Religion the number of people may have even diminished. The reason was that the economy was faltering, obliging families to put weddings off because they had trouble putting the capital together. As a result, by 1600, there were only some 19 million individuals within France's current frontiers, and only a million or so more by 1650.

It is true that in many respects these French demography trends did not differ from patterns observed elsewhere in Europe, even in England and Holland. There too marriages responded to the availability of resources. The only difference was that France's poverty reinforced most of the grim features of early modern demography. By the seventeenth century, for example, England had escaped the subsistence crises. Poverty in France also aggravated child mortality, and along with the lower productivity of French agriculture, it condemned the poor to a life of chronic malnutrition. If we trust evidence from the eighteenth century, some 15 per cent of the population may have been so weakened by hunger that they could not even work—a situation not unlike that found in the poorest countries today.

Agriculture

Yet another mark of France's underdevelopment was its rudimentary agricultural technology. Not that we would expect miracles in an age before tractors, reaping machines, and chemical fertilizers. But France did not seem to take advantage of all the possibilities already available in the technology that we can see portrayed in stained-glass windows and illuminated manuscripts such as *Les Très Riches Heures du duc de Berry*. Its failure to do so, so one could argue, was one of the reasons for its underdevelopment.

French historians have long distinguished between three great agricultural zones in France, each with its distinctive agricultural technology. At the risk of oversimplifying, the three zones were the

North, the South, and the West. In the North, farmers divided their holdings roughly into thirds each year. On one-third of the fields, they grew rye or winter wheat, and on another third, a spring grain, such as oats or barley. The remaining third—the fallow—was ploughed and fertilized for a year to prepare for winter grain production the next year and then oats the year after that. Each field would thus go through a cycle of fallow followed by wheat/rye and oats, yielding a crop only two years in three.

In southern France, the soil was lighter and drier, and the crop rotation went through a two-year cycle of fallow and then grain. Each field thus bore fruit only one year in two. The rotation in the West was more complicated. Typically, farmers raised livestock on pasture, commons, and waste, and at the same time cultivated certain fields intensively for several years, sometimes until they were depleted. They then abandoned the fields and reclaimed land from the surrounding waste.

This picture of three zones is something of an oversimplification because it leaves out the livestock that nearly all farmers raised, the meadows and pastures where they might mow hay or graze animals, and the orchards and gardens where they grew vegetables and experimented with new crops. It also overlooks wine. In early modern Europe, wine was not the same beverage we imbibe today. It was sold in barrels, not bottles, and drunk young and unclarified. But it was still enormously important. Grapes were cultivated throughout France, not just in regions such as Burgundy or the hinterland of Bordeaux. They were planted outside nearly every city to meet the needs of local consumers, and vineyards yielded wine for export in many parts of northern France where grapevines have long since vanished. Still, some regions were edging towards specialization in viticulture. Wine production in the West, for example, received an enormous boost after Dutch merchants arrived in the late sixteenth century. They began shipping local wine to northern Europe through ports such as Nantes and Bordeaux and thereby encouraged vintners to focus on the export trade.

Still, despite its omissions of wine, livestock, and orchards, the simple picture of three farming zones does allow us to understand some of the criticisms historians have levied against early modern French agriculture. One accusation is that farmers could have cultivated the fallow by planting new crops on it, such as vetch, peas, and artificial meadows. That would have meant additional fodder every second or third year and perhaps more fertile soil and higher grain yields.

Another charge is that French landlords should have consolidated their holdings and created larger, more efficient farms, which would have enjoyed the additional advantage of having fields enclosed by fences or hedges. The enclosures—so the argument goes—would have freed agriculture from the communal property rights that retarded progress. In particular, the enclosures would have kept out the sheep and other animals that grazed upon the fallow in the North and South of France, where arable fields lacked any fences. These grazing animals, it is said, retarded the introduction of artificial meadows and new crops in France. In England, where farming practices resembled those in the North and West of France, landlords had already begun to enclose in the early sixteenth century. Why did French property owners not do the same? Was it opposition from the peasant community, which had claims to grazing rights on the open fields?

One can ask similar questions about the very tools French peasants customarily used. Why, for instance, did French farmers not begin to harvest their winter grains—wheat and rye—with the scythe instead of the sickle? The scythe saved an immense amount of labour in what was the most time-consuming task in early modern agriculture, reaping grain. It was already in use for mowing hay and for cutting oats: indeed, one sees it in *Les Très Riches Heures du duc de Berry*. Why then was it not extended to the major food crops, wheat and rye? Was it an obstinate peasant mentality, which might also have explained why farmers failed to plant new crops on the fallow?

Many historians still believe that French agriculture was shackled by the lack of enclosures, by farms that were too small, by peasants who obstinately resisted new tools and new crops, and by landlords who failed to undertake the sort of improvements already underway across the English Channel. But recent research has cast doubt on these arguments. Enclosures, it turns out, added relatively little to agricultural productivity, either in England or in the places where they were tried in France. Larger farms were not that much more efficient either, and in any case most French farms were probably of the optimal size. Finally, the peasants were far cleverer than most historians have imagined. As we have seen, they planted vines for the export trade in the West, cleared land and shifted crops outside Paris; boosted yields and converted arable to pasture in Normandy, and introduced artificial meadows and expanded their livestock herds in the South. They were perfectly capable of innovation, even on small farms, and when farms were too small, they used sales and leases to achieve the appropriate size. They did not need enterprising landlords.

Even their failure to adopt the scythe has a ready explanation. To harvest wheat or rye, the scythe had to be wielded by a skilled reaper. It was particularly difficult to use on the deeply furrowed fields of northern France, and in the hands of the unskilled, it would simply knock the kernels of grain right off the stalk. Qualified reapers cost more and often had to be imported right at the moment when the grain was ripe—a difficult task in the hectic moments on the eve of the harvest. It was cheaper and thus more efficient to hire inexpensive women and unskilled men to bring in the crop with sickles. In short, as the example of the sickle demonstrates, the French peasants were not as hard-headed as historians have supposed, and one should look elsewhere for the real barriers to progress in French agriculture.

Our overview of French agriculture suggests that peasant farming was not what held the French economy back. Although complaints have long been made about the small size of the peasants' farms and about the lack of enclosures and of English-style landlords, none of that really mattered much. French peasants were cleverer than most historians assume, and the techniques they employed actually make considerable sense when we consider the problems they faced. The real causes of French economic retardation, it thus seems, must lie elsewhere.

Trade

Perhaps the causes are to be found in the workings of early modern French trade, for it too was tragically underdeveloped. As elsewhere in early modern Europe, trade was hampered by a number of obstacles—in particular, the high cost of transporting goods to market. Limited trade throttled economic development, especially in agriculture, where the costs of transportation loomed largest. More extensive trade could ignite growth in agriculture, by allowing peasants to reap the benefits of specialization. It did so in Normandy, where some farmers specialized in grain production while others raised cattle. It played the same role in the South, where productivity gains depended on specialization in viticulture or livestock. The key then is to understand the barriers that obstructed French trade and to learn what reduced these barriers in England and the Netherlands.

One of the hurdles, we have already noted, was the high cost of delivering goods to market, particularly bulky crops like grain. Over water, grain could be profitably shipped long distances—from the Baltic to Italy, for example, under the right conditions. But overland it was often too costly to transport it further than one day's journey (roughly 20 to 30 miles), whether it was hauled in a cart or carried in sacks on a horse's back. For a 60-mile trip, for example, the charges for conveying grain by road might be ten times what they would be by boat! Investment in canals and docks could thus be crucial, for it extended the reach of cheaper water transport and could thus invigorate trade. France's record of investment in canals before 1650 was not the worst—it certainly spent more, for instance, than Spain—but it paled by comparison with the Netherlands. Henry IV's minister Sully did begin construction of a canal linking the Loire and the Seine near Paris, and he envisioned further canals linking other rivers in France. But work slackened when he left office, and nothing came of the plan for additional canals. Meanwhile, the Netherlands was building a network of canals that cut the cost of transportation not just for farmers, but for manufacturers and merchants as well.

It was of course easier to build canals in the easy terrain of the Netherlands, but French efforts to build roads were also disappointing. Better roads made it possible to transport goods in carts and wagons, rather than on the back of pack animals. They also cut the cost of getting grain to the nearest navigable waterway. Although the French monarchy did briefly budget more for roads when Sully was minister, spending slackened after his departure, and France apparently lacked the private entrepreneurs who built toll roads in late seventeenth-century England. Another obstacle in France was the general distrust of middlemen, who would reorganize the land-based transport of grain to Paris in the century after 1650. Feared as speculators who might drive up the price of food, they faced legal and political obstacles that hampered their work around Paris, and around other large cities as well.

Although trade was underdeveloped in early modern France, we should not assume that it was non-existent. Even in agriculture there were well-developed local markets in grain and long-distance markets in livestock, which could walk to market. Few peasants were self-sufficient. The majority probably did not even come close to growing enough food to feed themselves (particularly after 1550), and they thus had to work if they wanted to eat. They toiled for neighbours—wealthier peasant farmers and noble landowners who lived in the countryside—and they earned enough money to buy what their gardens and parcels of land would not produce. They thus found themselves engaged in markets for goods, for labour, and also for the rental and sale of agricultural land.

Although the agricultural labour markets sometimes involved long-distance movement, the usual participants were peasants whose jobs took them no further than neighbouring villages and towns. Men laboured as farm hands, and young women worked as milkmaids and servants, while assembling a dowry for marriage. In late fifteenth-century Normandy, a half dozen or so of these farmhands and servants passed each year through the farm of the Cairon, a family of minor nobles. The problem for the Cairon and for the other farmers who hired them was that of sorting out the reliable workers—farmhands who could be entrusted with valuable livestock, for example, and milkmaids who would not steal. While servants who failed at their jobs were cast out, the successful ones were rewarded: they might be given a raise and kept on for another year. Alternatively, the nobles and wealthy peasant landlords who ran the farms might turn repeatedly to the same families when hiring, as if these families were sure to furnish servants who could be trusted. Over time, a relationship verging on clientage might even develop, in sharp contrast to the suspicion with which the farmers regarded most of their workers.

The same paradoxical mix of loyalty and mistrust characterized landlords' dealings with their tenant farmers, for understandable reasons. A bad tenant could destroy capital invested in vines and fruit trees; he could also let ditches silt up and deplete the soil of nutrients in his final year on a farm. A good one, by contrast, was to be cherished and protected, for he paid his rent on time and never damaged the farm. A landlord might therefore cut an exemplary tenant's rent, if frost or flooding wiped out his crops. He might advance him livestock or other agricultural capital. And he might forge an enduring relationship with him and his family, a relationship that could continue for generations.

In fact, in the countryside, loyalty and mistrust coloured nearly all economic dealings, and the same was no doubt true of cities and market towns, for nearly all transactions depended on informal credit. The Cairon family lent money to a local peasant and subsequently hired his daughter as a servant. On another occasion, they paid one farmhand's wages to his father, presumably to extinguish one of their own debts. Credit of this sort permeated the early modern economy. It depended on trust and a reputation for repaying debts, and failure to repay provoked suspicion and even violent retaliation in village after village and town after town.

But informal credit of this sort was itself an obstacle to the extension of trade. Typically, long-distance trade means anonymous trade, where goods are exchanged among parties who do not know one another. But when parties do not know one another, they will hesitate to extend one another credit; local reputations will not help at all. To extend trade—and thereby spur on economic growth—France had to develop the banks or middlemen who could provide the necessary credit.

The network of middlemen did emerge for textiles and especially for luxury goods. Merchants in Rouen, for example, offered the credit and organizational skills needed to integrate local textile production into the international market. And foreign merchants and bankers in Lyon used the city's fairs to finance long-distance trade in silk and spices. But in the more mundane field of agriculture goods, middlemen, we know, faced a number of obstacles, notably the government's suspicion and mistrust. As a result, most farmers had to do without the middlemen who could have cut the costs of transporting crops like grain. They had to rely on reputations and informal credit, which were themselves barriers to trade.

The only alternative was demanding cash in all transactions, but that was cumbersome. The only money in existence was coinage, and coins were scarce, particularly the copper or copper-silver small change that paid for the transactions of everyday life. One of the very reasons people in fact resorted to credit (whether it was the informal borrowing in villages or the bills of exchange used at Lyon's fairs) was to make the most of the small supply of coins.

The reasons why coins were scarce are complex. In any given locale, the supply of coins could be affected by trade flows, by events abroad, and above all else by policies of the royal mints. In the fifteenth and sixteenth centuries, silver began to be used as money in China, northern India, and parts of the Middle East; meanwhile, Europe was being inundated with silver from central Europe and the New World. Silver became cheap in Europe and dear in China, and European merchants discovered that they could buy silk and spices for a song in Asia. The resulting trade gradually drained away the Spanish silver, but not before it had helped bring on inflation.

As for mint policies, in the Middle Ages, local lords had minted coins, but by the early sixteenth century, the kings of France had achieved something close to a monopoly over coinage. (It is true that during the Wars of Religion, this monopoly would erode, like the monopoly over taxation.) The king maintained a number of provincial mints, and until the middle of the seventeenth century, he farmed out the rights to operate these mints to private contractors, just like other sovereigns in Western Europe. The mints turned out the three types of coinage that circulated in France: small change of copper or a copper and silver mix; silver coins that were used for larger transactions; and gold coins that served (along with many foreign coins that circulated in France) as an international medium of exchange.

It was difficult to keep three different kinds of coin in circulation, for reasons both technological and economic. Suffice it to say that states throughout Europe had difficulty mastering the task until the nineteenth century. One of the reasons they had so much trouble was that the mints produced a profit for the crown. When pressed for cash, the monarchy would try to squeeze more revenue out of the mints by manipulating the coinage, and French kings had a great penchant for such revenue-raising tactics, although they were hardly alone in doing so. By the sixteenth century, the monarchy had by and large achieved the power to dictate what coins were worth in what was called money of account: the king could say, for example, that a silver teston was worth 13 sous in all payments. But he could also change the valuation—declare the teston worth 16 sous, for example—which usually involved having people bring coins to the mint to be reminted. The operation was more profitable for silver than for the small change of copper or copper silver, and mints therefore spent more time reminting silver coins than producing small change that was needed for much local trade. (It was more difficult to manipulate the gold coinage because of its role into international trade.)

France was not the only country to manipulate its coinage, but it is clear that the monarchy's actions did dry up small change, making everyday buying and selling arduous. They also made it difficult to arrange long-term loans, because long-term debt contracts had to be specified in money of account, at least after 1602. A lender who made a long-term loan therefore risked repayment in debased coinage—a risk that undermined the sort of long-term credit that might pay for urban construction or the establishment of a business.

Even when entrepreneurs could raise funds for commercial ventures, they confronted yet another barrier in many French cities—guilds. Not that the guilds were opposed to trade—far from it. But where they existed (they were absent in many parts of France, particularly in the south) they limited competition among manufacturers and thereby kept prices high, a disadvantage for merchants who wanted to export French goods. Circumventing them was not easy, because the guilds had the support of the monarchy, which allowed them to raise prices and then siphoned off a portion of their profits in the form of taxes. One way to get around them was 'putting out': shifting production to the countryside, where there was a surplus of cheap agricultural labour, particularly in the winter. In Rouen, for example, merchants organized rural production of stockings, and weavers moved their looms to neighbouring small towns. Entrepreneurs began experimenting with such putting out in the sixteenth century, and it grew even more common after 1600. Still, even with putting out, many French exporters had to clear an extra hurdle in order to keep their goods competitive.

The various obstacles to trade did take a toll on the early modern French economy, for they impeded commerce that would have raised incomes and consumption. Here the monarchy must bear at least some of the blame, for it spent relatively little on the roads and canals that would have cut the cost of getting goods to market, and it distrusted the middlemen who could have extended trade in the countryside. It also supported the guilds, and by manipulating the coinage, it undermined financial markets and made it difficult for people to do business.

France overseas

Did France lag economically because it failed to develop the sort of colonies and commercial empire that helped enrich England and the Netherlands? Was that the reason why the early modern French economy proved so sluggish? If so, it might explain why France seemed to fall behind in the seventeenth century. That was the era when the Netherlands assembled a commercial empire and dominated international trade, at least for the first two-thirds of the century. It was also the period when the Netherlands became the richest country in Europe. And it was the time when English colonies initially flourished and when, at the end of the century, the English finally overtook the Dutch as a commercial empire—a prelude, perhaps, to England's subsequently becoming the first country in the world to industrialize.

If this line of reasoning is correct, France might have prospered had it created colonies and a commercial empire, like England and the Netherlands. France certainly had a chance to do so, for it did not lag behind England and the Netherlands as a colonial power at the end of the sixteenth century. In the Americas, for example, the only successful colonies in 1600 belonged to Spain and Portugal; England and the Netherlands as yet had none. By 1663, however, France had dropped far back. In North America, the English now had some seventy thousand colonists and the Dutch ten thousand. The French could count only four thousand, and France played second fiddle to England and the Netherlands in international trade too.

Such a lacklustre performance is surprising, for France could boast of intrepid sailors and able explorers from an early date, and it had even tried to establish colonies back in the 1500s. In the first half of the sixteenth century, French corsairs preyed upon Spanish and Portuguese shipping throughout the world, with the support of important shipowners such as Jean Ango of Dieppe. And within six years after the 1498 discovery of the Grand Banks fishing grounds, French boats were there bringing in cod, a catch with great appeal in Europe, since it could be eaten on the many days when meat was forbidden for religious reasons. The French were in fact the only fishermen who dared to set out for the Grand Banks in winter. Leaving as early as January, they filled barrels with enough salted cod to return to France by May. They could then go back to the Banks a second time in the same year. By 1519 they were placing crew members on shore to dry cod in the sun, making it easier to pack in the hold, and by 1542 cod fishing had grown so important in Brittany and Normandy that sixty boats sailed to the Grand Banks from Rouen alone.

Fishing also gave rise to a lucrative trade in Canadian furs. It happened when sailors drying fish on shore began selling beads, utensils, and tools to Indians in return for furs, which were used for hats, coat linings, and ceremonial trim back in France. Demand for the pelts was so high that the fur trade eventually overshadowed the fishing—so much so that by the end of the sixteenth century French merchants were setting up companies to specialize in it alone.

France also had significant explorers. In 1524, with the support of King Francis I, merchants and Italian bankers in Rouen and Lyon raised the money to send Giovanni Verrazano on a search for a northern passage to the Far East—a goal that tantalized explorers at the time. The aim seems to have been finding a water route that would cut through North America and shave time off the long and treacherous journey through the Straits of Magellan. Although no such passage existed, Verrazano became the first European to explore the east coast of the United States north of Florida, and his voyage gave France a claim (albeit a contested one) to much of the eastern seaboard of North America.

Verrazano was not alone. In 1534 Francis I commissioned Jacques Cartier to search for a northern passage and for precious metals in the newly discovered lands of North America that were unoccupied by Spain and Portugal. Cartier explored the Gulf of Saint Lawrence, traded with various Indian tribes, and was allowed to take two sons of an Iroquoian chief, Donnaconna, back to France with him so that they could interpret on his next visit. Returning to Canada in 1535, he built a base camp near Quebec City and travelled up the Saint Lawrence River as far as Montreal. Having decided to pass the winter in North America, he lost 25 of his men to scurvy, but the deaths and brutal cold did not dampen his enthusiasm. He believed that the Saint Lawrence was the passage to Asia, and his convictions were reinforced when Donnaconna and other Iroquoians told him about a wealthy kingdom further inland in Canada, a fabulous kingdom called Saguenay, where 'white men' supposedly lived and 'gold and rubies' abounded.[2]

This was just the sort of tale early modern Europeans were ready to swallow. Donnaconna and the other Iroquoians had fashioned it to curry favour with Cartier and perhaps to gain his help in an intra-tribal dispute. But it convinced Cartier to take desperate measures, in part because he misinterpreted the Iroquoians' own dispute and feared that they were about to attack him and his crew. On 3 May 1536, Cartier kidnaped Donnaconna, his sons, and two other Iroquoians and took them all back to France so that they could tell Francis I about the marvels of Saguenay.

Donnaconna's story persuaded Francis I, but it was not until 1541 that Cartier returned to Canada. War with Spain caused some of the delay, as did diplomatic problems after the fighting stopped in 1538. The Spanish and Portuguese feared that France aimed to set up colonies in the New World, which they claimed was entirely theirs, and the Spanish in fact tried to stop the French from sending another expedition to North America. But Francis I rejected their claims, particularly to land that Europeans had not yet settled, such as Canada. Having decided that he needed his own colony to bolster his own claims in North America, he put a nobleman, Roberval, in charge of Cartier's next expedition to the Saint Lawrence, in 1541. Their task was not only to search for Saguenay but to establish a settlement in what the French believed was a western extremity of Asia. The mission, however, proved to be a severe disappointment. Cartier of course never located Saguenay, and he spent another miserable winter near Quebec City, this time under attack by the Iroquoians, who not surprisingly had become hostile. Worse yet, Roberval, who was supposed to follow on his heels with supplies and more settlers, did not reach Canada until June of 1542, just as Cartier was leaving in disgust. Roberval then spent his own disastrous winter in Canada, and failing to find Saguenay, he and the survivors abandoned their encampment and headed back to France in 1543. For decades thereafter, permanent settlement in Canada was deemed hopeless. As an

[2] Charles A. Julien, René Herval, and Théodore Beauchesne (eds.), *Les Français en Amerique pendant la première moitié du XVIe siècle: Textes des voyages de Gonneville, Verrazano, J. Cartier et Roberval* (Paris, 1946), p. 175.

inscription on a 1550 map said, 'It was impossible to trade with the people of that country because of their austerity, the intemperate climate . . . and the slight profit.'[3]

France did try to found early colonies in the warmer climates of Brazil and the south-eastern coast of the United States, but these efforts proved to be spectacular failures. In Brazil, the French were attracted by brazilwood, a tree used in making textile dye. Merchants and shipowners such as Jean Ango sponsored expeditions to cut the wood, beginning early in the sixteenth century. They persevered despite Portuguese attacks on their ships and trading posts, and by mid-century they were getting greater support from King Henry II, who commissioned the chevalier de Villegaignon to set up a colony in Brazil in 1555. Villegaignon embarked with some six hundred sailors and colonists and established the colony on an island in Rio de Janeiro Bay, where he built a fortress. Several hundred additional settlers arrived in 1557, but in 1560 the encampment was bombarded by Portuguese warships, while Villegaignon was away seeking military reinforcements in France. Lacking naval support, the civilian colonists succumbed after a three-week siege, and thereafter the French monarchy made no further efforts to colonize South America.

The settlements on the south-eastern coast of the United States met a similar fate, this time at the hands of the Spanish. The French crown organized three expeditions to the south-east between 1562 and 1565, setting up a fort in South Carolina and a second stronghold and colony (Fort Caroline) in Florida. The aim was to lay claim to a region not yet occupied by Spain, but the Spanish feared that the French would use the settlements to plunder their treasure fleet, which brought them mountains of silver from South America. Their fears were understandable. Since the 1550s French corsairs had stepped up their assaults on Spanish shipping in the area, and Fort Caroline would make an excellent base from which to attack the silver fleet. Winds and currents forced it to sail nearby, through a narrow channel between Florida and the Bahamas that left little room for escape. The Spanish therefore mounted a major effort to wipe out the French installations. In 1564, they destroyed the fort in South Carolina, which the French had abandoned, and in 1565 they took

---

[3] Samuel Eliot Morison, *The European Discovery of America: The Northern Voyages A.D. 500–1600* (Oxford, 1971), pp. 451, 454, 462.

Fort Caroline by surprise, slaughtering all the men they captured. The defeat ended French attempts to colonize the south-eastern coast of the United States.

It was not until the early seventeenth century that France finally set up successful colonies. The delay resulted, at least in part, from the disruptions of the Wars of Religion. It may have also reflected Spain's continuing naval power in the Americas, which only began to wane at the end of the sixteenth century. When France did finally succeed in establishing lasting colonies, it was often in locations that were not easy targets for aggression, such as Guadeloupe and Martinique. Occupied by French colonists in the 1620s and 1630s, the two Caribbean islands were difficult to attack from Spanish bases because of the direction of prevailing winds. They only prospered, however, in the second half of the seventeenth century, after Dutch merchants introduced the cultivation of sugar cane. Having come to dominate shipping in the Caribbean, the Dutch transported the sugar to European consumers and furnished the African slaves who did all the work.

The territory that the French settled in Canada in the early seventeenth century seemed relatively safe from military assault too, but it did not remain so for long. In Canada, the French established their colonies around the Bay of Fundy (French Acadia) and in the Saint Lawrence Valley. Acadia, however, was claimed by England, and it ended up passing back and forth between French and English rule. Though more remote, the Saint Lawrence Valley ultimately faced its own English attacks, but the fate of the settlements there depended less on military prowess than on the business that attracted the French—the fur trade. Growing numbers of French merchants had been buying furs there since the 1580s, and after the explorer Samuel de Champlain founded a colony in Quebec in 1608, he helped unite the merchants in a trading company. He also consolidated their alliance with the Indian tribes who sold the furs. The fur trade expanded, but it still proved impossible to support a large colony. The reason was simple. The fur trade simply did not require much French labour. It relied upon the skill of Indian hunters, and to keep it going, all one needed was a handful of merchants and interpreters. The same was true of fishing. Other colonial goods—the tobacco grown in the English colony of Virginia, for example—might employ scores of colonists, but they were unsuited to the Canadian climate. It is no wonder then that by 1663 the English and the Dutch had many more colonists that the French.

Early modern France did not develop large colonies or a commercial empire, but was this failure ultimately what held its economy back? Answering 'yes' assumes that colonial trade was the engine of growth in the successful early modern economies of Netherlands and England, but historical research in fact argues to the contrary. In the Netherlands, the traffic in sugar and slaves with the Caribbean did not generate huge profits. Dutch commerce with Asia did somewhat better, but the resulting profits were still smaller than the traditional trade in grain and timber with Northern European ports. And in general, foreign trade did not stimulate much growth of Dutch manufacturing.

The same conclusions hold for England. England had successful colonies and a commercial empire, but they did not bring on the Industrial Revolution. Though trade with the colonies was sizeable by the standards of the day, it was too small a part of the English economy to have enormous consequences. In the middle of the seventeenth century, for example, shipments to English colonies amounted to only 10 per cent of all exports from London. Furthermore, had the colonies and commercial empire not existed, the same goods would have been easy to sell within England itself.

Finally, if colonies had been the engines of economic advancement, then Spain, with the biggest colonial empire of all, would presumably have experienced the most rapid economic growth in all of Europe. But the Spanish economy actually shrank in the early modern period. The Spanish colonies were in fact a financial drain until large silver shipments from Latin America began in the 1540s. Thereafter, Spanish living standards stagnated, agriculture and manufacturing collapsed, while the silver was squandered on warfare. All too often in early modern Europe, colonies provided little more for the economy than the tales of Saguenay; they were not motors of growth.

Change despite the lack of economic growth

Economic stagnation did not mean that the French economy was stuck in a rut of tradition and that nothing changed—far from it. Although productivity did not rise and average incomes did not grow, economic outcomes varied widely from century to century and across regions and social groups. We have already seen how Lyon rose to prominence in the sixteenth century as a centre of trade and mercantile finance. But at the end of the century Lyon lost its role as a major European financial centre, as merchants and bankers fled taxes, warfare, and devastating government defaults. Misfortunes obviously struck agriculture too. In the late sixteenth century, farmers outside Paris were devastated by the Wars of Religion; they suffered again in the middle of the seventeenth century, victims of higher taxes, lower prices, inclement weather, and the military operations of the rebellion known as the Fronde.

Economic change extended well beyond swings of fortune. In the sixteenth century, prices rose throughout Europe, and new financial techniques emerged in France and other countries. As the century drew to a close, trade leadership began to shift from the Mediterranean to the Atlantic, and resources started to move from the countryside to cities, a trend that would continue well past 1650. But the biggest change of all was the monarchy's fiscal policy. The crown pushed taxes to unheard of levels and borrowed heavily, all in an effort to meet the rising costs of war. The consequences for the early modern economy were enormous.

The clearest of these trends was the increase in taxes: it protrudes clearly despite the murky fog of early modern statistics. Under King Charles VII (1422–61), the crown collected roughly two million *livres* a year in regular taxes—taxes on land, salt, commerce, and trade. That was enough to buy two or three million hectolitres (7 to 8 million bushels) of wheat or to hire 12 to 16 million labourers for a day. By 1640 Louis XIII had nearly 80 million *livres* a year at his disposal. Prices had of course risen over the intervening two centuries, but the tax burden had still grown three or four times, if we measure it in terms of wheat, and seven or eight in terms of labour. The figures trace out the same dizzying climb if we look at central treasury receipts. They include a wider variety of taxes, though they do omit the huge sums that were collected and spent locally. In any case, they show that per-capita taxes shot upward too and demonstrate that the increase was steepest in the 1630s, when France entered the Thirty Years War (Figure 1).

It was warfare and new military technology that drove the monarchy to pile on more and more taxes. Most of the money the crown

Figure 1. Central treasury receipts, 1560s to 1660s

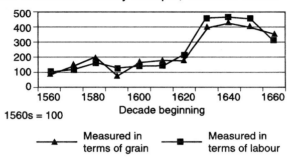

1560s = 100

Central Treasury Receipts, 1560s to 1660s. The central treasury receipts do not include huge amounts of taxes that were raised and spent locally, but they do give a crude measure of how much taxation rose, particularly in the 1630s, when France entered the Thirty Years War. In the graph, the receipts are measured in terms of bushels of grain and days of labour, using Parisian prices for wheat and unskilled labour. The grain and labour equivalents have been converted to indices, with the value 100 in the 1560s. The receipts themselves are annual averages for each decade.
Source: Philip T. Hoffman and Kathryn Norberg (eds.), *Fiscal Crises, Liberty, and Representative Government, 1450–1789* (Stanford, Calif., 1994), 238.

collected went for armies and defence, for subsidies to allies, or for interest payments on loans that had financed previous wars. Spending on justice, the arts, roads, education, and even palaces paled by comparison to direct and indirect military expenses. Warfare absorbed the money because military technology had changed. First came bows and pikemen and then mortars, cannon, and muskets. The use of artillery necessitated stronger and more extensive fortifications, at enormous expense. Meanwhile, armies swelled in size, from 14,000 men in peacetime in the late fifteenth century, to 72,000 in peacetime in the 1660s, and perhaps double that in war. Early modern states battled almost constantly, and France found itself trapped in a particularly difficult position, threatened as it was on either side by the Habsburgs, arguably Europe's greatest military power in the sixteenth and early seventeenth centuries. It was hardly a surprise then that the crown did its most to extract tax revenue from its subjects.

Not that the king kept all the tax money under his direct control. A considerable portion of the tax revenue might be collected and spent locally on troops controlled by the great nobility—a form of patronage for grandees. Still more might remain in the hands of local financial officials. And during the Wars of Religion, much of the tax revenue slipped from the king's hands, when military commanders from each camp seized the local tax administration.

Despite the huge tax increases, the revenues did not suffice. Once war broke out, expenses skyrocketed, and tax increases could not keep pace. The only solution was to borrow. As in the other European states, the cost of war forced France to experiment with new forms of government credit. In the 1540s, the crown began raising money systematically at the Lyon fairs, via short-term loans from foreign bankers. It sought long-term financing as well, by issuing *rentes*, perpetual annuities that promised an unending stream of income to a lender and his heirs in return for a loan. First peddled in 1522, the *rentes* proved popular with members of the elite who wanted to assure their children of income and to protect their estates from profligate heirs. But perhaps the most fateful sort of loan the monarchy employed was the sale of government offices, a practice that grew increasingly common in the 1520s. In return for the purchase price—in effect a loan—the government paid interest in the form of *gages*, the holder's earning from the office. Since France, like other states in Europe, was a risky borrower—it repeatedly defaulted on its debts—it faced a higher interest rate when borrowing than private parties did. Confronted with such a high cost of borrowing, the monarchy found the sale of offices appealing, for the lenders (the office holders) did not demand as much in interest payments as the monarchy's other creditors. The reason was that they also enjoyed the honour and the emoluments of their positions; in addition, they came to form powerful pressure groups that could resist government default. It is thus easy to see why the crown yielded to the temptation to sell offices: doing so released it from the cash squeeze provoked by the costs of war. In the process, though, the monarchy was not getting something for nothing. Borrowing by selling offices may have cost less in terms of cash, but it meant selling off bits of the crown's authority.

Could the monarchy have found another way to raise funds? Could it have borrowed at low interest rates, as the Netherlands eventually managed to do? That would have necessitated some sort of guarantees for creditors. The *rentes* were perhaps a step in this direction: they had the backing of powerful municipal governments such as

Paris or Lyon and they were to be repaid with specially earmarked tax revenues, all of which would have diminished the risks of default. Yet following in the Netherlands' footsteps would have required further assurances for lenders. In particular, it would have meant giving them real power over the purse. In the Netherlands, they had this power, because a number of the government's creditors were prominent members of the representative body, the estates. But it seems doubtful that the king of France would have shared so much of his authority.

The increase in taxes and government borrowing was not the only change that disturbed early modern France. The country also had to contend with inflation in the sixteenth and (at least in some parts of the kingdom) early seventeenth centuries. In France wages could not keep pace with the inflation, and while wage rates do not always translate into incomes, French wage earners probably suffered. They went from enjoying relatively a high real wage in 1500 to a much lower one in 1600. Meanwhile, rents on land increased. Nobles and other landowners, who had derived relatively little income from their property back in 1500, were now profiting.

One of the causes behind the inflation was the influx of silver from the Americas: it increased the money supply. But in France, as elsewhere in Europe, the inflation went beyond what silver imports can explain. One cause was population pressure on the food supply, which drove up the price of food faster than that of other commodities. There were also signs of financial innovation, of money turning over faster than in the past, which would help account for rising prices. One bit of evidence for the innovations was the slow decline in the interest rates that merchants and other private borrowers faced, as if money to lend were becoming more plentiful. The fairs in Lyon and a similar market for bills of exchange in Antwerp were the places where these financial innovations could be found: the bills of exchange allowed merchants to transact business without having to use cash. The innovations, though, did have their limits, at least in France. We already know that the credit they provided did not extend to agriculture, and even French merchants were reluctant to use bills of exchange in the sixteenth and early seventeenth centuries. They left such novelties to the foreigners trading in Lyon.

Beginning in the late sixteenth century, the French economy felt the effects of yet another trans-European trend, the shift of trade leadership from the Mediterranean to the Atlantic. Italian manufacturers—long the technological masters of Europe—lost their competitive edge, and Italian merchants gave up their role as Europe's leading traders too. They were supplanted by the English and above all else by the Dutch, whose ships ranged from the Baltic to the Mediterranean, and off to Asia and the Americas. The Dutch began to appear in larger numbers in France's Atlantic ports, and they helped bring prosperity to Rouen, Nantes, La Rochelle, and Bordeaux. On the Mediterranean itself, Marseilles actually prospered, as its merchants took the place of some of the Italians in trade with the Near East. The trade shift, though, did hurt Lyon seriously, for it had depended on resident Italian merchants and bankers to import silks and spices from the Mediterranean. Lyon shifted into manufacturing silks and lost forever its claim to be a major European banking centre.

The late sixteenth century also witnessed the onset of another economic trend that involved movement of wealth and prosperity— the gradual shift of resources from countryside to city. This trend would continue well past 1650, and it probably increased the fraction of the French population living in cities, although figures here are still a subject of debate. Cities grew, as wealth and jobs attracted migrants from the countryside. The growth of Paris was perhaps the most dramatic: it doubled in population between 1550 and 1700, from perhaps 250,000 to over half a million.

The transfer of resources had a number of causes. Prominent among them was the increase in taxes, for the fisc bore down more heavily on the politically weak peasantry, and the tax revenues were in turn spent in cities. The growing number of officials who collected the taxes and disbursed the revenues lived in cities. So too did the monarchy's burgeoning corps of judicial officials. Soldiers resided in cities too, at least when they were not fighting, and in any case they were usually outfitted by urban merchants. The fisc was thus taking more and more money from tax-paying peasants and giving it to city dwellers, many of whom were in fact tax exempt.

Cultural and religious changes accelerated the movement of resources. Rural nobles started to spend more and more time in cities, spending the revenue from their rural property in town, rather than in the countryside. This cultural shift was only beginning and it had a long way to go, but it did bring more money to cities. Similarly, during the Catholic Reformation, cities throughout France found themselves with newly founded religious houses. Since the money to support the religious houses came from rural property, the cities benefited again.

Finally, the tax exemptions that many urbanites enjoyed allowed them to buy up increasing amounts of farm land from impoverished, tax-paying peasants. They then rented the land out and thus added to the stream of revenue flowing from countryside to cities. The city dwellers who did this might be nobles, officers, or bourgeois; in any case, they served as the model for the rentier—the city dweller who lived from his investments. It was worth their while to purchase the land because they could farm it out and neither they nor their tenants would bear the full burden of the increased taxes, at least before tax reforms of the eighteenth century. For the tax-exempt city dwellers, rural property was thus a vast tax shelter, and every tax increase made it more attractive.

Rural property had the added advantage of serving as a hedge against the effects of inflation and currency manipulations. The reason was that alternative investments—long-term loans to private individuals, for example, or government *rentes*—had to be specified in money of account, at least after 1602. The noble, office-holder, or wealthy merchant who wanted to make such a loan thus risked losing his investment to inflation, which was still a problem in parts of France in the early seventeenth century, or, worse yet, to one of the government's frequent debasements of the coinage. But if he bought rural property, he could collect the rent in kind or revise it every nine years or so when leases were renewed. He was thus protected against the devastating effects of inflation and debasement.

While the French economy may not have grown, French society was nonetheless buffeted by economic change. Prices soared in the sixteenth century, and in the seventeenth the Atlantic replaced the Mediterranean as the locus of trade. But the greatest change in the early modern period was no doubt the enormous increase in taxes. They soared, and the government borrowed unheard of sums, all to fight wars and pay the costs of a military revolution.

The tax increase pulled money out of the countryside and trans-ferred it to France's cities. At the same time, the cities were beginning to benefit from the Catholic Reformation and from the nobility's decision to spend more time in urban quarters. The cities' population grew, and with more and more wealth in their hands, tax-exempt urban elites bought up rural land, tightening even further the cities' grip over the countryside.

Economic and political choices

What then were the ultimate causes of economic stagnation in early modern France? Why did France not keep pace with England and the Netherlands? Why was France unable to sustain economic growth for long periods of time and across the entire economy? Historians have advanced a number of seemingly plausible explanations, only to see them evaporate under the glare of recent research. Of the causes that remain convincing, some involved historical accidents, or geographic handicaps that France could have done little to change—for instance, the extraordinary advantage that Amsterdam extracted as a centre of trade and finance in the seventeenth century. The others, however, reflected political choices that the monarchy made. Had the kings fought less—admittedly, a difficult choice in early modern Europe—France might have developed a stronger economy.

We have already encountered some of the explanations that recent research has now rejected; again, many of them focus on agriculture, the largest sector of the economy in France and in any underdeveloped economy:

- Stubborn and suspicious of new crops and techniques, the peasants cared only about growing enough for their own consumption. What France needed were landlords like those in England, who would lead an agricultural revolution.
- Communal property rights blocked innovation. What France lacked were English-style enclosures that would wipe out the peasants' rights and create the necessary conditions for innovation.
- Farms in France were simply too small. As the population rose—as it did in the late fifteenth and sixteenth centuries, farms were fragmented still further. Again, English style enclosure and farm consolidation were the answer.

Again, recent research has undermined every one of these claims. The French peasants did innovate, when conditions were right, and their technology made more sense than a superficial glance would lead one to suppose. Furthermore, increased productivity in England was not the work of landlords, but of yeomen, the equivalent of the large-scale tenant farmers who tilled the soil in much of northern France. Similarly, enclosures are vastly overrated as a source of higher productivity in early modern agriculture. They contributed little to the advance of English agriculture and even if they had been attempted throughout France, they would not have contributed much to agricultural productivity. The reason is that the communal property rights were rarely the obstacle to innovation that historians once supposed. New crops—artificial fodder, for example—were introduced in many parts of France, despite communal property rights. The real obstacle lay elsewhere, with barriers to trade and insufficient demand.

As for the size of peasant farms as a cause of backwardness, it too has been exaggerated. Large farms did not have higher grain yields— one of the hallmarks of higher productivity—and although they may in some instances have saved on labour, French farmers had no difficulty putting together the appropriately sized farm. Minuscule farms were not the reason for lagging agricultural productivity in early modern France.

Beyond agriculture, one might point to France's lack of colonies and of a commercial empire as the reason for its lacklustre economic performance. But colonies and commercial empires were not the secret of England's or the Netherland's economic success and they certainly did not propel Spain, the early modern period's greatest colonial power, into economic growth.

Another traditional explanation for France's economic stagnation reaches back to the famous German sociologist, Max Weber. He maintained that Protestantism—and specifically Calvinism—created the 'capitalist spirit' that ushered in modern economic growth, by encouraging savings, discipline, devotion to work in the world, and a rational pursuit of profit. France never partook of this spirit—so the argument would go—because of the triumph of Catholicism. As a result, it lost out in the race for economic development. Weber's work has generated a huge, and seemingly unending debate in history, sociology, and economics. But it has fared badly in recent research on early modern religion. This research demonstrates that the traits Weber located in Calvinism permeated Counter-Reformation Catholicism as well. They were hardly peculiar to

Protestantism and were in fact characteristics of the early modern period as a whole.

Yet another weakness of the Weber thesis is that it has rarely had to endure empirical tests. One test—the one most relevant to economic history—would be to see if Calvinists who lived alongside Catholics grew richer than the members of the rival confession. If Weber is correct, and if the Protestants enjoyed the same opportunities as the Catholics, then they would presumably accumulate more wealth, for their faith will drive them to save and to pursue gain relentlessly. Just such a test has been conducted in the southern French city of Montpellier, which happened to be home to roughly balanced communities of Catholics and Protestants. The test was done for the years between the Wars of Religion and the 1660s, a period before Louis XIV's measures began to bear down upon the Calvinists. What the test reveals is that while Protestants generally had more wealth, they showed no tendency to grow richer over time, as the Weber thesis would suggest. Here too the Weber thesis seems to fail.

If Weber cannot account for early modern France's economic stagnation, what about the behaviour of the French bourgeois—the city dwellers and merchants who dominated trade and manufacturing? They have been accused of 'treason', of having abandoned commerce for government offices or for the profits of tax farming. They have also been blamed for not adopting the business techniques that foreign merchants and bankers employed in Lyon, such as bills of exchange. Did their behaviour retard the French economy?

Treason, though, is too harsh a word here, and if merchants leave commerce, the blame ultimately lies elsewhere. Merchants did forsake business for government offices, for tax farming, and for the purchase of rural property and seigneuries; and if they remained in commerce, it was their children who departed. Examples abound: the de Morlaix family in Nantes, the Gadagne in Lyon, and even Montaigne's ancestors. But was that really a sign of a character flaw peculiar to French merchants? The same pattern of behaviour crops up nearly everywhere in Europe—in Italy, and even in England. Only the Netherlands is a possible exception. And all the merchants were doing was responding to incentives, incentives that in large part were the monarchy's creation. If they lent money to the crown (as in sixteenth-century Lyon), it was because they were drawn by the profits of doing so. If they bought government offices and rural seigneuries, it was because these investments were attractive. As we know, the offices promised a return, plus prestige and the possibility of ennoblement. The rural land and seigneuries offered a hedge against inflation and currency manipulations, and a tax shelter as well, at least for the numerous bourgeois with tax exemptions on their rural holdings. Societal attitudes and above all else the government created these incentives, and here the crown must bear the responsibility for the merchants' defection. If the government had not sold offices, manipulated the coinage, or raised taxes, fewer merchants would have given up trade.

It is also difficult to assign French merchants all the blame for their failure to utilize the bills of exchange. Foreigners did monopolize the market for bills of exchange in sixteenth-century Lyon, but it was not simply ignorance or lack of training that kept the French out. When these Italians and Germans settled their accounts every three months at the Lyon fairs, they figured out who owed money to whom, and they wrote new bills of exchange to carry the credit of those who still owed money. They would only extend credit to merchants and bankers whom they knew well: other Italian and German merchants and bankers who could be trusted to settle their debts. The same sort of trust underlay the sale of the bills of exchange; only bills from known firms with a reputation on the exchange could easily be sold.

In a way, the Lyon fairs resembled the informal credit that financed village transactions. And as in the villages, it was nearly impossible to extend credit to newcomers whose credit histories were unknown. How could they be trusted? It is thus easy to understand why French merchants did not use bills of exchange, for they simply could not break into the market. They were unknown and had no way to create a reputation for trust.

In the other great financial centre of sixteenth-century Europe—Antwerp—merchants faced a similar problem, but they discovered a way to break free from the confines of a credit market based on reputation and personal knowledge. Over the course of the sixteenth century, they developed a different sort of financial market, one in which bills of exchange and other financial instruments were traded much as cheques are today, via the practice of endorsement. The whole process was slow and depended on a number of legal changes. But it created a financial market that was open to newcomers in a way that the Lyon market was not. All sorts of outsiders could finance their trade in Antwerp, and when the same practices were transferred to Amsterdam and pushed even further, they gave the Netherlands a great financial advantage in the seventeenth century. Amsterdam in fact became the European market for financing trade.

Could French merchants have developed such a financial market back in sixteenth-century Lyon? Probably not. The trouble was that the existing system—the closed market of foreign merchants and bankers—functioned too well. Although it was in foreign hands, it did successfully finance international trade. There was also less incentive to innovate than in Antwerp, for largely accidental reasons: Antwerp had more newcomers pressing to get into the market, and legal decisions made it difficult for the established merchants there to rely on the sort of financial system that worked in Lyon. In short, it is unfair to blame French merchants for failing to imitate Antwerp. And once Amsterdam had perfected its financial market, French merchants had even less reason to innovate, for they could now depend on Amsterdam. It was now the financial centre of Europe, the storehouse of goods and of information about trade between Europe, Asia, and the New World. French merchants would have been fools had they attempted to build their own financial system. It would have been as quixotic as creating a new operating system for modern PCs.

The remaining causes of France's economic stagnation all involve politics, and they suggest that the monarchy bears much of the blame for France's failure to keep up with England and the Netherlands. We have already noted that the monarchy devoted far less to canals than the Netherlands. Its spending on roads was also disappointing, and in contrast to England, there was no body of private road builders who could pick up the slack. The result was a higher cost of transportation, and government suspicion of middlemen only compounded the problem. The consequences were particularly severe for farming, which depended on low transport costs for growth.

The crown's foreign policy—in particular, the wars it waged—were even worse for the economy. Some of the effects were indirect. If merchants abandoned trade, it was in large part because of the incentives created by rising taxes, by the sale of offices, and by currency manipulations—all financial measures chosen by the monarchy to meet the rising costs of warfare. Similarly, French merchants might have had a greater hand in trade with the New World if the crown had given them greater support. But doing so would have necessitated changes in a foreign policy that was dictated by interests in Europe.

The damage that war did to the French economy was terrible. Warfare, especially civil war, could bring commerce and manufacturing to its knees. The Wars of Religion halted the export of wine and salt from Brittany and hobbled textile manufacturing in Amiens. The harm went beyond suspended shipments and idled looms. When the French government borrowed to finance warfare and then defaulted on its loans—as was the case in sixteenth-century Lyon—it helped drive away the foreign merchants and bankers who had made the city a centre of European finance. But the economic injuries war inflicted were greatest in agriculture. The rising taxes that paid for the wars bore down most heavily on the countryside, where tax collectors seized grain and livestock—essential agriculture capital—when peasants fell into arrears. Marauding troops, even when they were French, made similar exactions, and often farmers fled when armies approached. With farms abandoned and fields unploughed, weeds grew up and turned to brush, as farm land reverted to waste. In relatively short times, years of labour invested in reclaiming land would be lost, and in an era before steel ploughs, it could take a generation to recover.

The risks could drive nearly a whole generation of farmers to the edge of bankruptcy—as near Paris in the middle of the seventeenth century—and thus wipe out skills that were difficult to replace. Worse yet, these risks discouraged the survivors from undertaking new investments. One might think that the situation elsewhere would not have been much different, but across the English Channel, it turns out, the dangers were far less. Is it any wonder then that English farmers soared ahead of their French counterparts?

Economic stagnation did not mean a complete lack of change in the early modern French economy. Outcomes varied greatly from region to region and across the centuries, and a number of economic trends reshaped French society: the great increase in taxation, the rise of the Atlantic, and the gradual shift of resources from city to countryside. Stagnation did reinforce, though, the grim demographic patterns of hunger and mortality that were common to all of Europe. Because the French economy did not grow, the French were poorer than the Dutch, and, unlike the English, they had to wait until the eighteenth century to escape subsistence crises.

No doubt the French would have fared better if the monarchy

tempered its appetite for wars and if the country had never been riven by the Wars of Religion. Total peace was perhaps unthinkable in early modern Europe, particularly in a country surrounded by enemies and divided between two hostile confessions. Still, it might have been possible to do without some of the wars: the invasion of Italy, for instance, or the denouement of the Thirty Years War and the prolongation of the struggle with Spain. And one might even imagine France's escaping the worst excesses of the Wars of Religion. In such an imaginary world, the French would have been much better off.

4

Gender and the family

Barbara B. Diefendorf

Images of the father as sovereign in his family and of the king as father to his subjects flowed naturally from the pens of sixteenth- and seventeenth-century political theorists. Paternal authority was not merely an analogy for monarchical authority, it was considered the necessary complement to the king's powers in the well-run monarchical state. Jean Bodin summed up this view in his *Six Books of the Commonwealth*, first published in 1576, when he wrote that 'the family, which is the source and origin of all republics, is the principal member of it'. It followed for Bodin that the ideal family, like the ideal republic, was authoritarian and patriarchal. Governed by commandment and obedience, strong families were the building blocks of a strong state.

Enshrining the family as the very foundation of the state, early modern political philosophy justified royal intervention into aspects of private life previously left to individual agreement or, because marriage was a sacrament, to the supervision of the Church. It also reinforced traditional gender hierarchies. The idea that the female sex was naturally inferior to the male was at least as old and deeply ingrained in Western philosophical traditions as the analogy between father and king, and the head of the early modern family was in theory at least presumed to be a male.

The realities of family life were necessarily more complex than patriarchal theory would suggest. In practice, family relationships and gender roles both affirmed and subverted the hierarchical and paternalistic lines of authority that in theory governed them.

Emotions within the family ran strong, and mutual affection, even passionate love, coexisted with negative feelings born of the demand to subordinate individual desires to the common good. This chapter will examine the internal dynamics of early modern French families from four perspectives. It will look first at the legal structures governing marriage, inheritance, and property-holding; second at the domestic economy and in particular women's formal and informal role in this economy; and third at the impact of religious change on family relationships, child-rearing practices, and gender roles. A final section will take up the problem of social deviance as viewed through the prism of gender expectations and their violation. In each case, we will see that theories of patriarchal authority shaped but did not dictate actual behaviour.

Marriage and inheritance in French law

For the Catholic Church, marriage was first and foremost a sacrament, a mystical union of two individuals before God. Ecclesiastical courts adjudicated broken promises of marriage, cases of adultery, and other actions deemed to threaten the sacramental bond between husband and wife. But marriage was not just a private union. It joined families in a complex web of economic and social relations. That is why, at least among the middling classes and elites, arranging marriage was the business of parents and guardians and not of the young couple to be wed. That is also why the signing of the contract that set out the financial rights and obligations of the respective parties to a marriage was often as momentous an occasion as the wedding celebration itself.

In rural France, and especially in the South, married men sometimes continued to live under the roof—and hence under the authority—of their fathers. It was more common, however, for a married man to set up his own household. Within this household, he exerted an unquestioned authority over not only his children but also his wife. Married women had no independent existence within the law. They could not testify in court or buy and sell property in their own name. A woman was expected to bring money and domestic goods as a dowry when she wed. If she came from a wealthy family, she might also bring lands. Once married, her husband assumed responsibility for her property, and she could not dispose of it without his consent. Early modern legal treatises tended to justify women's legal incapacity with statements about the inherently weak, frivolous, and light-headed nature of the female sex. These misogynistic statements reflected both the medical view that women were imperfect, or defective men, and the Biblical idea that Eve was responsible for Adam's fall. When pressed, however, most jurists were willing to admit that married women had no legal capacity because they were married and not because they were women. The real basis of the laws requiring them to submit to the authority of their husbands lay in the belief that the household, like the state, could have but one head.

Ironically, the same hierarchical principle that gave husbands dominion over their wives very often allowed a woman, once her husband died, to step into his role as head of the household and assume responsibility for managing her own and her children's affairs. Men showed the confidence they had in their wives' practical intelligence in the frequency with which they chose them, rather than male relatives, to administer their estates and oversee their children's inheritances if they died. In the South, where Roman law traditions gave the head of the household much more freedom in disposing of his estate than did the customary law traditions of northern and central France, we even quite commonly find wills in which a man designated his wife as his universal heir, explicitly trusting her to manage the family's finances and provide for their children's education, marriages, and careers. And if in theory the children came into their paternal inheritance when they came of age at 25, in practice some widows retained control of the paternal estate throughout their lives. This could be a cause of tension between mothers and their adult children, as Montaigne pointed out when he deplored the 'error of judgment in some fathers . . ., who are not content with depriving their children during their long lifetime of the share they naturally ought to have had in their fortunes, but afterward also leave to their wives this same authority over all their possessions and the right to dispose of them according to their fancy'.[1]

---

[1] Michel de Montaigne, *The Complete Essays of Michel de Montaigne*, trans. Donald M. Frame (Stanford, Calif., 1958), p. 288.

Obviously, the freedom that Roman law traditions permitted in the naming of heirs could be an important source of tension between fathers and their children and a cause of envy and conflict among siblings as well. The few studies that have been done of actual practice nevertheless suggest that, among commoners at least, parents often tried to moderate these tensions by establishing a rough parity among heirs rather than favouring one or another child. Even when parents chose to keep their lands intact by passing them to just one child, usually a son, they frequently required the favoured heir to compensate his siblings by paying them a cash portion or annuity. There is less evidence than one might expect that this testamentary freedom was used to favour sons over daughters and the eldest over younger sons.

In areas subject to customary law, the strict rules that governed the division of family properties may have helped reduce inter-generational tensions by removing the element of personal whim. The fact that one's inheritance was largely dictated by law did not, however, necessarily appease the jealousy felt by children whose sex or order of birth entitled them to a smaller share of the parental estate than other siblings received. These jealousies would have been relatively mild in areas where egalitarian tendencies were strong, with laws that gave only a moderate advantage to the eldest son in noble families and otherwise treated sons and daughters alike. In the region of Paris, for example, among commoners, all of the children in the family had an equal claim to their parent's estate. Even married daughters might share in the estate by deducting the amount they had previously received as a dowry from their share of their parents' wealth. In aristocratic families, the eldest son received two-thirds of the family's noble lands if he had but one sibling and half if there was more than one, but he received exactly the same portion of non-noble lands and personal properties as his siblings. While still favouring the eldest son, these inheritance practices encouraged aristocratic families to establish all of their children well and created broad networks of collateral kin whose influence and favours could be used for the benefit of all.

By contrast, Norman law limited the share of the estate that could go to daughters. All of the daughters together could receive no more than a third of the estate, and no daughter could receive more than the smallest portion given to a son. On the other hand, the law mandated strict equality among the sons. Even in noble families, the only advantage given the eldest was the right to choose one of the family's fiefs in place of the share of properties he would otherwise receive. If he failed to exercise this option, it passed to the next brother in turn. In this way, Norman law achieved a compromise between the very high value it placed on fraternal equality and the desire to maintain an aristocratic family's dignity by keeping intact its principal estate.

The variation in local inheritance practices was much debated among sixteenth-century jurists, some of whom favoured creating a common code of private law that would apply to all of the kingdom. In the end, however, the weight of inherited tradition proved too strong. Believing that local practice was the very foundation of the law, French jurists settled for recording as yet unwritten local customs and amending antiquated compendiums of laws that no longer conformed to actual practice. They did not attempt to change or unify the laws themselves.

But if jurists refused to tamper with local traditions of private law, French monarchs did not show the same restraint. Between the mid-sixteenth and the mid-seventeenth centuries, they repeatedly issued edicts intended to reinforce parental control over marriage. They justified their intervention into a domain previously considered to belong strictly to the Church on the grounds that family honour and family fortunes were endangered by the insistence of Roman Catholic theologians that, as the sacramental union of two individuals before God, marriage required only the consent of the parties wed. At the heart of the issue was the fear of misalliance—the fear that children from good families would destroy their parents' expectations by running off with unworthy suitors or socially unacceptable brides.

François Rabelais captured well this pervading fear when he wrote that the situation permitted any 'scoundrel, criminal, rogue, or gallowsbird' to 'snatch up any maiden he chooses—never mind how lovely, rich, modest or bashful she may be—out of her father's house, out of her mother's arms, and in spite of all her relations'. Grieving with the brides' stricken parents, Rabelais mourned the ruin of their carefully nurtured plans to marry their daughters to 'the sons of their neighbors and old friends' and their eager anticipation of 'the birth of children from these happy marriages, who would inherit and preserve not only the morals of their fathers and mothers but also their goods and lands'.[2]

The idea that virtue was an inherited quality was central to the emphasis on good breeding, or lineage, that pervades sixteenth- and seventeenth-century demands for laws that would increase parental control over marriage. Coupled with the related notion that strong families were essential to a strong state, the belief served to justify the crown's progressive attempts to regulate marriage. The first royal intervention into marriage occurred in 1556 with an edict allowing parents to disinherit children who wed without their consent. The law applied to sons up to the age of 30 and daughters to the age of 25, after which they were still required to seek their father and mother's advice but could nevertheless marry without their consent.

. Separating for the first time the civil effects of marriage from its sacramental character, the 1556 law nevertheless failed to satisfy irate parents, who wanted not just to disinherit disobedient children but actually to have their wedding vows annulled. Annulment, however, was the prerogative of the Church, and French kings had to tread lightly here. When the Council of Trent closed in 1563 without handing down a strict ruling against clandestine marriage, there was new pressure on the king to take such step. Henry III responded in 1579 with an ordinance requiring greater publicity for marriage and threatening the death penalty for anyone who eloped with a minor, regardless of whether the minor claimed to have consented to the elopement. The ordinance also threatened to punish priests who performed clandestine marriages as accessories to the crime of abduction (*rapt*). These laws were repeated on several occasions, and in 1629 Louis XIII took an additional step towards nullifying marriages that lacked parental approval by declaring them not validly contracted. Ten years later, yet another law further reinforced earlier provisions against illicit marriages. Recognizing that parents often-times dropped their opposition to a child's elopement in the face of the returned child's tears, the law insisted that seducers be punished by death notwithstanding any later consent the parents might give. It also visited the effects of clandestine marriage on the next generation by declaring that the children born from such unions should forever

---

[2] François Rabelais, *The Histories of Gargantua and Pantagruel*, trans. J. M. Cohen (London, 1955), pp. 419–20.

be deprived of any claim to the family estate. Although still careful not to intrude upon the sacramental nature of marriage, French kings had by 1639 nevertheless gained an important role in regulating its civil effects. Responding to pressure from French elites determined to protect their social position and wealth by tightening controls over the next generation, the kings had gradually acquired the power to intervene in marriage even over a family's opposition.

The laws against clandestine marriage gave mothers and fathers equal authority over the alliances formed by their children, but a set of contemporaneous laws concerning second marriages shows a clear bias against women. A 1560 edict accused widows who remarried of failing to recognize that they were sought more for their wealth than for their persons. The law claimed that, showering their new husbands with extravagant presents, these women deprived their children of their rightful inheritance and thereby undermined both the family and the state. The same law applied to widowers, but, explicitly framed in terms of the 'infirmity' of the female sex, it was women, not men, who stood accused of allowing their new love to overcome their sense of family responsibility. A 1567 edict limiting the right of mothers to inherit property from deceased children similarly presumed that, in remarrying, a mother was likely to place a new husband's wishes above her children's rights. Still, we should be wary of placing too much emphasis on the misogynistic rhetoric in these laws. Remarriage—particularly the remarriage of widows—had always provoked family tensions and fears that new family ties would come to supplant the old. And yet, in practice, remarried widows continued to be favoured as guardians of the children of their previous marriages. If they shared the responsibility for managing the children's inheritance with anyone, it was more likely to be their new husband than one of the deceased husband's kin.

Household management and the domestic economy

In the realms of household management and the domestic economy, the respective roles of husband and wife were also more flexible in practice than we might assume from patriarchal theory. A woman was expected to contribute to the household economy through the dowry that she brought to her marriage and the labour that she supplied thereafter. This labour might exist only within the confines of the household, where it received little recognition and no financial compensation, but its contribution to the family's welfare was no less crucial on that account. Rural wives typically tended the barnyard animals and the fruit and vegetable gardens. The butter, eggs, and produce they marketed in neighbouring towns provided an essential part of the family's cash income. Women also helped with threshing, harvesting, and other tasks customarily performed by men. Unless a family was relatively wealthy and its holdings extensive enough to provide all of the income the family required, its male and female members alike supplemented the income from their own lands by hiring themselves out to neighbouring farmers.

Among the nobility, women had long been responsible for managing the family's estates while their husbands were travelling, at court, or at war. Their domestic skills necessarily included knowledge of the seasonal work necessary upon the land. Even if a hired manager oversaw the daily labours of the peasants on the estate, the lady of the manor needed to insure that both he and the peasants were serving her well. This meant understanding the nature and timing of work on the land, the care of livestock, property and tax laws, and family finances. Noble women living in fortified castles also had to understand armaments and, in the absence of their husbands, to be prepared to organize the castle's defence.

By the sixteenth and seventeenth centuries, the tendency of urban notables to purchase large estates outside their towns meant that the wives of magistrates and even bourgeois had to assume many of the same responsibilities as the wives of country gentlemen. A letter from Anne Baillet, the wife of a prominent Parisian magistrate, asking her daughter-in-law, Jeanne Luillier, to tend to certain affairs on her estates shows the broad range of responsibilities that might be considered women's work. Baillet instructed Luillier to inspect her house and mills at Bourneville, supervise some construction in progress there, and interview a new manager for the estate. She also asked her to superintend the winemaking on another property, inspect the accounts of her managers at two other estates, insure that her woods were well guarded and problems with poaching had ceased, draw up an inventory of the furnishings for one manor house, and make a list of the poor deserving charity on two of the properties. Baillet's son, also a magistrate, was heading out to the country at the same time, but for him she had only one request. He was to see that the officers of seigneurial justice on her estates were fair and honourable in their decisions.

In the cities, it is also often difficult clearly to separate women's work from their domestic responsibilities. Although many women worked independently in the crafts or trades, very often married women's work was an extension of that performed by their husbands. If the head of the household was a master craftsman or merchant whose business was run out of the family home, he frequently enjoyed considerable assistance from his wife. Just how much help she gave depended on how much time she had available (which in turn depended, among other things, on the age and number of children the family had) but also on the nature of the husband's work. Wives provided less help, for example, in blacksmithing and other forms of metalworking than they did with provisioning and textile trades, which 'could sometimes involve the woman so much that she took on a joint work identity with her husband'.[3] The wife of a baker, for instance, might run the shop while her husband and his journeymen mixed the dough, tended the ovens, and baked the bread. Women also sometimes worked alongside husbands who were printers and barber-surgeons, although guild rules and limits on women's education meant that their participation in these trades was more limited than where preparation of foodstuffs or textiles were concerned. Wives of merchants might also be heavily involved in their husband's business, especially when it required extensive travel on his part. Thus we find a number of wives and even some daughters of wood merchants representing their husbands and fathers at a civic assembly in Paris held to discuss a grave shortage of firewood during the cold winter of 1571.

Not all women, however, worked at home or in association with the men in their household. Midwifery was a classic women's trade, passed on through formal or informal apprenticeships, at least until 1560, when royal legislation began to move the trade under the

[3] Natalie Zemon Davies, 'Women and the Crafts in Sixteenth-Century Lyon', in Barbara A. Hanawalt (ed.), *Women and Work in Preindustrial Europe* (Bloomington, Ind., 1986), p. 174.

supervision of the male barber-surgeon's guild. Women also worked independently as linen merchants, tavern keepers, and traders in grain, among other commercial activities. Licensed as 'public merchants', they were freed from the legal restrictions that normally applied to women and could buy and sell freely in their own names. In smaller scale commerce—retail shops and city markets—women were a constant, if not a dominant presence. One Italian visitor to Paris in 1596 commented that women, more than men, seemed to run the city's shops.

There were far fewer organized crafts for women than for men in the sixteenth and seventeenth centuries, and their range was generally more limited. Rouen and Paris each had four exclusively female guilds, all of them associated with the manufacture and sale of clothing and women's finery. Girls also, however, learned artisanal skills while working as household servants or in their parents' home. Whether or not they continued to practise these skills after marriage depended largely on their husband's occupation and whether or not the household was better served by assisting with his trade or continuing an independent one.

The work options available to widows were also largely dependent upon the occupations of their deceased husbands. Many guilds allowed widows to continue to practise their husband's trade, although they were forbidden to take on new apprentices and sometimes had to employ journeymen to assist in their work. Charlotte Guillard carried on her deceased husband's printing trade for more than twenty years, employing as many as twenty-five or thirty workers at any given time. Wealthy widows unable to carry on their husband's profession invested their revenues at interest, thereby playing an important role in both local and royal capital markets. Of course many, if not most widows were not wealthy. Like other poor women, they found work where they could. They peddled cheap trinkets or foodstuffs, took in washing, and joined with men in seeking daily or short-term employment as unskilled labourers. Where possible, they enlisted on public relief rolls, which always contained a high proportion of female names. As a last resort, they defied laws against public begging and sought handouts in church squares and city streets.

Did women's economic role change between the early sixteenth and mid-seventeenth centuries? This is hard to judge, because economic activity was traditionally measured in terms of households and not individuals. There is some evidence to suggest that women did play a greater part in commercial and financial transactions in 1650 than they had a century and a half earlier. They took advantage of the expansion of the market economy in the sixteenth century to assume a greater economic independence. This development was not, however, entirely favourable in its consequences. One historian has suggested that women's assumption of a larger public role provoked a negative reaction. 'As long as the household remained the central economic unit', he explains, 'the critical role played by the woman of the household was effectively disguised behind her public powerlessness. What is more, her private importance did not threaten the patriarchal power structure'. As soon as women did attempt to assume a greater economic independence, the patriarchal order responded by attempting to limit women's opportunities and sphere of activity. A more repressive atmosphere resulted, further increasing the disparity between women's public powerlessness and the private importance of their economic contributions.[4]

Women, the family, and religious change

If sixteenth-century economic changes reinforced the apparent contradictions between women's public and private roles, so too did the religious changes brought about by the Protestant and Catholic Reformations. Noblewomen helped spread the Protestant Reformation in France by offering their protection and patronage to evangelical preachers and exposing their husbands and sons to the new faith. Jeanne d'Albret, queen of Navarre, is the most famous but not the only aristocratic woman who used her right of high justice to establish Protestant churches on her lands—just as her son Henry of Navarre is the most famous but not the only son of a Protestant noblewoman who took up arms for the Huguenot cause. It has been suggested that Protestantism's appeal for these women derived largely from the sense of autonomy they gained from the Protestants'

---

[4] James B. Collins, 'The Economic Role of Women in Seventeenth-Century France', *French Historical Studies*, 16: 2 (Fall 1989), 436–70 (quote on 467).

emphasis on reading the Bible for oneself and from the doctrine of justification by faith.

These aristocratic women, however, already enjoyed an unusual degree of independence as a result of their wealth and status as the wives and daughters of powerful noblemen frequently absent in the service of the king. Did Protestantism bring the same sense of autonomy to ordinary women? Probably not. Except among elites, few women living in the sixteenth-century could read the Bible—or any other book—for themselves. Reading and writing were skills acquired by far more men than women in the sixteenth century. Virtually all peasants and women from the urban working classes were illiterate, as were many women from artisanal families. Literacy was much more common among daughters of merchants and men in liberal professions, but even here it was far from complete.

Even if women could read, moreover, they were not encouraged to interpret the Bible themselves. Men also were urged to leave the interpretation of scripture to trained ministers, but women in particular were reminded of St Paul's injunction that they should remain silent in church. These passages of the Bible were used effectively to silence the small handful of women whose enthusiasm in the early days of the Reformation led them to speak publicly or to write on theological matters. French Calvinists taught that women should help provide young children with their first education in the faith, but they made the male head of the household ultimately responsible for his family's religious education and practice.

Abolishing the ideal of a celibate clergy, Protestant preachers praised the virtues of family life. Encouraging married men and women to seek companionship from their spouses, they placed a new emphasis on the emotional bonds of marriage and, some historians have suggested, thereby helped valorize women's domestic role. On the other hand, Catholic humanists also praised companionate marriage, so this development was not unique to the Protestant faith. The idea of companionate marriage, moreover, was not inconsistent with female subordination. Neither Catholic nor Protestant preachers envisioned marriage as a partnership of equals. They continued to view it as an association in which the husband, as teacher and leader, retained the dominant role.

If Protestants helped valorize married life as a praiseworthy vocation for women, they closed off the celibate life of the cloister as a valid option. In this way women lost the measure of independence from male domination that the cloister provided, as well as the opportunities the exclusively female convent community offered to learn and exercise leadership roles. They also lost certain reassuring rituals and forms of collective worship—confraternities, pilgrimages, and processions—castigated by Protestant reformers as superstitious and full of error. They could no longer address their petitions to the Virgin Mary, the sympathetic mother they had been taught to venerate from earliest childhood. Nor could they call out to St Margaret when the pains of childbirth grew too strong to bear. The saints had no place in Protestant worship, and the Holy Family was reduced to its male members—Father and Son—alone.

Throughout much of the sixteenth-century, convent life in France was in such disarray and disrepute that it might be said to have better served the propaganda purposes of Protestant reformers than its Catholic nuns. Stories of nuns entertaining clerics (and laymen) and giving birth to their illegitimate sons were often but not always fables spun by Protestant propagandists intent upon discrediting Catholic religious life. And if such stories were most often exaggerations, if not outright lies, religious houses were nevertheless filled with nuns who lacked a true vocation. A great many convents had fallen away from their original rule.

Convent life in sixteenth-century France was largely the preserve of elites. Few new houses had been founded in the later Middle Ages, and the old abbeys and convents in the French countryside had long since fallen under the domination of aristocrats who viewed them as an extension of their power and wealth. They installed their daughters as superiors in order to profit from convent revenues and, allowing religious standards to decline, permitted the houses to become the refuge of surplus daughters whose families preferred the lesser dowry required to enter religious life to the greater one required for a socially acceptable marriage. Fulfilling their religious obligations unenthusiastically, if at all, many nuns refused to abandon luxuries they believed appropriate to their social station for the poverty promised in their religious vows. They wore habits tailored of fine fabrics instead of the coarse cloth prescribed by their rule, lived in comfortably furnished apartments instead of simple cells, and ate delicacies in private instead of sharing simple fare in the convent's refectory. They blatantly violated the rules of strict cloistering by leaving the convent to visit their families or take part in urban processions and welcomed visitors with a complete abandonment of rules that required all but the closest of kin to speak only through a heavily shrouded grille.

Exposed to evangelical preaching by priests who had embraced the Protestant reforms, some nuns did leave their convents and married or returned to their families. Others, subjected to the same teachings, refused to convert and fiercely defended their way of life. Protestant attacks on monastic life made it more difficult for Catholic reformers to enact programmes for change for fear of getting caught up in accusations of heresy. It was easier—and safer—to defend the principle of monasticism and ignore any abuses in its practice. When orthodox Catholics did call for reforms in convent life, moreover, many nuns initially resisted the call for change. For some, it was a simple question of preserving a privileged style of living doomed to disappear with any reform. For others, resistance to reform was inseparable from a will to avoid outside interference and protect a cherished autonomy.

Only at the very end of the sixteenth century did momentum gain for the reform of old convents and the creation of new houses where a high ideal of religious life could be put into effect. The decades of civil and religious war, in particular the crisis of the Holy League, spurred apocalyptic fears and a penitential piety that in turn prompted the creation of new monastic institutions where lives of ascetic penitence might be the rule. The founding of austere new contemplative convents was just the first stage in a broader renewal of Catholic devotional life that began in the early seventeenth century. We shall return to the subject of women's participation in this Catholic revival (often referred to as the 'Catholic Reformation' or the 'Counter-Reformation') in a later chapter, where we will consider their active role in founding new contemplative orders but also the beginnings of an active apostolate for women, who began to leave the seclusion of enclosed convents to provide nursing care, religious instruction, and other charitable services to the urban and rural poor. We cannot, however, abandon questions of gender without looking more closely at the problem of women who refused to conform to prescribed gender roles.

Gender and social deviance

For many people, Counter-Reformation convents are best known through popular treatments of the mass demonic possession that occurred among the Ursulines of Loudun between 1633 and 1640. The image of nuns suffering convulsions and contortions, obscenely cursing their confessors and superiors, and otherwise behaving in a repellant fashion has left an indelible impression on many minds. And Loudun was not the only incident of its kind. Mass possessions also occurred at the Ursuline convent of Aix-en-Provence in 1611–13, among the Hospitalers of Louviers in 1643–7, and in various other French and European cities. Historians have most often diagnosed these incidents as the product of mental disorders—or 'hysteria'—brought on by the harsh conditions and boredom of convent life. But labelling these possessed nuns as 'hysterics' does not help us to understand why the incidents occurred. A more productive approach has emerged from recent research, which sees the cases as a rather more natural outgrowth of conditions within the convents that contributed to the nuns' vulnerability.

Even for girls who had a religious vocation, life in a Counter-Reformation convent was stressful, with its strong emphasis on ascetic renunciation as a path to God and the requirement constantly to scrutinize one's least thought and action for signs of sin. When this intense self-scrutiny was cultivated by women who from earliest childhood had internalized the message that their sex was weak and their bodies easily seduced by the devil's charms, the fear of being possessed by a malefic spirit could easily result. In a culture that accepted both positive and negative spirit possession as natural but was profoundly suspicious of female spirituality, demonic possession thus appears as a perhaps inevitable counterpart to mystical possession of a positive sort, or rapture in God. The male clerics responsible for examining cases of alleged possession among women found it easier to attribute their mystical experiences to the devil than to God. Conditioned to self-doubt, the women accepted this judgement and even began to act the part. One historian has recently suggested that the most bizarre symptoms, in particular the unrestrained sexuality, displayed by possessed nuns only appeared after their affliction was diagnosed as demonically possessed. Only after the exorcists had ruled out divine rapture did they begin to re-enact symptoms popularly associated with demonic possession. Oral tradition but also published accounts of alleged incidents of demonic possession may thus have inadvertently instructed disturbed girls in the behaviours that would confirm the suspicion that evil spirits were responsible for their unseemly actions.

The case of Nicole Obry in 1565–6, otherwise known as Nicole de Vervins, occurred outside a convent and did not set off a mass reaction—at least not an immediate reaction—and yet it too seems to fit this chronology. Nicole Obry's possession began at the age of 16 with visions of her dead grandfather, who begged the living to help free him from purgatory. Obry began to suffer some bodily symptoms shortly after her possession began. She suddenly fell and lay on the floor 'as stiff as a board'; she also complained that her dead grandfather threatened to twist her arms and legs if the family did not complete the prayers and pilgrimages he demanded of them. It was, however, only after the local priest decided to conduct an exorcism that the symptoms classically associated with demonic possession took hold, with prolonged fits, obscene utterances, and bizarre distortions of body and face.

The case also supports the theory that spirit possession allowed women to engage in the theological discourse from which they were normally excluded on account of their sex. More than 150,000 people witnessed one stage or another the exorcisms performed to rid Nicole Obry's tormented body of possessing demons over a more than six-month period. The episode coincided with the troubled period between the first and second Wars of Religion and was used by Catholic authorities to propagandize against their Protestant enemies. In addition to the exorcisms, they staged public processions around the possessed girl to demonstrate the diabolical nature of Calvinism and warn that tolerating heresy threatened to bring down the wrath of God. Through Nicole Obry's voice, the devil called out to Huguenot ministers, recognizing them as his minions. Through her gestures, in particular through her acceptance or rejection of the consecrated host, the truth of Catholic rituals was acted out. In this way, Nicole Obry gained a role in the on-going debate over the nature of religious truth that her sex would otherwise have denied her. And yet, precisely because of her sex, Nicole Obry's agency here—in fiction or reality—

was limited. She could not speak in her own voice; rather, demons spoke through her, and, however fierce the battles that raged in and through her body, the victories were attributed not to her own powers but rather to Christ.

Accepting the notion of spirit possession as a matter of course, both common people and elites found it entirely credible that an individual could invoke the devil's powers for the working of harm. The era of demonic possession was also the era of the 'great witch craze'. The same supposed susceptibility to the devil's blandishments that made women the victims of the large majority of accusations of demonic possession caused them to be identified as the perpetrators in a disproportionately large number of witchcraft cases. Unlike the possessed nuns, who were largely young and from middle-class families, however, accused witches were most often elderly and poor. They were typically aging peasant women, often widows who had fallen on hard times and were believed to be harbouring old grudges that, impotent to enact other forms of revenge, they avenged through evil spells and demonic malevolence. As with the possessed girls, then, women were targeted as witches because of special vulnerabilities associated with both their gender and their situation in life.

Witch accusations peaked during the last two decades of the sixteenth century and may be attributable at least indirectly to social dislocations brought about by the prolonged period of civil and religious war. The magnitude of the 'witch craze' in France has, however, frequently been exaggerated. Firm numbers are impossible, but the best recent estimate holds that only 500 convicted witches were put to death by French courts between 1560 and 1670. By contrast, more than 2,000 condemned witches were executed in the neighbouring duchy of Lorraine, which had close cultural ties to France but still lay outside the boundaries of the kingdom. As the figures from Lorraine indicate, the 'witch craze', if it existed at all, was largely a localized and sporadic phenomenon. Many areas of France appear to have escaped it entirely, although it is not clear how many accusations occurred on a strictly local level and were resolved through informal action or counter-magic without ever finding their way into the courts. Witch accusations occurred most frequently in rural and forest lands, where there was a marked reluctance to bring local affairs under the scrutiny of outside authorities. It is probable, then, that many if not most cases left no trace in written records. The execution of convicted witches dropped off, first gradually after 1610 and then more sharply after 1640, not because either people or magistrates ceased to believe in witches but rather because the educated men called upon to judge these cases became more sceptical about their ability to identify witches, given the lack of evidence usually associated with accusations of malevolent harm.

In fact it was not witchcraft but rather infanticide that was the crime for which women were most often executed between the mid-sixteenth and the mid-seventeenth centuries. Between 1565 and 1625 the Parlement of Paris, which served as a high court of appeal for more than half of the French population, sentenced 57 women to death for the crime of witchcraft but 625 women—eleven times as many—for the crime of infanticide. The historian whose exacting studies of criminal justice in the Parlement of Paris produced these startling statistics has further noted that at the height of the 'infanticide craze' (between roughly 1565 and 1690) the crime accounted for fully two-thirds of all death sentences meted out by Parlement to women and as much as one-third of all of the court's cases—both sexes considered—that resulted in the death penalty. 'For more than one hundred years,' he concludes, 'infanticide trials—not witchcraft trials ... constituted the major *legal* outlet for the misogynistic feelings so prevalent in early modern society.'[5]

Just what was the crime that the magistrates found so threatening? Almost all of the infanticide cases brought before the Parlement of Paris followed the same pattern. A woman conceived a child illegitimately, hid her pregnancy, and gave birth in secret, whereupon she killed the baby or let it die in hope of permanently concealing her shame. When caught, the woman invariably claimed that the infant had been born dead. In over 60 per cent of the cases the accused was an unmarried woman (very often a domestic servant), with the remainder consisting largely of young widows and married women whose husbands were absent. Only very rarely did the accused name an accomplice, and when she did it was more often her mother than the father of the child. Infanticide was thus the crime of desperate women in a society that identified women's honour above all with

[5] Alfred Soman, 'Anatomy of an Infanticide Trial: The Case of Marie-Jeanne Bartonnet (1742)', in Michael Wolfe (ed.), *Changing Identities in Early Modern France* (Durham, NC, 1997), p. 252.

chastity and offered few options once this honour was lost. In a period in which elites were increasingly preoccupied with raising standards of morality, women accused of infanticide served as scapegoats for a whole raft of other crimes involving honour, illicit sexuality, and other violations of social norms.

Infanticide had long been a capital crime in France, but until 1557 it was one that often escaped punishment because it was difficult to prove without a confession. Even with the application of torture, confessions were difficult to obtain. By the mid-sixteenth century, moreover, the Parlement of Paris was carefully regulating the use of torture in order to improve its own public image and that of the king as the fount of French justice. In February 1557 an edict of Henry II resolved the court's quandary by making infanticide a special case, or *crimen exceptum*, in French law. Thereafter, in the case of a dead baby, a woman found to have concealed her pregnancy and given birth secretly was automatically to be presumed guilty of child murder and sentenced to death. Torture could be eliminated because the court no longer required a confession. It needed only to convict the accused of having first failed to declare her pregnancy to a responsible person and then concealed the birth itself, so that no one could testify whether or not the infant was indeed stillborn.

The 1557 edict resulted in a dramatic rise in the rate of convictions for infanticide but also—as a consequence—in the number of cases brought before the high court. Obviously, lower magistrates had previously hesitated to prosecute cases of suspected infanticide because they did not want to waste time and money on a prosecution that appeared to have little chance of success. The 1557 edict on infanticide, like contemporaneous edicts on clandestine and second marriage, represents a new intrusion of monarchical authority into the private lives of French subjects. At the same time that it shows a broadening of royal powers, it demonstrates a greater willingness on the part of the magisterial elite charged with adjudicating these cases to use their legal authority to enforce more rigid codes of conduct in the kingdom. Inscribing gender roles in a natural order that reinforced their own sense of moral superiority, elite men justified and maintained their dominant role in a hierarchical and patriarchal society.

We must nevertheless be careful not to mistake the ideologies that justified this dominance for the more complex social realities they sought to contain. The same magistrates who enforced the laws that placed women securely under the authority of husbands or fathers, limited their rights to acquire or dispose of property, and attributed to them a moral weakness not shared by the male sex, depended upon their own wives' invaluable contributions to the domestic economy. They trusted them to manage the complex business of the country estates that often provided a large part of their income and frequently made them guardians of their children and administrators of their properties upon their death. Merchants and artisans too often worked in a partnership with wives that belied the public powerlessness of the female sex. For their part, women manoeuvred within the written laws and unwritten presumptions of a hierarchical and gendered society, sometimes victims of rules they did not make, but on other occasions profiting from the large measure of private power their public powerlessness concealed.

5

Religion and the sacred

Philip Benedict and Virginia Reinburg

Amid the patchwork of provinces that made up France in 1500, in a
world where country folk were very different from town dwellers, the
learned from the unlettered, and nobles from commoners, Christianity defined the country's common culture like nothing else. For
much of the Middle Ages the French kings had tolerated a small
minority of Jews, but they had been definitively expelled in 1394.
Small pockets of Waldensians (*vaudois*) lived in the hills of Dauphiné
and Provence. These dogged descendants of a heretical movement of
the twelfth century remained loyal to their *barbes* (lay preachers).
Their refusal to pray to saints, honour images, or submit to priests
they considered immoral brought them intermittently afoul of the
law. Still, they conformed to most features of the established religious
order, regularly attending mass and receiving the sacraments.
Nobody therefore lived entirely outside the Church, which reached
into every village and touched every household. The increasingly
elaborate national myths that took shape in the waning centuries of
the Middle Ages even linked France's prosperity and identity to its
exemplary attachment to the true faith. Legend asserted that France
had entered into a special covenant with God during Clovis's reign
according to which it would thrive so long as error never took root in
the land. 'I am famed for always having been Catholic, never having
nourished heresy, and I never will', an embodiment of France
declared in the fifteenth-century mystery play, *The Council of Basel.*[1]

---

[1] Quoted in Colette Beaune, *Naissance de la nation France* (Paris, 1985), p. 213.

Each new monarch swore at his coronation to extirpate heresy from the kingdom.

Precisely because attachment to the true Christian faith was so integral to both individuals and the nation, movements of religious renewal had a unique capacity to galvanize the mass of the population and to destabilize the political order. France experienced significant changes in many domains during the sixteenth and early seventeenth century, but none were as important as the storms that shook and ultimately transformed its religious life.

Religious life, c.1500

While the worship and doctrine of the established Church comprised France's common culture at the end of the Middle Ages, the same tendencies that were so strong throughout late medieval life towards local diversity, sharp distinctions of status and hierarchy, and the incomplete integration of overlapping chains of authority also characterized religious life. What we label with a singular noun 'the Church' was actually a network of loosely interrelated institutions—most of them local (parish, chapel, monastery, confraternity, school) or regional (archdiocese, diocese, religious order), some kingdom-wide (the theology faculty of Paris, clerical assemblies), a few with supraregional claims (cardinals, papal legates, inquisitors, centralized religious orders). As ecclesiastical institutions varied considerably by function, jurisdiction, wealth, and customs, so the clergy attached to them varied enormously in function, social position, power, wealth, and education. The central elements of ritual and worship were more widely shared, but here too significant variations existed from region to region, city to city, and village to village. Pious individuals participated in the common rituals of the Church in very different ways according to their degree of literacy, wealth, and the local traditions in which they were raised.

To judge by the evidence of its material culture, religious life flourished in what has been called the period of flamboyant Christianity between the end of the Hundred Years War and the early sixteenth century. As the kingdom recovered from the demographic and economic disasters of the previous century of war and epidemic disease, local communities everywhere began rebuilding ruined or ransacked churches, and constructing new ones to accommodate growing populations in both city and countryside. The churchwardens of prosperous parishes like Saint-Vincent in Rouen and Saint-Eustache in Paris, as well as smaller one-parish towns like Caudebec-en-Caux (Normandy) and Arcueil (Île-de-France), took the opportunity to design new churches in the flamboyant Gothic style of the day. Parishioners were proud of their church and its furnishings. Most parish churches were financed locally, through regular church dues and special assessments, so the wealth and generosity of parishioners largely determined how large and lavish a church could be. Of necessity some were modest, built perhaps of wood as in rural Champagne and Normandy, and equipped with an altar, pulpit, church bell, and a minimum of altar vessels, linens, perhaps a missal. Urban parish churches could also be humble, especially those serving neighbourhoods of artisans and wage labourers. Parishes in more prosperous urban neighbourhoods often owned land and buildings and benefited from the donations, loans, and assessed dues paid by their parishioners. Such churches could be very grand, built of stone, and equipped with carved and gilded altars, rich linens, stained glass, liturgical vessels made of precious metals, a full set of liturgical books, as well as multiple statues, paintings, tapestries, and reliquaries. Parishioners often formed strong attachments to the images and saints' relics displayed in their churches, donating funds to conserve them, praying before them, and participating in collective rites honouring them.

Late medieval building programmes were both a consequence and sign of the collective nature of Christianity and the central place of the parish in communal life. Most of the laity's religious activities centred on the parish church of their neighbourhood or village. There they worshipped on Sundays and feasts; got married; baptized their children; buried their parents, and too often also their spouses and children; celebrated local feasts; paid church taxes; and gave alms to support the parish's clergy and poor. In addition to being the smallest unit in the Church's administrative network of archdioceses and dioceses, the parish served as an administrative unit of local government. The pastor might announce new laws or taxes from the pulpit. Church buildings were regularly used for collection of taxes, meetings of neighbourhood or village assemblies, and local festivals.

Parishioners conducted all manner of business in or near the church. In his diary Gilles de Gouberville (c.1521–78), a Norman nobleman, regularly reports transacting business, enquiring about rents and land sales, recommending clients for positions, and issuing dinner invitations on the front steps of his parish church after Sunday mass. Trysting and dancing after dark in church or outside in the cemetery must have been common enough as well, to judge from regular admonitions in synodal statutes. The parish was the social centre of the community.

The parish community of the living was not the only collectivity of importance for late medieval Christians. Other communities also mattered deeply: the communion of saints, deceased men and women who by their virtuous lives had earned a place in God's heavenly kingdom and thus could intercede with God on behalf of others still seeking salvation; and the souls in purgatory awaiting the assistance provided by the living faithful through their prayers. Images and inscriptions on altarpieces and stained glass windows appealed to the living to pray for the deceased sinners who had commissioned them and invited supplicants to seek the intercession of holy people who had gone before them. Both the economy of salvation and collective religious life functioned through patronage, intercession, and reciprocity. Through art and ritual, local communities implored the aid of patron saints, gave thanks for past blessings, and negotiated future aid. In Poitiers, processions of magistrates, clergy, corporations, and guilds carried a beloved image of the Virgin Mary, together with relics of Sts Hilary and Radegonde, through the city's neighbourhoods, pausing frequently for display, prayer, and hymns. Parisians held frequent processions venerating the relics of their city's patron, St Geneviève, and imploring her aid against natural disaster and armed invasion. Nor was the patronage of Christ himself neglected, as images, rites, processions, and sermons honouring relics of his passion (Paris) and miracle-working hosts (Paris, Dijon) testify abundantly. Christ was particularly honoured at the annual feast of Corpus Christi, when a consecrated host was carried through the city by a solemn and elaborate procession led by the local bishop, with the participation of clergy, universities and schools, magistrates, guilds, confraternities, and parishes. The rite culminated in a mass, hymn singing, and special blessings. There could be no better demonstration of the belief that a community's collective welfare depended on the protection of God, the Virgin Mary, and the saints, and moreover that it was their task to appeal for that protection, and to thank God and the saints for assistance received.

Spectacular though processions may have been, far more common forms of public prayer were the sacraments and the mass. Late medieval Christians believed that in the sacraments—rites performed by a priest, received or witnessed by the faithful—God bestowed grace on the participants. Four sacraments marked significant stages of the life cycle. Baptism incorporated newborns into the Church and its promise of salvation after death, while exorcizing the devil from the child's body. Baptized children were sponsored by godparents (as many as six), chosen by the child's parents from networks of kin, neighbours, and patrons. Confirmation by a bishop marked the passage to adulthood, usually between the ages of 10 and 13, though before the late sixteenth century many Christians never received this sacrament. Marriage was also a sacrament, and weddings were increasingly celebrated in one's parish church. In extreme unction, the dying or gravely ill person was prepared for death, confessed sins and received absolution, and was anointed with blessed oil. Of the remaining three sacraments, only aspiring priests received ordination at the hands of a bishop. The other two sacraments, penance and the Eucharist, were meant to be received regularly throughout one's life. The Fourth Lateran Council (1215) had required all Christians to receive the sacraments of confession (penance) and communion (the Eucharist) annually in their parish church. In the rite of penance people confessed their sins aloud to a priest, either individually or collectively. He judged the seriousness of these sins and the sincerity of the sinner's contrition before granting forgiveness and requiring a penalty in the form of prayers or other good works. Penance was a key element in the spiritual jurisdiction the Church claimed over Christians and their salvation. According to the Church, only a sin forgiven by a priest (acting in God's place, with God's guidance) would be removed from a person's moral account. Pastors urged the faithful to confess often in order to protect themselves against the possibility of dying suddenly in a state of mortal sin, which put them at risk of eternal damnation.

The Eucharist was the most important sacrament, and the Eucharistic liturgy, or mass, was the heart of Christian life. It was key to the economy of salvation, and the most essential and familiar rite of the

faith. Since the Sunday parish mass gathered an entire neighbourhood or village in a shared rite of sacrifice, prayer, hymns, communion, and almsgiving, it was also central to collective religious
experience. Lateran IV had required weekly attendance at mass; the
evidence suggests that around 1500 most people heeded this requirement. Performed in Latin and thus understood in slightly different
ways by the presiding priest and attending congregation, the Eucharistic ritual commemorated Christ's Last Supper with his disciples
and his crucifixion, in which he sacrificed his life in exchange for the
redemption of humanity. Over the centuries theologians and
churchmen had studied, debated, and reformulated this rite that had
likely originated among the early Christians as a blessed, shared meal
accompanied by scriptural readings and lessons, until by the late
Middle Ages it had become a carefully scripted ritual sacrifice,
enacted by a priest before an altar, that could be carried out either
with or without the presence of a congregation. Central to the understanding of the ritual was the doctrine of transubstantiation, made
authoritative at Lateran IV, according to which Christ was rendered
'really' or corporeally present through the rite. When the priest took a
piece of unleavened bread (the host), and repeated over it Christ's
blessing at the Last Supper, 'This is my body,' the host was transformed in substance into Christ's body, though retaining the appearance of bread. Thus everyone attending mass witnessed Christ's real
presence in the Eucharist, whether or not they chose to receive and
consume a piece of the consecrated host at communion. In return for
the sacrifice offered him with and through the ritual, God bestowed
grace on all in attendance, on any donors who may have endowed a
particular mass, and on the individuals and communities for whom
they prayed.

By the late Middle Ages the Eucharist had taken on a range of
widely shared meanings, even if occasional critics questioned certain
of these. The mass had become a 'good work' offered to God in
exchange for his protection, help, and ultimately salvation. The number of and occasion for masses had multiplied, as has been docu-
mented especially well for the region of Avignon. Masses were offered
for the souls of the dead, who often were named specifically by their
surviving families, fellow guildsmen, and neighbours. Testators left
funds to support priests who would say such masses; some priests
without benefice supported themselves through these donations.

Masses were also commonly said for the benefit of the living: to help individuals who were ill, poor, or otherwise suffering, and to aid the local community in times of distress. An additional feature of popular Eucharistic practice that attracted some disapproval was devotion to the consecrated host, both inside and outside the mass. Participants at mass were encouraged to honour Christ's presence among them by venerating the consecrated wafer that had become his flesh—gazing upon it, kneeling, repeating prayers pledging dedication and allegiance to the crucified Christ. Like veneration of saints' relics and images, popular devotion to the Eucharist was an integral part of the religious culture of late medieval Christianity. The early fifteenth-century theologian Jean Gerson, while encouraging the faithful to adore Christ's body in the consecrated host, also cautioned against allowing such adoration to degenerate into 'superstition', criticizing especially the apparently widespread belief that anyone who gazed upon the host would not that day suffer blindness, sudden death, or loss of personal goods. It was precisely because the Eucharist had acquired such central religious importance, and consequently such symbolic power in public life, that it was available for intense, various, and (from the point of view of learned clerics like Gerson) potentially disorderly and uncontrollable uses by the faithful.

Since only an ordained priest could preach and perform the mass and sacraments, the clergy enjoyed an important spiritual and social status in relation to the laity. In addition to his liturgical duties, a parish's pastor (*curé*) maintained the parish's property, especially its relics, buildings, and cemetery. A steadily growing number kept records of births, marriages, and burials, especially after the 1539 ordinance of Villers-Cotterêt imposed this upon pastors throughout the kingdom. In large parishes, assistant pastors, chaplains, or priests paid by the rite often assisted the pastor. When it came to administering parish funds and property, from the thirteenth century onward the pastor usually shared the task with the *fabrique* (vestry or churchwardens), a group of lay men chosen from among the parish's heads of household. Their duties and jurisdiction included arranging for the design, construction, and financing of building programmes, and sometimes a role in appointing and supervising the parish's clergy.

The number of parishioners, scale of activity, and character and education of a parish's clergy varied according to local circumstances.

A large city like Rouen (pop. 71,000–78,000 at mid-sixteenth century) had some three dozen parishes, each staffed by multiple priests. The only slightly smaller city of Lyon (pop. around 60,000 c.1550) had but twelve parishes. The considerably smaller city of Dijon (pop. around 12,000 c.1500) had seven parishes, while residents of Aix-en-Provence (pop. around 12,000–15,000 c.1550) had only two parishes, but many chapels attached to convents and monasteries where they could worship. In the larger cities, a good percentage of pastors had attended university, but this was rarely true of village priests. Rural parish life had its own character. Many larger villages had but one parish to serve the entire population; several smaller villages and hamlets might well have to share a pastor, if not a parish. The parish's *fabrique* and the village's community of inhabitants were often the same group of men, whose parochial and communal functions intertwined; in some regions the word 'parish' in legal practice was synonymous with 'community of inhabitants'.

Parish clergymen were typically sons of their communities. Studies of Aix-en-Provence and Dijon have shown that parish clergy usually came from the same social groups they served. Merchants' sons served parishes in bourgeois neighbourhoods; in neighbourhoods heavily populated by officials and lawyers, the pastors were usually themselves sons and brothers of officers. Most rural priests were native to the region they served. In fifteenth-century Burgundy they were often peasant boys who had been tutored and mentored by the local pastor or schoolmaster, before going on to theological studies at the cathedral or monastic schools of Dijon or Langres. Priests remained local boys in other ways as well. In villages they continued to farm, in cities they sometimes participated in the family business or occupation. They inherited family property, served as godparents to kin and neighbours, and suffered financially when economic times were bad. They also drank in the local tavern, and not infrequently participated in local feuds and brawls.

Though they lived and worked alongside the people, parish clergy were also part of a larger network of ecclesiastical institutions. In 1500 France had fourteen ecclesiastical provinces; several more were added over the course of the sixteenth and seventeenth centuries as the crown acquired territories by war, diplomacy, and dynastic marriage. Within the fourteen provinces were 114 archbishoprics and bishoprics of varying size. The most reliable estimate puts the number of the kingdom's parishes at around 32,000. The vast dioceses of Langres and Le Mans had 843 and 736 parishes, respectively, that of Grasse just 25. The system of clerical appointments was exceedingly complex. In principle each candidate for ordination was required to prove possession of a benefice, an ecclesiastical office that would guarantee him adequate financial support. Benefices were acquired in much the same way any office was acquired: by right of assignment from a bishop, abbot, cathedral chapter, or secular lord, which usually meant through patron–client networks. Most bishops did not control the appointment of large numbers of clerics within their dioceses. The bishop of Rodez was highly unusual in having the authority to appoint men of his choosing to nearly half the parish benefices in his diocese.

Though many parish benefices were hardly large enough to support the priests who held them, great fortunes could be made at the higher levels of church office, especially among archbishops and bishops, but also to some extent cathedral canons and the abbots of powerful monasteries. Those angling for a lucrative appointment in the upper ranks of the Church were well advised to make their interest known with an obsequiously worded petition to the person who controlled the benefice and to keep the pressure on by enlisting the support of as many of those in his confidence as possible. Only sons of the aristocracy or members of the prominent Italian families that rallied to the French cause during the Italian wars could reasonably dare to hope for a bishopric or archbishopric. Italian exiles, *fuoruscuti*, received approximately one-fifth of all sees under Francis I. At least 85 per cent of the remainder went to noblemen. The effort required to land a bishopric or rich abbey was nonetheless handsomely repaid. The richest bishoprics brought revenues of 80,000 *livres* per year by the later sixteenth century. Great political prerogatives could also attach to the bishop's office; the archbishop of Narbonne, for instance, presided over the meetings of the Estates of Languedoc. Since pluralism was rampant in the upper reaches of the Church, a particularly accomplished courtier-churchman could accumulate a dozen or more abbeys to go along with two or three bishoprics and archbishoprics. François de Tournon (1489–1562) never held more than a single bishopric at once, but his successful career as a diplomat, royal adviser and, ultimately, cardinal allowed him to trade up the hierarchy of archbishoprics until he reached the lofty rank of 'primate of the Gauls' as archbishop of Lyon. Additional revenues from 23 abbeys and four priories provided him with enough income to support a retinue of 70 people and to have himself transported comfortably to and from Rome in a snugly fitted sedan chair.

Two important institutions operating largely outside the parish structure were the religious orders and the confraternities. Religious orders were congregations of men or women who lived, worked, and prayed in community. Members took vows of chastity, obedience, and poverty, and lived in convents or monasteries under the authority of a superior (abbot/abbess, prior/prioress). All nuns lived in cloistered convents, where they devoted themselves to prayer, contemplation, and work within the community. Men could join monastic orders, whose members generally followed the rules of St Benedict or St Augustine, and worked as teachers, scholars, administrators, or in various agricultural or artisanal occupations. Members of mendicant orders—the Franciscans and Dominicans—devoted themselves to preaching, teaching, and charitable work, tasks that sometimes brought them into conflict with bishops and parish clergy. Just as the relationship between religious orders and the dioceses was generally poorly defined, so also was the relationship between parishes and confraternities. By the late fifteenth century French cities had dozens if not a hundred or more confraternities, which were voluntary pious organizations dedicated to the patronage of a saint or shrine. Confraternity members (overwhelmingly lay people) worshipped together regularly, paid dues, elected officers from among their membership, hired chaplains, organized funeral services, and prayed for the souls of deceased members. These mutual aid societies performed vital social functions in late medieval and early modern cities, providing charity, sociability, and leadership opportunities for generations of young men. Feasts of patron saints were celebrated with mass and a lavish banquet, usually followed by a thanksgiving service or vespers. Ideally Eucharist and banquet were the spiritual and worldly sides of the commensality confraternity members shared as 'brothers and sisters in Christ'. In practice the banquets attracted criticism from civil authorities suspicious of 'factionalism' and lavish spending, and church authorities wary of organizations in which clerics and lay people—not to mention religious and secular events— mingled freely. Like the religious orders, confraternities were in theory subject to supervision by the parish and diocese where they were located. But in practice they often operated independently of clerical supervision.

Another grey area in late medieval religious life was preaching. In theory the bishop, and through him the parish clergy, were responsible for preaching and teaching. There was little preaching during mass, though there was a place for it in the rite. Most sermons were delivered by mendicant friars, in churches, cathedrals, cemeteries, or town squares, on Sunday afternoons, saints' feasts, and especially during the seasons of Lent and Advent. Preaching was overwhelmingly an urban phenomenon before the early sixteenth century. Preachers were generally hired by civil authorities, or sometimes by a parish's fabrique, though technically the bishop or pastor could withhold approval. Popular preachers could hold an audience's attention with a compelling message about the need for repentance, good works, and moral behaviour, but just as often preachers entertained with lively stories about miracles, heroic saints, and evildoers who came to a bad end.

That a city's central square or cemetery could provide the stage for regular sermons underscores the public nature of Christianity. Yet Christianity was not only a public matter, but also a matter of private conviction and devotion. The constellation of Christian beliefs, rites, symbols, and practices was sufficiently large that there was much room for individual interpretation and appropriation. Individuals understood Christian beliefs in varied ways, and embraced or interpreted even the Eucharist, saints' cults, and penitential practices in often highly personal terms. Some were particularly attached to patron saints or saints favoured by their families or parishes. Others confessed their sins frequently to a priest, or attended mass more often than every Sunday. The varieties of private devotion increased markedly over the fourteenth and fifteenth centuries, in tandem with the growing wealth, influence, and especially literacy of the nobility and bourgeoisie. Wealthy, educated lay people could endow masses, purchase and display images and rosary beads, and assemble impromptu shrines in their homes for private prayer and meditation. Humbler working people could acquire religious objects fashioned of less costly materials, or even craft their own rosaries out of cord and wooden beads. Especially widespread among the literate classes by the later fifteenth century was the purchase of a manuscript or printed book of hours. The book of hours was an adaptation for lay people of the clergy's breviary that offered daily prayers written in Latin (with increasingly large portions translated into French), individually designed for women and men who wished to have a personal or family prayer book to guide their religious practice. By the early sixteenth century elite lay avidity for what one historian has called 'the consumption of devotions' could breed a vigorous life of personal piety intertwined with the collective rituals of the Church.[2]

A commonplace of late medieval preachers held that women were more pious than men. 'Men presume too much in their abilities and trust in their reason,' as one preacher put it, but 'it is not that way with women. So we find they are more commonly devout than men.'[3] Whether or not this commonplace reflected the reality of women's piety, it is nonetheless true that women's participation in the religious activities of family, parish, and community had distinctive features. The Virgin Mary, St Anne, and St Margaret were perennial favourites of the women who owned images of them, prayed to them, and gave alms in thanksgiving for their assistance with pregnancy, childbirth, and motherhood. Wives and mothers played an important religious role in the family: supervising the household's observance of church fasts and feasts, providing for children's religious education, collecting devotional objects like rosaries and prayer books. On the other hand, women's participation in the institutions of collective life was limited. Barred from ordination, women were also normally excluded from parish vestries and confraternal offices. They were less frequently ordinary members of confraternities than men. Female convents were far less numerous than their male counterparts—by a ratio of 2:10 in Aix-en-Provence, for example. Wealthy convents nonetheless offered their aristocratic abbesses an opportunity to wield considerable power, both in the convent and beyond. Perhaps the best examples were the successive abbesses of Fontevraud Renée de Bourbon and her niece Louise de Bourbon, who between them spent nearly eighty years reforming the convent and its dependent communities, as well as managing an impressive array of property and assets that often required them to negotiate legal matters locally and in Paris. Aristocratic and bourgeois women could exercise

---

[2] Angelo Torre, *Il consumo di devozioni: Religione e comunità nelle campagne dell'ancien régime* (Venice, 1995).

[3] Quoted in Larissa Taylor, *Soldiers of Christ: Preaching in Late Medieval and Reformation France* (New York, 1992), p. 172.

considerable religious influence through their patronage of monasteries, parishes, and shrines. Even women from mercantile and arti-
san families left their mark by endowing altars and chaplaincies, or
donating liturgical books, altar vessels, and art to parishes and
convents.

Institutionally the French Church had obtained considerable
independence from Rome, but was falling increasingly under monarchical control. During the crises that shook the papacy during the late
fourteenth and early fifteenth centuries, Paris theologians asserted
the self-governing character of the Church and its independence
from papal control. Appeals of church court decisions and transfers
of revenues to Rome were curtailed, and in the Pragmatic Sanction of
Bourges (1438) the crown codified into law the principle that cathedral chapters and religious houses were to elect their bishops and
superiors free of papal interference. But this hardly settled the matter
of how high church offices and benefices were to be filled. In practice
the king often promoted his own clients for important church offices,
and elections were in effect negotiated between the crown and
religious communities holding the right of appointment. In 1516
Francis I negotiated with Pope Leo X the Concordat of Bologna,
which placed episcopal appointments in the hands of the crown,
subject to papal approval. The Concordat modified rather than over-
turned the Pragmatic Sanction, since many financial, judicial, and
doctrinal matters within the French Church continued to be decided
without reference to Rome. Nevertheless, the parlement of Paris and
the Paris theology faculty (the Sorbonne) fiercely resisted accepting
the Concordat, arguing that it threatened 'the liberties of the Gallican
Church' so well protected under the Pragmatic Sanction. But in many
ways the Concordat was more a claim to royal authority over the
offices, property, and activities of the French Church than it was an
effective policy of royal control. Leading churchmen and monastic
houses remained powerful lords with extensive seigneurial rights of
jurisdiction and control of key positions within provinces and cities.
And despite constant efforts by Francis I and Henry II to obtain
larger subsidies from the clergy and firmer control over church-
owned lands, high churchmen and ecclesiastical institutions were still
among the wealthiest individuals and institutions in the kingdom.

Doctrine was also increasingly a bone of contention among crown,
parlement, and Church as the Middle Ages drew to a close. The

Sorbonne claimed the authority to decide doctrinal questions throughout the kingdom, and in the early sixteenth century it often cooperated with the parlement of Paris in challenging royal and episcopal jurisdiction over heresy and dissent. By mid-century the parlement largely controlled heresy prosecutions. Thus, although crown, parlement, and Sorbonne would have agreed that the Gallican Church was by tradition and law free of papal authority, the precise lines of authority within the kingdom over offices, property, and doctrine were in dispute long before battles between Protestants and Catholics began in the mid-sixteenth century.

How shall we evaluate the state of religious life at the turn of the sixteenth century? One historian has called attention to what he terms 'the magnificent religious anarchy' of the era, emphasizing the diversity of views, beliefs, and projects within the Gallican Church. But he and others have also pointed out the frequent criticism of the Church's wealth, power, and corruption. Certainly abuses in the Church were on the mind of early fifteenth-century reformers like Gerson, who worked for decades to improve clerical and lay education. These calls for reform in many ways are a sign of the vigour of Christianity. Only those attached to the highest ideals of contemporary Christianity felt keenly its inability to live up to those ideals. Perhaps what stands out most is the growth of lay engagement in religious life. Parish fabriques, confraternities, the growing numbers of religious books available to the laity, large audiences for sermons, expanded donations to parishes, shrines, and other religious institutions: these are evidence of what Febvre called 'a tremendous appetite for all that was divine'.[4] They also betokened rising lay expectations of the wealthy Church establishment, and a certain degree of lay independence from clerical domination.

Currents of change

The early years of the sixteenth century witnessed formidable challenges to the Church from humanism. Like their Italian predecessors,

---

[4] Lucien Febvre, 'The Origins of the French Reformation: A Badly Put Question?' in *A New Kind of History: From the Writings of Lucien Febvre*, ed. P. Burke, trans. K. Folca (London, 1973), pp. 86, 65.

northern humanists were committed to making available purer and less corrupt versions of secular and Christian texts. Leading northern humanists also sought to join scholarship and piety in ways that would have profound consequences for both. Their central ideal might be summed up in Erasmus's term 'learned piety', by which he meant a lived Christianity that was scriptural, practical, and theologically serious. The ideal of an educated Christian laity, together with the humanist critique of the Church's wealth and power, provided an important foundation for the growth of Protestantism as well as the reform of Catholicism later in the sixteenth century.

Already by the 1510s the promise of a humanist Christian Renaissance inspired Parisian intellectuals and a few bishops. Here the central figures were two men whose scholarly profile and reputation were so similar that Francis I reportedly once spoke of one when he meant the other: Jacques Lefèvre d'Étaples (c.1460–1536) and Desiderius Erasmus (c.1467–1536). Lefèvre, professor of philosophy and the liberal arts in Paris, was an influential teacher and adviser to several generations of scholars, teachers, and clerics. After mastering Greek as a student and travelling to Italy, where he met the leading humanists of the day, he devoted most of the early part of his career to editing and commenting upon authors such as Aristotle and Euclid. From 1509 onward, he began to apply the tools of humanistic philology to the study of the Bible, which he believed should inspire all Christians. His close study of the text in the original languages led him to propose changes in the accepted Latin translation of several Psalms, to cease speaking of purgatory and the cult of the saints, and to question whether extreme unction or mandatory confession to a priest had biblical foundation. His understanding of salvation emphasized that Christ had given his life to redeem undeserving sinners, and that this was far more important than any good works on their part or prayers for them by others. But while the vision of Christianity that Lefèvre articulated departed in several ways from the practices of the Church of his time, he advocated keeping silent rather than being drawn into unnecessary disputes over such issues.

Erasmus, a native of the Low Countries, arrived in Paris as a student in 1495. Though he left the city permanently in 1511, he remained deeply engaged with French scholars and issues for the rest of his life. He shared with Lefèvre both the concern to apply the methods of humanist scholarship to biblical study and the unwillingness to split the Church over doctrinal quarrels. He parted company with him in placing more emphasis on the role of works in salvation and in being more committed to the humanist project of promoting elegant Ciceronian Latin, a cause that never attracted Lefèvre. Erasmus's *philosophia Christi* emphasized the importance of inward spiritual renewal and a life modelled on Christ's rather than the outward observation of laws and ceremonies. His satires were unsparing in their depiction of the greed and folly of the mendicant orders, even while he always claimed to attack only the abuses of monasticism, not the institution itself, and asserted that no vice was worse than sowing discord in the Church. He was enormously popular with French readers. Many libraries of educated clerics and laymen—especially lawyers, officers, minor nobles, and even a few humanist bishops—included copies of his oft-reprinted *Handbook of a Christian Soldier* (1503), his other works on piety, and his biblical paraphrases. His influence extended as far as the royal court: Francis I and Marguerite de Navarre reportedly read his works in French translation, and the royal library at Blois included a number of his books. Marguerite's distinctive brand of evangelical Christianity has been traced in large measure to the inspiration of Lefèvre and Erasmus, and Francis supported Christian humanist scholars throughout the 1520s and 1530s. Although Paris was the centre of Christian humanism in France, humanists in Lyon and Avignon also dreamed of a renewal of Christianity inspired by biblical study.

Humanism prompted practical efforts at church reform most directly in the diocese of Meaux, where shortly after his appointment in 1518 Bishop Guillaume Briçonnet launched a programme of pastoral reform. Briçonnet, son of a wealthy and prominent family of financiers and royal officials, had studied with humanist teachers in Paris, ascended through a series of increasingly important church positions, and helped Francis I negotiate the Concordat of Bologna. Soon after his consecration as bishop of Meaux, he moved to the diocese, an unusual step for a man with such a brilliant ecclesiastical career and one that signalled his intent to be a pastoral, reforming bishop. One of his first moves was to require the parish clergy to reside in the diocese (located near enough to Paris to tempt those holding clerical benefices to live in the more lively capital city). Briçonnet also introduced regular preaching of God's word through exposition of the Gospels and St Paul's Epistles. To help improve education and reform the liturgy and preaching, he summoned to the diocese in 1512 Lefèvre d'Étaples and some of Lefèvre's former students, including Gérard Roussel, Michel d'Arande, Martial Mazurier, Pierre Caroli, and Guillaume Farel. Many of the activities of these men revolved around making the Bible, liturgy, and Christian teachings more accessible to the faithful. Lefèvre translated the Psalms, the Epistles, and Gospels read during the mass, and eventually the entire New Testament into French, so that (as he said in the preface) 'the simplest members of the body of Jesus Christ can be as certain of the Gospel's truth as those who have it in Latin'.[5] By 1524 the reading of biblical passages in French had been incorporated into Sunday mass in the diocese. Roussel gave a daily exposition of St Paul's Epistles. Farel, d'Arande, and Caroli travelled the region, preaching during or after Sunday mass, and often on weekdays as well.

But quickly Briçonnet's reforms ran afoul of growing opposition from the Franciscans, who jealously defended their de facto right to preach in the diocese, and from the Sorbonne and the parlement of Paris, both of which claimed authority to determine and enforce orthodox Christian teaching. Here also the drama of Martin Luther, currently being played out in the Holy Roman Empire, made itself felt. In October 1517 Luther, an Augustinian monk and professor of scripture at Wittenberg (Saxony), had publicly criticized the Roman Church's teachings on intercession, indulgences, purgatory, and ultimately salvation. Citing St Paul's Epistle to the Romans, Luther argued that human beings were saved by faith in God alone, not by any effort of their own. Church authorities in Rome and elsewhere, correctly sensing a challenge to the notion of good works that justified and supported most Christian religious practices and institutions, pressed Luther to retract his views. He dug in and soon was calling for a reduction in the sacraments from seven to three (later two) and the abolition of the monastic orders, while denouncing the Church of Rome as hopelessly corrupt. Although excommunicated by the pope and condemned by the Imperial diet of Worms, he was protected by the Elector of Saxony. Thanks to the printing press, Luther's example and ideas galvanized widespread agitation for

---

[5] Jacques Lefèvre d'Étaples, preface to French translation of the Gospels (1525), text in *The Prefatory Epistles of Jacques Lefèvre d'Étaples and Related Texts*, ed. E. F. Rice, Jr (New York, 1972), p. 450.

change in the structure of the Church across the German-speaking world. Parisian booksellers also began to sell his writings to eager customers as early as 1519. The Sorbonne condemned Luther's teachings in 1521, and secular laws soon made possession of his writings a crime, but these measures did not stop several Frenchmen from echoing his ideas or seeking to learn more about them by travelling to Wittenberg.

The 'Luther affair' revealed the danger of allowing reformers to appeal to the Bible in opposition to prevailing church practices. Briçonnet sought to protect his experiment in Meaux from the taint of heresy by anathemizing Luther, forbidding criticism of the veneration of saints and the doctrine of purgatory, and revoking the licences of those who went beyond these limits in their sermons. Still, the Sorbonne and parlement continued to investigate the Meaux circle, and over the course of the next decade formally condemned many of the writings that emanated from it, as well as the reforms undertaken in the diocese. The king's absence at war, his capture at Pavia, and his subsequent imprisonment throughout most of 1525, combined with the hostility towards suspected heretics on the part of the king's mother, the regent Louise of Savoy, were particularly unfortunate for the Meaux reformers. In that year the leading members of the group were all called to Paris for interrogation. Most chose to flee to reformed Strasbourg rather than answer the summons. Lefèvre and Roussel returned to France a year later under Marguerite de Navarre's protection. Lefèvre was appointed librarian at Blois and tutor to the royal children, and later retired to Marguerite's seigneurial domain at Nérac. Roussel began a long stint as Marguerite's spiritual director and chaplain that ultimately led him to the see of Oloron (Béarn) thanks to her patronage. Farel, on the other hand, quickly absorbed not only Luther's outspoken critique of the Roman Church but also the Eucharistic views of those Swiss reformers who went beyond the Wittenberg reformer in their subversion of the practices and doctrines of the established Church by denying Christ's real presence in the Eucharist. He became a wandering 'preacher of the Gospel' spreading the call for a break with Rome throughout the French-speaking localities located just beyond the sixteenth-century boundaries of France from Metz to Geneva. In the eyes of the Sorbonne doctors, all of those involved in activities such as the Meaux experiments constituted what the sorbonniste Noel Béda called 'Luther's confraternity'. As the subsequent biographies of the members of the Meaux group reveal, their visions of reform in fact differed. Historians now tend to prefer the label 'evangelical' for all those involved in such movements since it emphasizes their shared commitment to renewing Christianity through a return to the Gospels while allowing for the very real differences among them that ultimately led them in different directions: some to break with the established Church, others to seek to reform it from within, others to retreat from all controversy over the contested issues of the day, and still others to develop personal religious views that would lead them to wander back and forth across Europe's increasingly variegated mosaic of confessions in search of a church that conformed to their ideals.

Despite the break-up of the Meaux circle and the continuing opposition of the Sorbonne and the royal law courts to all activity that smacked of 'Lutheranism', evangelical ideas kept filtering through France during the decades after 1525. Books, sermons, and even mystery plays were the vehicles of their dissemination. The gradual extension of accusations and trials for heresy throughout the country reveals the gradual penetration of these ideas into almost every corner of the land.

The surviving books and pamphlets of an evangelical character are our best guide to the changing mix of ideas associated with the cause. From around 1520 into the early 1530s, evangelical propaganda was dominated by vernacular editions, excerpts, and summaries of the Bible, and by books that combined short expositions of Gospel passages with prayers, such as the popular *Livre de vraye et parfaicte oraison*, which went through at least fourteen editions between 1528 and the 1540s. Luther was by far the most widely translated foreign theologian in this period, with his catechetical and spiritual works making their way into French more often than his controversial writings. Often fragments of his works were published or paraphrased without attribution in composite devotional pamphlets that also included pages from Erasmus and Farel.

The second phase of evangelical publishing began in 1533, when local reformations established Protestant worship of an uncompromisingly Swiss character in Neuchâtel and then Geneva. French language printers quickly set up presses there and began to produce polemical works of a more outspoken character. Antoine Marcourt's immensely successful catalogues of the defective goods sold by the

Church of Rome, the *Livre des marchans* (1533), was soon followed by the notorious placards, also authored by Marcourt and posted simultaneously in Paris and other cities in 1534, denouncing 'the insufferable abuses of the papal mass, invented in direct opposition to the holy supper of Jesus Christ'.[6] Borrowing from the sacramentarian ideas circulating in reformed Swiss cities, Marcourt's placards directly attacked the idea of the mass as the congregation's sacrifice to God: 'Every faithful Christian is and must be most certain that our Lord and only savior Jesus Christ, as eternal bishop and pastor ordained by God, gave up his body, his soul, his life, and his blood in most perfect sacrifice for our sanctification, which never can or should be repeated by any visible sacrifice.'[7] Two years after the affair of the placards, a young native of Noyon, Jean Calvin (1509–64), published the first edition of his *Institutes of the Christian Religion*, which evolved through subsequent revisions into the most forceful and successful exposition of Reformed Protestantism of the sixteenth century. Calvin established himself as the chief prophet and architect of the Genevan Church after 1541, and from 1543 onward he began to urge all those who had seen the light of Christ's Gospel in places that had not yet established a new Protestant church order to separate themselves from the abominations of Roman worship and, if possible, emigrate to a land where worship was pure. As growing numbers of French evangelicals heard this call and fled to Geneva, the number of Genevan presses multiplied, and clandestine networks were established for distributing their products throughout France. By the early 1560s Geneva housed 34 presses. No less than 178 French-language editions of one or another of Calvin's treatises, sermons, and commentaries appeared during his lifetime. His sharp critique of Catholic theology and worship and uncompromising call for separation from it increasingly dominated evangelical propaganda.

The ever more uncompromising tone of evangelical propaganda at once responded to and encouraged the stricter definition and enforcement of Catholic orthodoxy. The bitterness with which the placards of 1534 denounced the mass shocked Francis I, as did the organization that apparently lurked behind their simultaneous

---

[6] Text edited in Robert Hari, 'Les Placards de 1534', in *Aspects de la propagande religieuse* (Geneva, 1957), p. 114.
[7] Ibid., p. 115.

distribution in many cities. The scale of the legal repression that followed was unprecedented; two dozen people died in Paris alone in the months that followed, the largest total ever executed for heresy in one French city within such a brief period. The king himself took part in the grand expiatory procession organized to honour the consecrated host. He continued to protect those humanist evangelicals who did not denounce the mass and to mitigate the activity of the most zealous heresy-hunters within the Sorbonne and the law courts for another decade, especially when he was eager to win the friendship of the Protestant princes in Germany in his struggles against Charles V. But Francis's attitude towards heresy gradually hardened. In 1543 he ordered the Sorbonne to draw up a set of articles of the faith, which for the first time established orthodox positions on doctrinal and institutional questions. The document not only defended the traditional Catholic understanding of the mass as a true sacrifice and replication of Christ's sacrifice at Calvary, but asserted the value of pilgrimage, purgatory, and intercessory prayer, all of which had been the object of Erasmian ridicule as well as Protestant criticism. In 1544 the Paris theology faculty issued the country's first index of prohibited books, which included authors such as Lefèvre and Rabelais as well as Luther and Calvin.

The middle years of the 1540s were a difficult time for all those accused of heresy. The country's law courts displayed new severity in their treatment of the crime, and the volume of executions tripled between the first half of the decade and the second. Most tragically, Francis allowed the *arrêt de Mérindol*, a collective arrest warrant for the inhabitants of an entire village in the Luberon hills, to be carried out against the Waldensian inhabitants of this region on the border of Provence and the papal enclave of Avignon. Throughout the 1530s, the Waldensians had become the object of a series of investigations organized by papal inquisitors and the parlements of Toulouse and Aix that produced the interrogation and torture of arrested suspects in such an irregular fashion that the king finally intervened to put a stop to the repression. When he altered his position in 1545 and allowed the parlement of Aix to proceed with its warrant against Mérindol, a miniature crusade ensued in which royal troops joined local and papal militias to sack over a half dozen villages, killing more than 1,800 people. But even repression on this scale could not break the Waldensians or stop the spread of Protestant ideas, though it temporarily prompted greater caution on the heretics' part and increased the volume of flight to Geneva. By 1549 Waldensians were said to have returned to Mérindol, where according to one of their critics they 'lived worse than before, without an altar and without the sacraments, working on holidays and singing heretical songs'.[8]

Two confessions

In 1555 France's religious history entered a new phase, when Calvin began to encourage the scattered brethren in the country to form what he considered properly organized churches, with a duly selected minister, the regular administration of the sacraments, and a consistory of elders charged with overseeing the behaviour of the faithful and the operations of the church. To guide the formation of these churches, he sent out two Geneva-trained ministers—the first of approximately 220 such clergymen who went out from Geneva over the subsequent seven years. The first two churches were established in Poitiers and Paris. They were soon followed by dozens more.

At first these congregations met in secret—in members' homes, at night. As they grew, they often dared to gather in public, or even seize church buildings or public markets to hold their services. Their proliferation so alarmed Henry II that he agreed to mildly humiliating terms in the 1559 Peace of Cateau-Cambrésis so that he could devote more attention to the repression of heresy. But his unexpected death in a jousting accident during the peace celebration soon thereafter only made conditions more favourable for the new churches, for two young heirs followed him in rapid succession, and the political conditions that attended each one's accession were hardly conducive to the implementation of a forceful policy of repression. By 1562, upwards of a thousand congregations probably existed of what the members of these assemblies were beginning to call the 'Reformed religion'. Their enemies called it the 'so-called Reformed religion' (*Religion Prétendue Réformée*) and dubbed its adherents 'Huguenots', a name derived from the legend of the ghost Huguet or Hugon reputed to

---

[8] Quoted in William Monter, *Judging the French Reformation: Heresy Trials by Sixteenth-Century Parlements* (Cambridge, Mass., 1999), p. 102.

haunt the vicinity of Tours at night, and applied to the Protestants because of their clandestine nighttime gatherings.

While these churches initially sprang up independently of one another, their adherents soon took steps to knit them into a larger whole to ensure that they shared a common creed and order of worship. A synod assembled in Paris in 1559 drafted a confession of faith and laid down provisions for an ongoing network of local, regional, and national assemblies, each of which would gather at regular intervals to determine church policy. The erstwhile Waldensian communities integrated themselves into this network.

During the 1550s and early 1560s Protestant churches drew adherents from every social class, occupational group, and region of the kingdom. Stronger in cities and market towns than in the countryside, Reformed communities were especially numerous in Normandy, the Loire valley, and a crescent of provinces stretching from Poitou into Aquitaine and across Languedoc to Vivarais and Dauphiné. Any attempt to estimate their total membership is speculative, but a reasonable guess is between 1.5 and 2 million, roughly 10 per cent of the kingdom's total population. In the cities Protestantism reached its demographic height in the early 1560s. The Huguenots represented the majority of the population of a few southern towns (Nîmes, Montauban, Castres) by 1561. In Lyon they comprised about one-third of the population; in Rouen one-fifth; in Paris, significantly, less than a tenth. There have been many attempts to chart the social composition of Protestantism. Although personal conviction and individual will were perhaps the factors that most strongly determined confessional choice in these early years, still it is possible to find affinities between the new religious ideas and particular social groups. In the largest cities Protestantism attracted merchants, especially those from middling ranks of wealth. Artisans, especially from trades associated with high literacy rates and independent craft traditions, were the backbone of the movement. Evidence about lawyers and officials generally suggests that the upper ranks of these professions remained strongly Catholic, whereas the middle and lower ranks were overrepresented in Reformed churches. There were however a few cities—notably Toulouse—where a large minority of officers were identifiably Protestant. Only the lowest strata of urban society—unskilled workers, day labourers, and the poor—were largely indifferent to reformed ideas. In the countryside Protestantism did not have the same appeal it did in cities, where social and geographical mobility was greater and new ideas spread easily by preachers, books, and public discussion. The kingdom's peasants remained overwhelmingly Catholic, though here too we find exceptions in the strongly Protestant region of the Cévennes, as well as other clusters of villages closely tied to urban centres by trade and kin connections, or regions whose lords were staunch Huguenots. The nobility joined the movement in significant numbers during this period. Among their members were such figures of the high nobility as Louis, prince of Condé, Gaspard de Coligny, the admiral of France, and Jeanne d'Albret, Francis I's niece and queen of Navarre. In the late 1560s Jeanne would oversee a state-sponsored reformation in her little principality of Béarn, secularizing all church property, outlawing the mass, requiring participation in Reformed worship, and decreeing strict new morals ordinances.

The worship of the Reformed churches broke dramatically with Catholic practice. When existing church buildings were seized by the Reformed, they stripped them of all altarpieces, images, and elaborate decoration in accordance with their strict interpretation of the ten commandments' prohibition of graven images. When they built their own churches, they constructed simple auditoria for preaching, decorated with little more than a board with those commandments behind the pulpit. Believing that human beings were redeemed by God's saving grace, freely given without the need for any human collaboration in the form of good works, and that most of the rituals of the Roman Church were fraudulent inventions offensive to God, they replaced the liturgy of the mass and other collective rites with weekly services built around the proclamation of the word—soon known, significantly, as the *prêche*. A vernacular sermon on a biblical text was the central event of the service, and was supplemented by scriptural readings, prayers, and Psalms sung by the congregation. Afternoon catechism lessons and midweek sermons rounded out a simplified Christian calendar from which all saints' days were removed. The high points of the devotional year were the quarterly celebrations of the Lord's Supper, at Christmas, Easter, July, and Pentecost. Following scriptural readings, ordinary bread and wine were laid out on a wooden table facing the congregation, and the ministers and deacons distributed it to the faithful who filed past according to what was for the sixteenth century a relatively egalitarian order of reception, in which the minister, elders, and deacons received the sacrament before groups of magistrates, men, and women. Unlike the more radical sacramentarians such as Marcourt, or Farel in his earlier years, Calvin viewed the ceremony not simply as a memorial re-enactment of the Last Supper reminding the faithful of Christ's promise of salvation, but as an occasion when Christ truly joined with and refreshed the faithful in spirit. Though Christ was not substantially or corporeally present in the sacrament, as Catholics believed, Calvin nevertheless insisted that he was still 'truly' present in spirit, in the 'internal substance' of the sacrament that transcended flesh, bread, and wine. Communion manuals warned church members sternly that the ignorant and dissolute should not take part in the ritual lest they eat and drink to their own damnation, yet encouraged as many believers as possible to take part in the ceremony so that they might reap its real spiritual benefits. As Theodore Beza wrote in his preface to the Psalter published for the French churches in 1562, 'because it is done in the name of everyone, everyone must be a participant'.[9] In the eyes of the Reformed, their worship services honoured God by respecting his commandments scrupulously and following only practices that Christ himself had instituted. In Catholic eyes their services appeared pitifully impoverished and unspeakably cruel to the souls in purgatory abandoned without prayers to shorten their sufferings.

In a Church built around the proclamation of Christ's redeeming sacrifice, a ministry equipped to proclaim the word was essential. As congregations proliferated between 1559 and 1562, men who had received scarcely more than a few months instruction in Geneva had to be pressed into pulpits. More than a few of them were former Catholic priests or monks who had been persuaded of the truth of Protestant teachings, and joined the Reformed cause. However, Reformed theology schools were quickly established alongside the municipal colleges once the Protestants gained control of several major French cities. While little is known about the quality and formation of the Reformed clergy in the decades immediately following the initial establishment of the Reformed churches, it is clear that by

---

[9] *Les Cent Cinquante Pseaumes de David mis en rime françoise par Clement Marot et Theodore Besze* (Paris, 1562), preface (unpaginated).

the early seventeenth century a university education that included formation in Hebrew, Greek, and Latin, plus extensive instruction in theology, was the rule for all Reformed ministers. The leaders of the cause around 1560 already could boast considerable learning.

An essential element of these churches was their system of ecclesiastical discipline. In the eyes of the Reformed, truly believing that Christ had sacrificed himself for one's salvation inspired one to strive to follow his commandments as scrupulously as possible out of gratitude for his love. Church discipline at once allowed church members to work together for one another's improvement and to guard the Eucharistic community against being polluted by unworthy participants. Together, the ministers and elders were to watch over the behaviour of all church members. When members strayed, they were to admonish them privately, call them before the consistory to discuss their behaviour, or finally, if absolutely necessary, exclude them from the Lord's Supper in order to get them to mend their ways. The oldest surviving consistorial registers show that even in the first years of the churches' existence, when they gathered in secret to escape detection, consistories reprimanded members for sexual misconduct, gambling, dancing, and making liturgical items for Catholic churches. They also devoted much attention to reconciling quarrelling spouses or neighbours. Reformed authors soon regularly began to claim that the initial proliferation of churches sparked a dramatic transformation of the morals of those who joined them, so that 'one could recognize a member of the Reformed Religion at twenty paces by his countenance, his words, and his deeds'.[10] Such claims undoubtedly contained a good measure of exaggeration, the better to highlight the subsequent declension. Still, great hopes of a reformation of manners unquestionably accompanied the sudden upsurge of support for the Reformed cause, and there can be no doubt that the act of joining a Reformed church in these years implied a conscious commitment to a specific doctrine and way of life that might entail estrangement from family, friends, and home. The new identity as God's chosen assumed by members of this church was often proclaimed publicly through the choice of Old Testament names for children in place of the previously popular saints' names.

By 1561 the kingdom's population had become increasingly

[10] Daniel Toussaint, *The Exercise of the Faithfull Soule* (London, 1583), dedication.

polarized around religious questions. To some Catholics the sudden proliferation of Reformed churches was alarming. 'This entire country is so full of heretics that if our Lord does not have mercy and does not intervene this year then everything is finished', a Jesuit wrote from Toulouse in 1561.[11] The Reformed movement's disproportionate appeal to town dwellers and the nobility further heightened its appearance of strength. 'The truth is that the Protestants surpass the Romanists in weight, if not in number', crowed a Reformed pamphlet in 1562.[12] But while some 'Romanists' despaired at this situation, others rallied around the cherished symbols of their faith that the Protestants mocked in their propaganda and increasingly in their deeds as well. New confraternities were founded to honour the Blessed Sacrament. Crowds gathered before street-corner images of the Virgin Mary and forced passers-by to join them in singing canticles. Protestants who ostentatiously challenged Catholic preachers or ignored processions found themselves the objects of angry attack. This rallying around Catholic symbols was encouraged by outspoken mendicant preachers who denounced the errors of the Reformed and reminded the authorities of their sworn obligation to extirpate heresy.

Not all French Christians recognized their religious aspirations in either the new practices of the Reformed churches or the traditional devotions of flamboyant Christianity. Recent scholarship has begun to call attention to those who fell between these camps: the so-called *moyenneurs*, who hoped that certain concessions to Protestant doctrine and a moderate reform of the Gallican Church might close the widening breach, or individual searchers like Pierre Caroli, an original member of the Meaux group, who passed back and forth several times between Geneva and the Catholic Church in his quest for a form of worship that conformed to his understanding of the Bible. For a brief time in 1561, the aspirations of the *moyenneurs* guided royal policy. During his reign from 1547 to 1559, Henry II pursued the legal repression of heresy with more consistent diligence than his father. However, by the later part of his reign, as Reformed churches

[11] Quoted in A. Lynn Martin, *The Jesuit Mind: The Mentality of an Elite in Early Modern France* (Ithaca, NY, 1988), p. 90.
[12] 'Exhortation aux princes et seigneurs du Conseil prive du Roy, pour obvier aux seditions qui semblent nous menacer pour le fait de la Religion', in *Mémoires de Condé*, ed. D.-F. Secousse (London, 1740), pp. 900–1.

began to multiply, his courts buckled under the task. Several parlements grew reluctant to impose death sentences, either because some of their members themselves inclined to Protestantism, or because the judges recognized the futility of trying to eliminate heresy by force. Many of those arrested and condemned for heresy were rescued by their co-religionists before their sentences could be executed. After Catherine de Medici took control of a regency government for the 10-year-old Charles IX in December 1560, she abandoned the policy of repression and turned in the direction of the *moyenneurs*. Bishops were encouraged to seek an accommodation with ministers of the new religion in their area, and a colloquy was convoked at Poissy in September 1561 between leading Catholic and Reformed spokesmen in the hope that common ground between them could be found. These efforts at reconciliation only revealed that the views of the Reformed were as far from those of the majority of French bishops 'as heaven was from earth', to use the analogy with which the Reformed spokesman Theodore Beza shocked most of those in attendance by telling them how far away Christ's body was from being in the consecrated host. Catherine then tried a second policy of compromise: granting legal toleration to two churches rather than trying to reunite them both in a single entity. The Edict of Saint-Germain (17 January 1562), commonly known as the Edict of January, gave the Protestants permission to hold organized worship anywhere in the kingdom except within walled towns, while at the same time forbidding the clergy of each faith to insult the other. Astonishingly, just seven years after the formation of the first Reformed congregations on the model of Geneva, the practice of two different forms of Christianity had become legal within the 'most Christian kingdom', 'famed for never having nourished heresy'.

6

The wars of religion, 1562–1598

Philip Benedict

When Catherine de Medici granted Protestantism legal toleration by
the Edict of January 1562, she broke dramatically with the prior traditions of the French monarchy and made France the first Western
European kingdom to grant legal recognition to two forms of Christianity at once. She also quickly learned that legislating religious co-
existence was far easier than making it work. Within three months,
violent Catholic rejection of the legitimacy of toleration combined
with Protestant hopes for the imminent triumph of their faith to
plunge the country into the first of a deadly cycle of civil wars that
would recur eight times over the next three decades. So frequent and
gruesome were the massacres accompanying these conflicts, so sear-
ing the sieges, and so numerous the assassinations of leading political
actors, that the events of the 'time of religious troubles' burned themselves into French and European historical memory for centuries to
come. From one point of view, the wars may be seen as the country's
gradual, painful working out of an equilibrium between the two
religious parties and of a set of legal terms governing their co-
existence that allowed religious plurality to function in a land whose
deepest traditions rejected it, but where two faiths had become too
deeply rooted to be eliminated. At the same time, the wars sparked
such intense questioning of the conditions under which subjects
owed obedience to their rulers and of the nature of the French constitution that they were critical to the entire subsequent evolution of the
French monarchy.

The root cause of these conflicts must be located in the clash between two antithetical systems of sacred symbols and in the violently hostile images of the other faith that came to be attached to these. The preceding chapter has highlighted the sharp contrast between the rituals and beliefs of the Reformed churches and those that prevailed within the established Catholicism of the day. These were beliefs with deadly consequences. New converts to the Reformed cause often brimmed with indignation at what they saw as the shameful idolatry of the Catholic Church, with its veneration of saints and a 'god of dough'—the consecrated host. Its prelates, they believed, had perpetrated centuries of frauds against innocent believers by inventing unnecessary rituals and dispensations, most requiring monetary payment. The faith's spread was accompanied by numerous incidents of iconoclasm that expressed the urge of eager converts to restore the purity of God's ordinances and to expose venerated images of the Virgin or saints as nothing more than wood or stone. Often, as the cause grew in strength, monastic houses and clergymen came under attack as well. But to believing Catholics of a traditionalist bent, smashing images of patron saints, blaspheming God's holy body, and attacking those who dedicated their lives to prayer, preaching, and works of charity placed the community in mortal danger, for how could God not respond with anger to such events? Floods, plagues, and earthquakes were all attributed by clerical chroniclers to the 'horrible abominations' of the Calvinist image-breakers, who since frequenting their *prêche* 'have become so depraved that all virtue has deserted them'.[1] The long-standing national myths that tied France's prosperity and survival to its loyalty to the true faith reinforced these sentiments; any concession of freedom of worship to the Protestants represented a betrayal of the crown's sworn obligations. If the crown could not fulfil its duty to punish such dangerous and depraved souls, ordinary Christians had to do it for them, by violence if necessary. Catholic violence in turn generated an increasingly aggressive Protestant response in the name of self-defence. Once the cycle of civil wars began, memories of past injuries and suspicion of the other side's intentions added still more fuel to the fire. After fifteen years of extreme instability, a measure of equilibrium began to return, as bitter experience and hard negotiation forged a set of legal terms

[1] *Relation des troubles excités par les calvinistes dans la ville de Rouen depuis l'an 1537 jusqu'en l'an 1582* (Rouen, 1837), pp. 11, 15.

governing the co-existence of the two faiths that allowed them to share the land. But less than a decade after this fragile victory was achieved, the vagaries of dynastic succession cast everything in doubt again. The military leader of the Protestants became the heir presumptive to the throne. Renewed Catholic mobilization and a final sequence of civil wars rapidly followed.

Aristocratic rivalries and grievances also contributed their deadly share. For more than sixty years prior to 1559, the Italian adventures of the successive Valois kings had enabled a warrior aristocracy still attached to chivalric ideals to pursue its quest for glory and command safely outside the kingdom. Francis I and Henry II had distributed favours among the leading families deftly enough to keep in check the jealousies that inevitably arose when ambitious families gathered at court in search of power and preferment. But by the time the crown agreed to the Peace of Cateau-Cambrésis, the growing cost of sixteenth-century warfare had all but bankrupted the king. A particularly sharp contraction in royal pensions accompanied the troop reductions brought by the peace, leaving many aristocrats feeling inadequately rewarded for their wartime service. The fatal wounding of Henry II during the jousts celebrating the peace then deprived the kingdom of an adult male ruler. His immediate successor, the 15-year-old Francis II, was related through marriage to the house of Guise, whose leading members immediately assumed predominance within the royal council and became the lightning rod for all dissatisfactions. Within months, the first major conspiracy against them had taken shape. By the time Francis II died seventeen months later, to be succeeded by a regency government headed by Catherine de Medici—a woman, and a foreigner to boot—aristocratic vendettas were taking on a life of their own. The numerous occasions for violence and betrayal offered by the subsequent civil wars then intensified them, while the regular recurrence of religious warfare enhanced the ability of provincial governors and military commanders to reinforce their clienteles and pursue their families' interests.

From the conspiracy of Amboise through the peace of Saint-Germain, 1560–1570

The sharply contrasting sets of beliefs and attitudes that fuelled the outbreak of the civil wars had already incited regional conflicts and moved both religious parties to mobilize armed men prior to January 1562. Inside France's burgeoning Reformed churches, those who drove the course of events between 1555 and 1562 dreamed of the total overthrow of the Catholic Church and were quick to see the hand of God behind events that advanced that. The pamphlets that greeted the accession of both Francis II in 1559 and Charles IX in 1560 called upon them to emulate Josiah, the Old Testament boy-king who purged Judah of its idols, and to reform the national Church, as Jeanne d'Albret would soon do in Béarn. When they failed to oblige, many members did not hesitate to take direct action to help topple the pope from his perch. Although Calvin and Beza urged the faithful to respect authority, their simultaneous encouragement of the forma-tion of Reformed churches without official sanction incited disregard for law and its agents, as local officials discovered when their orders to cease assembling were ignored. In many localities, furthermore, members of these churches soon passed beyond simply meeting in secret for worship. They raided royal prisons to save arrested co-religionists from the stake. They took over public buildings for their assemblies. They posted armed men around these assemblies to pre-vent them from being broken up. In a number of cities in southern France in 1561, they occupied the local churches, stripped them of their altars and images, forced the closure of convents and monaster-ies, and brought the saying of the mass to a halt. By the end of that year, a civic reformation had made Nîmes, Montpellier, Montauban, Castres, and a number of smaller towns entirely Protestant. By the end of 1561 as well, several provincial synods had created a system of military units attached to each church that could be mobilized as necessary to defend the cause against the 'popular mutinies' and 'undertakings of priests' that the Protestants identified as urgent threats to their security.

Aristocratic discontent also blended with Protestant enthusiasm to spur anti-Guise plotting throughout 1560. As early as August 1559, a number of Protestant ministers and publicists began to advance a legal argument that gained wide support despite its rather dubious foundation, namely that kings were subject to the oversight of a regency council established by the Estates General and princes of the blood until they reached their full majority at age 25. Calvin accepted the claim and urged the first prince of the blood, Antoine of Navarre, to assert his rights in this regard, believing him to be favourably inclined towards the Reformed cause. For a brief while in the summer of 1560, when it appeared that Antoine was about to act decisively, Calvin even helped raise men and money to support a projected rising on his behalf. This foundered when Antoine hesitated to become involved. Even before this plot aborted, other Reformed ministers within France were involved in the 'Conspiracy of Amboise', a confused mixture of a sworn conspiracy to seize control of the king by force and mass petition campaign to present him with the recently drafted Reformed confession of faith that was the most important mobilization of opposition to the policies of Francis II and the Guise. The chief participants in the plot to remove the king from the control of the Guises came from the ranks of recent aristocratic converts to the Protestant cause, including in all likelihood Louis, prince of Condé. The court got wind of their machinations and was able to arrest many of those involved as they assembled in the woods near Amboise castle. As many as a hundred conspirators were summarily executed. Condé's status as a prince of the blood and the intervention of his powerful relatives narrowly preserved him from the same fate. When the then 8-year-old Agrippa d'Aubigné passed through Amboise some months later, the heads of the conspirators still hung from the castle battlements in grisly warning. His father recognized the features of several former comrades and solemnly adjured the future Huguenot soldier, poet, and historian to avenge their deaths.

For those strongly attached to the Catholic cause, events such as the Conspiracy of Amboise appeared to confirm what the Roman Church's defenders had been proclaiming from pulpits since the first traces of Protestant heresy had appeared in France: a faith that asserted that layfolk could understand the Bible as well as Sorbonne-educated doctors and cast aside time-honoured rules about fasting and clerical celibacy was a levelling, libertine creed. Catholic mobilization proceeded as quickly as Protestant. In Provence, a group of townsfolk aroused by a Franciscan friar attacked the chateau of a

nobleman who sheltered a Protestant preacher late in 1559, precipitat-
ing a series of raids and counter-raids by armed bands of both parties
that troubled the province for much of the next year. In the south-
west, as Protestant iconoclasm spread in the autumn of 1561, the
Catholics of several regions established sworn associations to defend
the Church. At court, three of the realm's leading noblemen, the
constable of Montmorency, the duke of Guise, and the *maréchal* of
Saint-André, joined ranks to oppose the spread of heresy. Ever since
the early part of the century, certain Sorbonne theologians had advocated the view that government rested on a pact among citizens to
procure certain social benefits and had suggested the theoretical possibility that rulers whose actions imperilled those benefits violated the
contract that undergirded their power and justified disobedience. As
the crown moved to embrace a policy of toleration for Protestantism,
Parisian preachers began to apply these theories to current events.
Late in 1561 one defended the proposition that the pope could
excommunicate kings who favoured heretics and free their subjects
from their obligation to obey them. Violent attacks stained the streets
of Cahors and Carcassonne with Protestant blood. The Huguenots
feared that their enemies sought their total extermination.

In this situation of growing polarization and mobilization, it only
took a spark to ignite a conflagration. This came less than two
months after the Edict of January. On 1 March 1562, a confrontation
between the entourage of the duke of Guise and a group of Protestant
worshippers assembled inside the walls of the small town of Vassy
escalated into an affray that left 25 to 50 people dead. Was this the first
act of a Catholic plan to subvert the Edict of January and destroy the
faith? The Reformed Church of Paris and Beza circulated letters
urging all congregations to be on their guard and to raise as many
armed men as possible. The duke of Guise was summoned to court to
explain his actions, but he went instead to Paris, where he received a
hero's welcome and pledges of men and money from the pro-
Catholic municipality. Catherine turned to the prince of Condé and
urged him to take the young king, then at Fontainebleau, under his
protection, but he refused to do so. The Catholic 'Triumvirs', Guise,
Montmorency, and Saint-André, did so instead and obliged Charles
and Catherine to return to Paris with them. Condé went to Orléans
where he issued a manifesto declaring that the king had been illegally
kidnapped and calling upon his compatriots to join him in defending

the king's authority and God's honour. Over the next month, the Huguenots seized control of roughly one-third of the kingdom's sixty largest cities. Wherever they took control, iconoclastic violence and the prohibition of the mass soon followed. Such Catholic-controlled towns as Sens and Gaillac witnessed further massacres of Protestants. Although the Huguenots claimed to be acting in the name of the king, they refused to let representatives dispatched from court into the towns they had seized. Catherine desperately tried to negotiate a settlement but ultimately was obliged to send troops against them.

The crown and Catholic forces had a significant numerical and logistical advantage in this as in future conflicts, and they benefited from the assistance of Spanish troops that Philip II dispatched across the border to help fight the Protestants, but they were unable to deliver a knockout blow. Where the Huguenots controlled a locality, they seized church property and revenue, established a political council, and appointed military commanders to lead the troops they were thus able to raise. In the heavily Protestant *pays d'états* of Languedoc and Dauphiné, they convoked their own meetings of the provincial estates and took control of regional tax collection. Queen Elizabeth sent 6,000 troops and a large loan. The royal forces won several pitched battles and recaptured many Huguenot-held towns, but the going was slow, and the costs were high. Anthony of Navarre and Saint-André died of wounds incurred in battle. Montmorency and Condé were each taken prisoner by the other side. After the last of the Triumvirs, the duke of Guise, was slain in an ambush while besieging Orléans—the family subsequently blamed his killing on the admiral Coligny, thus beginning a bitter vendetta—the way was finally clear for Catherine to negotiate the peace she had pursued at regular intervals throughout the conflict. The terms of the peace restricted Protestant rights of worship to a specified universe of localities, while ordering the re-establishment of Catholic worship throughout the land. Many Protestant ministers denounced this restriction of their rights of worship as a betrayal of the cause, but its military men saw that the peace represented the course of political wisdom. The war, not the peace, was the disaster for the Protestants, for it ended the dramatic numerical expansion that they had previously been experiencing. 'If the first war of 1563 had not taken place,' the Venetian ambassador subsequently reported, 'France would now be Huguenot or almost entirely so, because the people were rapidly changing their faith. . . . But when they passed from words to weapons and began to rob, destroy and kill with great cruelty, the poor people began to say, "What kind of religion is this? They claim to understand the gospel better than anybody, but where do they find Christ commanding to steal your neighbor's cloak and kill your fellow man?"[2]

The new peace held for more than four years, thanks in large measure to the vigorous efforts of the queen mother and the chancellor Michel de L'Hôpital to ensure that its terms were respected, to elaborate laws to regulate new points of dispute between the two parties as they arose, and to demonstrate through both word and deed that their goal was to maintain a 'just balance' between them. To rekindle loyalty to the crown, they also took the now teenaged king, who was declared of age to rule in 1563, on a 27-month-long journey around the kingdom, during the course of which they hosted the queen of Spain and the duke of Alva for two weeks in Bayonne. Huguenot suspicion of Catholic extermination plots bordered fatally on paranoia, however. Several events in 1566–1567 intensified Protestant mistrust, notably the renewed growth of Guise influence at court, the passage of Spanish troops along France's eastern border en route to the Netherlands, and the crown's refusal to grant Condé the high military command he had been promised. Rumours developed that the queen mother had made a pact with Alva at Bayonne to eliminate the faith, and that Swiss troops were on their way to Paris and Orléans to implement this. To forestall these phantoms, Condé and Coligny attempted to separate the king from his Swiss guard as he travelled near Meaux. By dint of hard riding, Charles IX escaped their clutches. The Protestant chieftains then briefly besieged the capital. Catherine could not understand what seemed to her an unprovoked attack that sabotaged her policy of equilibrium. She subsequently mistrusted and disliked the Protestant commanders.

The civil war that followed the surprise of Meaux was brief, but so was the peace signed six months later, for the renewal of hostilities so intensified the suspicion and hostility between the rival parties that each used the peace primarily to rearm. The uneasy truce collapsed in October 1568. Condé and Coligny, again fearing a joint Spanish-Catholic plot against their lives, fled in the direction of La Rochelle,

---

[2] Eugenio Alberi (ed.), *Relazioni degli Ambasciatori Veneti al Senato*, 15 vols. (Florence, 1839–63), lst ser., iv. 185–6.

mobilizing men and seizing towns along the route. With the moderate L'Hôpital ousted from the chancellorship, the crown fought Protestantism vigorously, revoking all legal toleration of Reformed worship, ordering the faith's ministers to leave the country within fifteen days, and launching extensive campaigns across the south-west that lasted for fully twenty-two months. Again its efforts were inadequate to crush a determined minority that had reinforced its hold over the portions of the kingdom in which it was strongest. Ultimately, exhaustion led to still another edict of pacification in August 1570 that restored toleration of Reformed worship while allowing the Protestants to retain control of several of their fortified towns as points of refuge in the event of further hostilities. Catholic opinion was hardly pacified. Over the following year, some of the largest incidents to date of anti-Protestant mob violence broke out in Amiens, Rouen, and Paris against those Huguenots who dared to return home in accordance with the provisions of the peace.

The St Bartholomew's massacre and its consequences

The escalating spiral of confessional antagonism reached its crescendo in the massacre that broke out in Paris on St Bartholomew's Day (24 August) 1572 and spread from there to a dozen provincial cities. The occasion was provided by the festivities to celebrate the marriage of Henry of Navarre to Marguerite of Valois, which brought the better part of the aristocracy to Paris. As the Admiral Coligny returned to his lodgings from the Louvre on the night of 22 August, a hired killer fired a shot. The would-be assassin's aim was poor. The shot merely grazed the admiral. As Coligny's co-religionists angrily demanded a judicial investigation and punishment for the attack, Charles IX was torn between fury at the challenge to the peace he was trying to reinforce with the royal marriage and fear over the possibility of a new civil war. A meeting with a few of his closest advisers convinced him that the leading Protestant noblemen threatened his authority and needed to be eliminated. He gave the order to kill a specified group of them, beginning with Coligny himself. A detachment of the royal guards led by the young Duke Henri of Guise dispatched the admiral on the 24th and flung his body into the street, where Parisians mutilated it, dragged it triumphantly through the city, and hung it from the Montfaucon gallows. As those dispatched to do the killing went about their business, rumours distorted the nature of the king's instructions, and the controlled operation against the leading Protestant noblemen grew into a vast bloodletting by ardently anti-Protestant members of the civic militia, who had allowed themselves to believe that the king had finally sanctioned the long-hoped-for eradication of all Huguenots. Groups of killers sacked Huguenot houses and butchered their inhabitants for four days in the capital, despite reiterated proclamations over the final three that the king wished the killing to end. From Paris, the violence spread to at least a dozen provincial cities over the next days and weeks. Perhaps 10,000 victims died in all. As terrified escapees streamed into Geneva, the situation appeared worse yet. 'Fifty thousand people have been slaughtered in France in the space of eight or ten days. The Christians who remain wander by night in the forests. I hope that the wild animals there show them more clemency than those in human form,' wrote one.[3]

Since the key decisions behind the two attacks on Coligny were taken in secret, and since in their aftermath every party involved had strong incentives either to cover up their culpability or to claim undue credit for a deed that many Catholics greeted with glee, responsibility for the events that precipitated the massacre remains murky to this day. In the midst of the events themselves, Charles IX initially blamed the violence on a 'sedition' sparked by the Guises, then took personal responsibility for the killing of the Huguenot aristocrats, claiming that it was necessary to prevent a Protestant conspiracy. Much of the Protestant polemical literature of the subsequent years directed its opprobrium against the wicked Italian queen mother and her Machiavellian advisers. By the nineteenth century, it had become received wisdom that the protective Catherine had ordered Coligny killed because she was jealous of his increasing influence over her son and fearful that he was leading him into intervention on behalf of the Dutch rebels against Philip II, a policy that risked disaster. Recently, historians have reopened the question. Given

[3] Quoted in Scott M. Manetsch, *Theodore Beza and the Quest for Peace in France, 1572–1598* (Leiden, 2000), p. 34, n. 18.

current sensibilities, most, unsurprisingly, have tended to attribute the suspicion of Catherine to misogyny and xenophobia, arguing that a queen who had worked so long for peace between the rival religions would not have been likely to incite the first attack on Coligny. It nonetheless bears noting that several of the diplomats at the French court whose business it was to sort fact from fiction, including some Italian ones, reported to their superiors that Catherine had grown jealous of Coligny's influence and was responsible for the attack on him. She certainly does not appear to have been dismayed by the outcome of the massacre, for she burst out laughing when Henry of Navarre attended mass in its wake. The Guises, Coligny's sworn enemies since the ambush of the elder duke of Guise in 1563, certainly were involved. The king's younger brother, the future Henry III, may also have been.

If the exact division of responsibility for the massacre may never be apportioned with certainty, its broader ramifications are clear. First, it precipitated a massive wave of defections from the Protestant cause. In the wake of the killing, Charles IX forbade the Reformed from gathering for worship—to protect them against violence, his edict proclaimed, but also because he undoubtedly realized that the massacre might end the Protestant problem once and for all. Even in many areas where the Huguenots formed a majority of the population and had disregarded the 1568 prohibition of Reformed services, they were now so alarmed that they dared not disobey. In certain Catholic-controlled towns such as Tours or Toulouse, defections had already begun to eat away at the cause from 1562 onward. As the Indian summer of provincial massacres stretched into October, thousands more Protestants lost heart, fled abroad, or sought refuge in a few strongholds within France. As one Catholic priest gloatingly recorded in his diary, 'The Huguenots who remained after the seditions, both in Paris and in the rest of France, except for those of La Rochelle, Sancerre and Montauban, all went to mass, . . . and it seemed as though they had never left or been separated, so cheerfully did they behave, going not by ones or twos but in large groups to sing in the churches.'[4] Ultimately, the Protestants were able to defend themselves and regain legal rights of worship, but when their

[4] Quoted in Philip Benedict, *Rouen during the Wars of Religion* (Cambridge, 1981), p. 148.

churches began to gather safely again in the later 1570s, they were often a shadow of their former selves: just 1,500–3,000 in Rouen, a church which had had boasted about 16,500 members around 1565, or 3,500–4,000 in Caen, where almost 11,000 people had worshipped between 1564 and 1568. In many cities such as these, where the Huguenots had taken control in 1562 or been a large and threatening minority presence throughout the 1560s, they now were transformed into a cowed and docile remnant. Kingdom-wide, for every person killed in the St Bartholomew's massacres, dozens returned to the Catholic fold or fled abroad.

That any Reformed churches were able to worship legally in France after 1572 testifies to the desperate resistance that the Protestants mounted from their greatest strongholds, such as La Rochelle, Sancerre, and Montauban. While their co-religionists elsewhere fled, abjured, or ceased to assemble for worship, the inhabitants of these cities closed their gates to the king's officials and disregarded the prohibition of Reformed worship. In Rouergue, the Vivarais, and the Castrais, Huguenot noblemen re-established the military organization they had used in previous civil wars. The crown responded with force and took Sancerre after a five-month siege that so depleted the resources of the besieged city that incidents of cannibalism were reliably reported. However, a still larger combined land and sea operation against La Rochelle bogged down into eight months of fruitless attacks on the fortified port that cost the ill-supplied royal army over 40 per cent of its commanding officers. Ultimately, the crown had to raise the siege and concede new rights of worship to La Rochelle's Protestant inhabitants, as well as those of Montauban and Nîmes. But the Huguenots did not let their guard down after this triumph. Instead, delegates from the different regions where they had established local political and military organizations were summoned to a succession of larger political assemblies likened to Estates-General. The first two of these, which met in Millau in December 1573 and July 1574, established guidelines for the subsequent convocation of such gatherings and named a protector of the faith to take command of the Protestant military forces. For the next half-century, Huguenot political assemblies of this sort gathered intermittently to deliberate about the cause's interests and organize its defence. A second consequence of the St Bartholomew's massacre was thus that it prompted the Protestants to develop a supra-regional system of political organization and military defence that enabled the party to defend its interests with an effectiveness out of all proportion to its reduced numbers.

The massacre also prompted a flurry of publications about the limits of obedience to royal authority that made the years after 1572 one of the most fertile periods of political reflection in all of French history. In 1573 Genevan printers brought out the first published editions of two daring works written before 1572. Étienne de La Boétie's *Discourse on Voluntary Servitude*, already two decades old but never previously printed, was a reflection on how men, who were created by nature free and equal, had come to accept and even take pleasure in the chains of government. It did not advocate throwing off these chains by force, instead urging the truly wise to cultivate inner freedom. Its bold, proto-Rousseauian contrast between humanity's original freedom and current oppression nevertheless cast the prevailing systems of political rule in a dark light. The *Francogallia* of the Huguenot jurist François Hotman, largely written in 1567–8, then offered a historical account of the declension La Boétie had reflected upon more abstractly. Exploring the institutions of French government both prior to Rome's conquest of Gaul and during the early Middle Ages, it suggested that a public council, the ancestor of the Estates-General, had once actively shared in the country's government and effectively limited the authority of its rulers. In the last centuries of the Middle Ages, however, these ancient checks on royal power had been destroyed by the advance of Roman law, ecclesiastical ultramontanism, and other forms of corruption. The demonstration was so powerful that the moderate Catholic lawyer-diarist Pierre de l'Estoile recorded that it was 'well regarded and well received by all men of learning and good Frenchmen ... [except] some corrupt Macchiavellists and Italianized Frenchmen'.[5]

Two tracts written after the events of 1572 soon followed. Theodore Beza's *On the Right of Magistrates over their Subjects*, anonymously published in both Geneva and Heidelberg in 1574, asked whether subjects had any recourse against a ruler who had become a tyrant. While private citizens did not, it argued, the magistrates of inferior jurisdictions such as town councils did. Having been given a share in

[5] *Journal de l'Estoile pour le règne de Henri III (1574–1589)*, ed. Louis-Raymond Lefèvre (Paris, 1943), p. 89.

government, they could legitimately resist unjust orders from their superiors. Indeed, they bore an obligation to summon a general assembly that could moderate the ruler's tyranny, uphold the law, and exercise the authority granted to the Estates-General under France's ancient constitution. The work thus offered a theoretical justification for the Huguenot assemblies. At the same time, it omitted reference to recent events and couched its arguments abstractly in terms of tyranny and the ancient constitution, so that it could appeal to Catholics as well as Huguenots dissatisfied with the current state of affairs. A still more copious but similarly abstract justification of resistance by lesser magistrates to unjust rule soon followed with the anonymous *Vindication of Liberty Against Tyrants*, most often attributed to Philippe du Plessis Mornay and/or Hubert Languet. Written in 1575–6, it circulated widely in manuscript before being first published in Basel in 1579. More than a dozen further printings, including English translations that appeared in 1648 and 1689, made it the most enduringly important of these 'monarchomach' justifications of armed resistance against rulers who violated their covenant with their subjects.

While these treatises provided powerful new arguments for those who had already begun to suggest prior to 1572 that unjust rulers could be legitimately resisted and that the French monarchy was properly a mixed constitution, they generated critics as well as admirers. None would prove more influential than the judge and polymath Jean Bodin. His 1576 *Six Books of the Commonwealth* had already begun to take shape prior to 1572 as part of his larger attempt to build a new science of jurisprudence on the study of universal history. Crucial features of the work were nonetheless shaped to respond to the recent treatises justifying resistance to unjust rule, which he regarded as so many invitations to 'a licentious anarchy . . . worse than the harshest tyranny in the world'. Bodin particularly insisted that sovereignty within any state involved a bundle of attributes among which the right to make laws was paramount, where earlier theorists had tended to see the law as something that existed independently of the ruling authorities, which they merely confirmed or clarified. He further argued that this 'high, absolute and perpetual power over the citizens' had to reside in a single locus; any system of overlapping authority involved fatal contradictions. Theoreticians of absolutism in the early seventeenth century would draw heavily on this new definition of sovereignty, which they, like Bodin, saw as vested fully in the king in France. The political reflection of the years 1572–6 thus contributed to subsequent absolutist as well as constitutional thought.

The character of the civil wars also changed in the wake of the St Bartholomew's massacre. The element of crowd involvement in the 1572 butchery, at once a re-enactment of numerous previous incidents of religious violence, yet on a scale without precedent since the king was believed to have condoned the killing, proved to be both the crescendo of popular religious rioting and its catharsis. Episodes that had become common during the previous twelve years—Protestant attacks on holy images or religious processions; Catholic attacks on Protestants returning from worship or seeking to bury their dead; the cold-blooded slaughter of neighbours of the opposite faith—all but disappeared from most corners of the kingdom after 1572, in part in revulsion against the sheer scale and horror of the events of that year, in part because the tense balance between the rival religious groups that had prevailed in many localities before that date gave way to the clear domination of one side or the other. But all fighting did not cease. In parts of the south and west, pockets of Protestant strength interlocked with bastions of Catholic fidelity. Here small-scale warfare became nearly permanent for much of the 1570s, as garrisons from each side's strongholds mounted raids against the other's, obliging communities caught in the middle to raise their own armed men in self-defence. Documents from the small towns of these regions reveal a proliferation of military captains who supplemented their peacetime income with the booty of local command.

Meanwhile, at the national level, intensifying aristocratic discontent combined with the Protestant desire for more extensive rights of worship to keep the cycle of violence turning. The last of Henry II's four sons, François, duke of Alençon (later Anjou), grew embittered after being denied the title of lieutenant-general on the 1573 departure of his older brother Henri to become king of Poland. He soon was the point man for a series of plots at court. The Huguenots of several provinces seized a series of towns early in 1574 and proclaimed themselves defenders of the 'public good', awakening echoes of the fifteenth-century League of the Public Weal against Louis XI. Among the 'Malcontents' who came over to the side of the opposition was the powerful Catholic governor of Languedoc, Henri de Montmorency-Damville, who had been angered by his brother's imprisonment in connection with the plots around the duke of Alençon. Damville soon forged a union with the Protestants of Languedoc that promised toleration for both faiths and gave rise to a self-convoked 1575 'Estates-General of the Provinces of the Union' that met in Nîmes. Amid the agitation of these years, Henry of Navarre escaped from court and returned to the Reformed faith, while the powerful and turbulent viscount of Turenne joined the faith in a particularly self-interested conversion. So strong were the forces aligned against the crown that Henry III could not avoid another war soon after returning to the kingdom in the wake of Charles IX's death in 1574. The war went disastrously for the new monarch. After two years, he was forced to accept the so-called 'Peace of Monsieur', brokered by his brother. This granted the Protestants freedom to worship anywhere in the kingdom except within two leagues of Paris or the court, granted them eight fortified strongholds and special courts to hear their lawsuits, and conferred a modest compensation on families of the victims of the St Bartholomew's massacre. It also called for the rapid convocation of an Estates-General and transferred several provincial governorships to prominent Malcontents.

So generous were the terms of this peace that it provoked the more zealous Catholics and those noblemen who stood to lose commands to organize in opposition. As we have seen, sworn associations dedicated to defending the Catholic faith had taken shape in parts of the south-west as early as 1561. Such organizations spread to many other regions over the subsequent years. The 1576 League of Péronne, founded by a group of Picard noblemen threatened with ouster from local captaincies by the nomination of Condé as provincial governor, combined the crusading rhetoric of these associations with the constitutional aspirations increasingly associated with aristocratic discontent. Its early manifestos spoke of a 'holy and christian union' to defend the Roman Church against 'Satan's ministers' and of restoring provincial liberties 'as they were in the time of king Clovis'. Efforts were made to spread the League to other provinces and to establish a supreme commander, ideally the young Henri, duke of Guise, whose military exploits had already won him the wound of his glorious nickname, 'le Balafré' (i.e. 'Scarface'). Those favourable to the League proved so menacing and so successful in the elections for the Estates-General convoked in accordance with the Peace of Monsieur that

Henry III placed himself at the head of the movement, revoked toleration for Protestant worship, and sought to convince the Estates to vote substantial new taxes for another war against the Huguenots. In keeping with deeply rooted myths about the extent of wasteful spending at court and the ability of kings to 'live of their own', the delegates refused to vote any such taxes, insisting that economies at court and proper fiscal oversight were all that was required to produce the money for a larger army. The sixth civil war that followed lasted only until September 1577, so ill-supplied and eager to negotiate were both sides. The Peace of Bergerac that ended it scaled Protestant rights of worship back to a fixed set of localities, as had been the case from 1563 to 1568 and 1570 to 1572. It also confirmed the Protestant control of eight strongholds, special courts divided between Protestant and Catholic judges to hear their lawsuits, and tax reductions for the families of victims of the St Bartholomew's massacres.

Amid the turbulent events of the period 1572–7, one final development may also be glimpsed: a growing, if still begrudging, acceptance of the argument that religious toleration was less of an evil than endless warfare. In the immediate aftermath of the St Bartholomew's massacre, many Catholics exultantly imagined that the blow had put an end to Protestantism in France once and for all. As Huguenot resistance revived and it became clear that even this stunning a blow had not wiped out the faith or put an end to fratricidal warfare, some who had previously opposed toleration began to accept it. One of the most ardent Catholic warriors during the early civil wars, the duke of Montpensier, stunned his fellow noble deputies at the 1576 Estates-General with a speech that declared that the events that he had experienced and the misery he had observed among the population had convinced him that sufferance of 'those of the new religion' was the only proper course for the kingdom until all could be reunited in a single Church. Despite vigorous royal lobbying at the gathering, only a bare majority of the Third Estate voted in favour of repealing the Peace of Monsieur and renewing the crusade against Protestantism. The next year's Peace of Bergerac broke down briefly in 1580, but its key provisions endured for eight years, longer than any previous religious peace. They might have endured far longer, if only Henry III's procreative efforts and political decisions had proven less spectacularly ill-fated.

The tragedy of Henry III

While Charles IX, who was just 23 when he died, scarcely had the opportunity to emerge from his mother's shadow and cast his personal stamp on events, Henry III's personality and politics placed him at centre stage for the sixteen years of his reign. Less than two years younger than his brother, he came to the throne already a military hero in Catholic eyes for having participated in several successful battles against the Huguenots, but he proved to be anything but the military champion of the faith that so many Catholics longed for as king. Although spectacularly pious—he founded and participated in the rituals of one of the companies of hooded Penitents that began to proliferate across France in these years—he distanced himself from the warrior code by which most of upper French aristocracy still lived. He preferred dancing and tennis to hunting and jousting, publicly sported matching pearl earrings and an open neckline 'like the ladies at court wear', and founded and took part in a palace academy at which leading humanists led discussions about moral philosophy. With the royal coffers dangerously depleted, he raised the *taille* sharply and had recourse to the sale of public offices on an unprecedented scale. The leading grandees grew more undisciplined and assertive than ever, with the duke of Alençon/Anjou pursuing an endless round of schemes and the Guises claiming a share of the royal succession; a genealogy of the house of Lorraine published in 1580 traced the family's roots back to Charlemagne. Under these circumstances, Henry relied heavily on a small coterie of favoured advisers whom he raised up from noble families of the second rank and to whom he became fondly attached, most notably the dukes of Epernon and Joyeuse. He sought to impose a new ceremoniousness on the notoriously informal French court, promulgating successive etiquette regulations, dining on a raised platform separated from the rest of the court by a balustrade, and insisting upon being called 'Your Majesty'. All of these policies and personality traits made him the object of considerable criticism, about which we are exceptionally well informed thanks to L'Estoile's extensive diary, which includes every scrap of gossip and propaganda on which its compiler could lay his hands. At the same time, many of his policies may be judged to be necessary responses to the difficult situation in which he found himself. During the central years of his reign strong patches of light began to emerge amid the darkness. The commerce of key ports such as Rouen and Marseille flourished during the later 1570s and early 1580s. Henry's solicitation of advice about how to reform government gave rise to an important revision of the country's law codes. For these reasons, a number of historians have recently sought to revise the highly negative assessment of Henry's rulership that long dominated the depiction of his reign, echoing L'Estoile's own judgement that he could have been a good king in a better time.

In monarchical polities, however, biology is destiny. For all of both Henry's strengths and weaknesses as a ruler, he had one unquestionable failing: he and his queen, Louise de Vaudémont, could not beget an heir. Since sixteenth-century monarchs had very little privacy, we know that they tried as hard as possible. Reports inform us that they made love every night for a solid month. They gathered advice from the leading fertility consultants of the day. They had special prayers inserted into the liturgy of the kingdom's cathedrals for an entire year. Nothing availed. Their infertility became a national crisis when the duke of Anjou died in June 1584, still unmarried himself (Elizabeth of England was among those he had vainly courted). The heir-presumptive as most people reckoned the succession became the king's twenty-first cousin Henry of Navarre, the military commander of the Protestant party, although it was also possible to advance a legal case for Henry's twentieth cousin once removed, the Catholic cardinal of Bourbon. The threat of a Protestant succession suddenly loomed. Since elsewhere in Europe the accession of a Protestant king had typically been followed by measures making Protestantism the obligatory religion of state, the relatively successful settlement of the religious question defined by the Peace of Bergerac now seemed to be cast into doubt, even though Navarre hastened to stress in print that he had always tolerated Catholic worship in his ancestral lands and would do so as well if he became king.

In response to the new threat of a Protestant king, a number of Catholic aristocrats led by the duke of Guise revived the League of Péronne and won a pledge of assistance from Philip II of Spain. Parisian Catholics organized an affiliated network of cells in the capital and sought to extend branches into provincial cities as well. A manifesto issued by the cause in March 1585 articulated a series of goals: the cardinal of Bourbon should be named heir-apparent; Catholicism should be re-established as the sole religion of the realm; taxes should be reduced to the levels of the reign of Charles IX; the nobility should be restored to the full enjoyment of its privileges; and an Estates-General should be summoned every three years. The League mobilized troops, gained control of a number of border towns, and won its first great victory when the alarmed Catherine de Medici negotiated an agreement with it that committed the crown to outlaw Protestant worship once again. A royal edict of July 1585 rescinded permission for Reformed services and required all subjects to profess the Catholic faith or leave the kingdom within six months. Predictably, the Huguenot strongholds vowed their defiance, mobilized troops, and obtained the assistance of foreign Protestant princes. Civil war began again.

The years 1586–7 were perhaps the worst France had yet experienced in the century. Two consecutive bad harvests brought famine to much of the country, leading an English ship captain returning from Rouen to report in August 1587, 'they dye in evrie streete and at evrie gate, morning and eveninge, by viii or xii in a place.'[6] Plague swept across much of the south-east, carrying away over half of the population in some towns, accompanied by hallucinatory scenes. In Die (Dauphiné), according to a local chronicler, those stricken with the disease dug their own graves and lay down in them to await death. Such instances of God's wrath, at least one pamphlet suggested, stemmed from the continued presence of heretics in the land. Henry III, however, moved slowly to punish Huguenot resistance in the south, awakening doubts about his commitment to eliminating the faith. Queen Elizabeth's execution in February 1587 of Mary Stuart, once Francis II's wife and thus France's former queen, further shocked Catholic opinion and intensified fears about the fate that awaited them if a Protestant acceded to the throne. Against this backdrop of anxiety and suffering, Henry III finally dispatched two important armies late in the summer of 1587 to combat the Protestants and the German mercenaries who had marched to their aid: a larger one under the duke of Joyeuse, and a smaller one under the duke of Guise. Contrary to his evident expectations, the larger force was defeated and Joyeuse died in battle, but Guise triumphed over the

---

[6] Quoted in Benedict, *Rouen during the Wars of Religion*, p. 173.

reîtres at Auneau and burnished his reputation as Catholicism's great champion.

During the winter lull after the German mercenaries had been driven out, a family council of the house of Lorraine gathered at Nancy and adopted a new set of terms that they pressed upon the king: the removal of Epernon from the king's council; implementation of the decrees of the Council of Trent; the creation of inquisitorial tribunals in every province to stamp out heresy; new taxes to pursue the war against the Huguenots, with all who had been Protestants at any point since 1560 contributing fully at a third of their property; and permission for the heads of the League to fortify a number of garrison towns, just as the Huguenots had previously been permitted to have their strongholds. While Henry considered these demands, he ordered the duke of Guise to stay away from Paris, knowing how intensely the Catholic capital longed for action against heresy and seethed with hatred against the 'politiques' and 'atheists' who refused to subordinate every consideration to this goal. In May 1588 Guise defied the king's orders and entered the capital, an action that appears to have been determined in consultation with the Spanish ambassador and timed to coincide with the sailing of the Armada against England, so that Henry III could not think of assisting the English or blocking off Channel ports to Spanish ships needing shelter. Henry responded by marching twenty units of his guards into Paris. Rather than forestalling an insurrection, this action triggered one. As the Swiss guards began to fan out around the city, they found the Left Bank, the centre of League militancy, already in arms. Their arrival elsewhere in the city prompted the erection of barricades across the major intersections, for outside troops were always hated and feared in sixteenth-century cities, which jealously guarded their rights to assure their own defence. Several brief skirmishes convinced the Swiss that they had no choice but to lay down their arms and accept the duke of Guise's offer of safe escort from the city. The king fled the agitated city the next day. Immediately thereafter, the League took full control of the municipal government and city militia. This 'Day of the Barricades' (12 May 1588) revealed how great a threat to royal authority the League had become.

Soon after fleeing Paris, Henry convoked a new Estates-General that he apparently hoped would be the occasion for him to rally his supporters, or at least to explain the immense fiscal problems that stood in the way of new military campaigns against the Protestants. The League rallied its supporters and, after electoral assemblies that often became the scenes of tense battles between the two sides, assured the election of many delegates committed to it. The Parisian militants advocated dramatic modifications of the kingdom's constitution, urging that it be recognized as fundamental law that the consent of the Estates-General was required for all taxation or decisions of war and peace, that the Estates-General had the power to depose kings who violated the rules of law or equity, and that when it was not in session, it could establish a special committee to ensure that its ordinances were upheld. As the vast Spanish fleet made its way around the country's west coast, the king's power seemed to reach its nadir. On 15 July he swore the 'Edict of Union', reportedly sobbing as he did so. He vowed to fight heresy without cease, agreed that a heretic could never succeed to the French crown, and amnestied all those involved in the events surrounding the Day of the Barricades. Soon thereafter Guise won appointment as lieutenant-general of the kingdom. The dispersal of the Spanish fleet gave Henry a bit more room for manoeuvre. He demonstrated a new determination to rule as his own man by firing the team of secretaries of state who had served both him and his mother for the preceding decades. Within two days of the opening of the Estates-General at Blois in October, however, the suspicious deputies forced him to elevate the Edict of Union's prohibition of a heretic king to the status of a fundamental law of the kingdom. The assembly then took up a range of grievances while refusing to see the need for anything other than economizing on the king's part to finance the war against the heretics. By December Henry was convinced that the only way to restore his authority was to have the duke and cardinal of Guise killed. The royal guards carried out the task inside the chateau of Blois on 23 December. 'I want to be king, and no longer a prisoner and a slave,' he told his mother when the deed was done.[7]

To the large fraction of Catholic opinion that reacted in shock, these killings made Henry a tyrant, not a king. Preachers competed with one another to denounce the villainy of the 'wicked Herod' who had martyred the faith's greatest defenders. The theology faculty of Paris met in solemn conclave and declared that his subjects no longer

[7] Quoted in R. J. Knecht, *Catherine de Medici* (London, 1998), p. 267.

had to obey him. Woodcuts depicted the man they now simply labelled 'Henry of Valois' as a hermaphrodite, a debauchee who commandeered nuns from convents for his sexual pleasure, and a devil in penitential disguise. Emotional processions wound through the streets of Paris imploring God to temper his wrath.

Uprisings followed in many provincial cities. In some, the same exalted religious atmosphere that prevailed in Paris contributed to the League takeover. In others, militants for the cause profited from the play of local factions and rivalries, the influence of locally prominent noblemen, or a desire for increased municipal autonomy. Where the Huguenots had seized roughly one-third of the kingdom's sixty largest cities in 1562, the League by March 1589 controlled slightly more than half, including Paris and the four largest provincial cities: Rouen, Lyon, Orléans, and Toulouse.

Henry III still might almost have succeeded in carrying off what early seventeenth-century political writers called a 'coup d'état', i.e. sudden blow against an overmighty subject that served to restore royal authority. After disposing of the Guises, he allied himself with Henry of Navarre and asserted anew that the Béarnais was the true heir to the throne. Together, the two Henries directed their troops towards Paris and placed the city under siege. Whether they might have retaken it and put a prompt end to the revolt throughout the country will never be known. On 1 August 1589, just two days after Henry had arrived at Saint-Cloud, the Dominican friar Jacques Clément went to the royal camp, gained an audience with the king, pulled a dagger from beneath his robe, and fatally stabbed him. League treatises justified the killing of tyrants by private individuals and hailed Clément as a divinely inspired martyr. The last acts of Henry's reign were bathed in as much blood as a Shakespearean tragedy.

The war of the Bourbon succession

Matters now came down to a war of succession to the vacant throne between Henry of Navarre and the various candidates who would emerge from the camp of the League. Initially, the outcome of the struggle was anything but certain. On learning of Henry III's assassination, the normally decisive Navarre vacillated between heading immediately for his strongholds south of the Loire and presenting himself to the captains of the royal army as their king, so unsure was he that Catholic noblemen would accept the legitimacy of his succession. He chose the latter course, and after some early hesitations, more noblemen rallied to his standard than entered the armies of the League. The percentage of nobles who tried to remain out of the conflict was higher yet, however, and the League initially controlled the majority of the larger cities and several vast provinces. Queen Elizabeth sent aid to Navarre, but the duke of Savoy, the duke of Lorraine, and the crack Spanish troops of the duke of Parma all intervened at various points on behalf of the League. If Henry IV ultimately triumphed, his victory was anything but easy or sure. Four considerations chiefly explain it.

First, the battle-hardened Béarnais was a far better general than any of the League's commanders. Within eight months of his accession, he twice engaged the new head of the Guise family, the duke of Mayenne, in direct combat. In both instances, at Arques in September 1589 and at Ivry in March 1590, he won major victories despite being outnumbered. In an age that was quick to see the hand of providence in events, these victories reinforced his claim to being the kingdom's legitimate ruler and were loudly trumpeted in royalist propaganda.

Second, and perhaps most importantly, the League was internally divided and never managed to provide a unified counter-force to Henry IV. First off, it was divided between its aristocratic and urban wings. The Council of Sixteen that controlled Paris advocated calling an Estates-General as promptly as possible and sought to establish a standing committee to oversee the war effort until the Estates-General could take charge. The chief military men did not relish the possibility that an assembly of their social inferiors might dictate policy to them. They made no initial effort to convoke an Estates-General. Cooperation between the two groups was always strained. The tension between them erupted into open conflict in 1591, when the Sixteen arrested three members of the parlement of Paris whom they suspected of secretly aiding Navarre and condemned them to death. This attack on the judges of the land's highest court shocked Mayenne, who came to Paris, oversaw the arrest and execution of four of those responsible, and packed the city government with men loyal to him.

The League also rapidly divided over the question of whom to support for the succession to the throne. The cause's initial candidate, the elderly cardinal of Bourbon, had been taken into custody when the duke and cardinal of Guise were killed. He never escaped from his prison cell and died on 9 May 1590. With no direct successor to pick up his mantle, a series of claimants stepped into the breach, including the duke of Mayenne, the duke of Lorraine, the duke of Savoy, and the Spanish Infanta, who as the sole child of Philip II and Elizabeth of Valois was Henry III's closest blood relative, but whose claim required setting aside the Salic law prohibiting the French royal succession from passing through the female line. Factions formed around each claimant. Their ambitions prevented them from working effectively together. The full extent of the cause's divisions stood pitilessly revealed when its leaders finally consented to convene the long-awaited meeting of an Estates-General in order to elect the legitimate successor. The small body of delegates that was able to overcome the insecurity of travel and assemble in Paris in January 1593 broke up in confusion eight months later without ever resolving the issue. The League never effectively settled the problem of the succession, while the campaign of the Infanta's supporters to secure her claim to the throne made the cause appear to be a tool for Spanish conquest.

By the time the Estates-General broke up in August 1593, a third factor was also swinging opinion in Henry IV's favour. The war of the Bourbon succession was by far the most devastating of all of the civil wars. Where the campaigning of most previous conflicts had been confined to portions of the kingdom and had rarely lasted long, the war of the Bourbon succession reached into almost every province and lasted up to nine years in some. Few of the country's major rivers or roadways were controlled by one party for their entire length, so commerce dwindled to a trickle, except in a few peripheral ports such as La Rochelle. In 1590, after defeating Mayenne at Ivry, Henry IV besieged Paris for four months and reduced its inhabitants to grinding up the bones of the dead for nourishment. Only the diversion of a large force of Spanish troops from the Low Countries saved the city and forced Henry to raise the siege. In 1591–2 it was Rouen's turn to undergo five months of siege and starvation before being relieved by the Spanish, just as rioters within the city were beginning to demand peace or bread. By late 1593, peasant leagues were forming to agitate for peace in several provinces. With the League unable to unite behind a single claimant to the throne, Henry IV seemed more and more to be the only person who could restore the order people increasingly longed for.

The astute policies that Navarre embraced as the country tired of war were the final cause of his triumph. Most famously, as war weariness grew, he let it be known that he wanted to receive instruction in the Catholic faith. After a suitable period of tutoring, he publicly abjured his Protestant beliefs in July 1593 at Saint-Denis. This act can be seen as his implicit acceptance of the principle defended by the League that the king of France had to be Catholic. At the same time, it removed the primary obstacle that kept many of his subjects from recognizing him as king. Within a year, Paris, Lyon, Rouen, and dozens of lesser cities all proclaimed their allegiance to him and opened their gates. Henry also showed himself to be exceptionally generous towards his former enemies. He granted large pensions to prominent League chieftains to induce them to recognize him as their ruler, and proved willing to work with all who had formerly opposed him so long as they now were loyal and helpful. The Spanish noted with rueful admiration that the king fought like the devil and forgave like a god. In personality, furthermore, Henry IV was the virtual antithesis of Henry III. A bluff, hearty man of the saddle, he never stood on ceremony and lavished his substantial charm on those of all stations and both sexes. When royalist propaganda figured him as the Gallic Hercules or the French Perseus saving the country from the hydra of sedition, the image was convincing.

Opposition to Henry IV hardly withered overnight. Die-hard League preachers warned that the conversion of a man who had already relapsed once into heresy could not be trusted. Their call for a second Jacques Clément to strike down the feigned convert inspired several assassination attempts, one of which nearly succeeded in December 1594. Brittany's powerful League chieftain, the duke of Mercoeur, battled on determinedly. The Spanish threw increasing aid behind their League allies, signing a formal alliance with Mercoeur in 1594 and sending troops into Picardy and Burgundy as well. In retaliation, Henry IV formally declared war on Philip II early in 1595. More and more the conflict came to appear a war of resistance against the ancestral Habsburg enemy. The Spanish war machine was still not too exhausted to capture Calais in 1596 and to surprise Amiens early in

1597. These, however, proved its last gasps. Henry IV rallied enough men to retake Amiens six months later. With both sides running out of men and money, Mercoeur finally laid down his arms in March 1598. Peace was signed with the Spanish at Vervins on 2 May 1598.

The Huguenots used these final years of fighting to extract concessions from a king who was no longer their co-religionist. In the wake of Henry III's death, Navarre's greatest concern had been to convince France's Catholic majority that his accession would not endanger their religion. His public pronouncements during the first two years of his reign consequently stressed his commitment to maintain the religious status quo as he found it on his accession, although he quietly allowed Protestant worship to resume in towns taken by his troops. In July 1591 he repealed the 1585 prohibition of Protestantism and restored the terms governing religious co-existence defined by the 1577 Peace of Bergerac. Despite these measures on behalf of the faith, a number of Huguenot grandees who had been his long-standing rivals for pre-eminence within the cause complained that he was not protecting its interests sufficiently and agitated to replace him as protector of the faith. His conversion then came as a bitter blow to all those of the faith. In its aftermath, the Protestants resumed their political assemblies. A succession of ever longer and larger gatherings demanded rights of worship throughout the kingdom and subsidies for their schools and ministers. The leading Protestant military commanders ignored Henry's call to come to his aid in fighting the Spaniards in Picardy. As the king's victory over the League and Spain finally grew certain, he moved to placate his erstwhile co-religionists with a revised edict of pacification. The result was the Edict of Nantes, issued in April 1598. This continued to confine Protestant worship to a specified number of localities but increased that number by comparison with 1577. It confirmed the existence of the special chambers of the parlements first established in 1576 to provide impartial justice for Protestant litigants. A further set of secret articles that were never submitted to the parlements for registration and thus enjoyed less force of law granted the Protestants control of 84 garrisoned towns and modest subsidies for their schools and worship. Many of the kingdom's parlements dragged their feet at registering the edict, but the king insisted upon its implementation.

The sources are too scanty to permit a definitive assessment of the economic costs of the civil wars. The demographic expansion of the first six decades of the sixteenth century undoubtedly slowed or came to an end, but since the wars prior to 1588 tended to be short and localized, their overall impact may not have been as great as one might initially imagine. The 25 larger cities for which good population estimates are available around 1550 and 1600 experienced no significant aggregate change in size. Some declined, notably Lyon, which lost its position as the country's leading money market and banking centre. Others grew, especially Marseilles, whose port boomed. It seems clear that the last decade of the conflict extracted the heaviest toll across the largest portion of the kingdom. Agricultural production was badly disrupted. Where 75 Italian merchant families were still active in Lyon in the 1560s, just 21 remained in 1596–7, carrying out sadly diminished enterprises. In brigand-ridden Lower Brittany, packs of wolves marauded across the countryside as the century drew to a close, their taste for human flesh reportedly whetted by the unburied corpses on which they had been able to feast.

Such scenes were hard to forget. For several generations afterwards, the epoch of the League stood as a particularly fearful object lesson. Not only had much of the kingdom been reduced to desperation. A king had been assassinated to hosannas of praise from prominent clergymen, a gathering of the Estates-General had claimed the power to elect his successor but failed miserably, and the Spanish had almost taken over the land. The tale became a standing warning against the danger of political theories advocating anything other than strict obedience to an absolute monarch. Earlier events were also regularly recalled. Toulouse staged a public procession every 17 May for centuries to commemorate its preservation from the attempted Huguenot takeover of 1562. The Protestants memorialized the victims of St Bartholomew in their *Book of Martyrs*, integrating their story into the saga of suffering of those who witness for Christ that became the sustaining epic of their lost cause. Many of both faiths drew the lesson that where two religions were so deeply rooted in a single country that even violence could not exterminate them, a measure of toleration was preferable to the costs entailed in trying to restore religious uniformity, although no French author was as yet willing to defend freedom of worship as a positive good under all circumstances. Still later, during the Enlightenment, the Wars of Religion became evidence of the harmfulness of religious fanaticism, and

Voltaire claimed to run a fever every year on St Bartholomew's Day. The events of these troubled years were subsequently recalled and judged in many ways. They were not soon forgotten.

7

Catholic reform and religious coexistence

Barbara Diefendorf and Virginia Reinburg

Until the middle of the sixteenth century, Christianity had been a
major source of France's common culture. But the dramatic growth
of the Protestant movement, the division of French Christians into
two separate confessions, and decades of civil war had undermined
that collective identification with Christian symbols and practices.
The Edict of Nantes, decreed by Henry IV and registered by the
parlements, established a truce between Catholics and Huguenots,
within the framework of Catholicism as the kingdom's majority and
officially established religion. The wording of the edict's preamble
refers obliquely to the collective religious life of all the king's subjects.
The king expressed the wish that God 'be adored and prayed to by all
our subjects', and though it was not yet 'in one form and religion',
that it at least be done 'with the same intention', that 'we and this
kingdom may always conserve the glorious title of most Christian,
which has been by so much merit so long since acquired'.[1] The edict
established neither parity between the confessions nor genuine toleration of the Protestant minority, at least not in the contemporary
understanding of the term. Yet however imperfectly, the peace Henry
negotiated did secure the legally sanctioned observance of two separate, competing, and sometimes mutually hostile forms of Christianity
within the kingdom's borders—at least until the last decades of the
seventeenth century.

---

[1] English text of the Edict of Nantes in Roland Mousnier, *The Assassination of Henry
IV: The Tyrannicide Problem and the Consolidation of the French Absolute Monarchy in
the Early Seventeenth Century*, trans. J. Spencer (New York, 1964), p. 317.

The Catholic–Protestant struggle determined much of the course of national events during the second half of the sixteenth century and continued to preoccupy the kingdom until the late 1620s. It also shaped the character of religious life within both churches. French Reformed piety was deeply influenced by the Huguenots' status as a small minority of the population, constant encroachments on their religious freedom, and their never-ending need to resist Catholic pressures to convert. Projects to reform the Catholic Church, though obviously stimulated by the Protestant movement, built on earlier reform currents and drew inspiration from the larger movements of renewal that transformed all of Catholic Europe in the wake of the Council of Trent. At the same time, the crusading spirit that infused the Catholic revival guaranteed that the religious peace worked out at Nantes would continue to be an uneasy one. Both Protestants and France's small Jewish population were made continually to feel the limits of the toleration accorded them. Moreover, differences of opinion between devout and moderate Catholics over the nature of true piety and the role that religion should play in both domestic life and foreign affairs helped to undermine the unity of the dominant faith.

Pastoral reform and Catholic religious life

The League had for a few years presented the image of a strong, organized party determined to establish Catholicism as the single faith of the realm, and yet the Catholic Church itself emerged from the religious wars in a state of disarray. Throughout the kingdom there were neglected or destroyed church buildings, absentee clergy, uncollected revenues, and church property that had been usurped by Huguenots or local lords. After the defeat of the League, the Edict of Nantes set the terms for religious coexistence in the kingdom. The edict granted members of the Reformed Church full civil rights and limited freedom of worship, but it also provided the conditions for rebuilding and strengthening Catholicism in relation to the Reformed Churches. The edict ordered that Catholicism be re-established in every jurisdiction of the kingdom, destroyed churches rebuilt, and seized ecclesiastical properties and revenues returned. The Catholic Church was to collect the tithe from Catholics and

Huguenots alike. Precisely how the edict's terms were to be carried out had to be negotiated at the local level, with royal commissioners overseeing the work of civil and religious authorities. After four decades of war, peace was welcome, even among League supporters. But Catholic opinion was divided on the question of allowing Protestants freedom of worship. Perhaps most would have agreed with the bishop of Agen, who supported the settlement as 'provisional', satisfactory for the present 'while awaiting a better one'.[2]

Without doubt the Protestant movement and religious wars stimulated reform within the Catholic Church. The Protestants' success had called into question many features of Catholic belief and practice. Particular sore points were some glaring institutional problems: immoral and absentee prelates; uneducated parish clergy; corrupt monasteries; an inaccessible liturgy; uninstructed congregations. This widespread criticism, from Protestants and Catholics alike, was coupled with an ever-increasing lay engagement with the life of the Church expressed in confraternity membership, pious bequests, patronage, and avid acquisition of religious books. Yet in the early modern Catholic world institutional reform could only proceed with significant episcopal leadership. Some of the bishops were genuine pastoral leaders. Although Henry IV and Louis XIII continued their Valois predecessors' tradition of granting episcopal sees to political supporters, they also devoted new care to choosing learned and pastorally committed bishops. Episcopal pluralism virtually died out under Henry IV. By the accession of Louis XIV nearly all bishops had studied at university, and the percentage boasting a degree in theology had risen from 26 to 40 per cent, although canon law continued to be the most common field of study for future bishops. The Council of Trent (1545–63) had made the episcopate the linchpin of church reform. The Tridentine ideal of the pious, pastoral bishop was perhaps best exemplified by Milan's Archbishop Carlo Borromeo, whose work was well known in France. Gallican opposition blocked Trent's decrees from becoming part of French public law. But provincial councils gradually adopted many of the decrees, and the assembly of the clergy approved them in 1615. The endorsement of these bodies signalled the bishops' approval of the basic outlines of Tridentine

---

[2] Quoted in Marc Venard, 'L'Église catholique bénéficiaire de l'édit de Nantes: Le Témoignage des visites épiscopales', in M. Grandjean and B. Roussel (eds.), *Coexister dans l'intolérance: L'Édit de Nantes (1598)*, (Geneva, 1998), pp. 301–2.

reform. Even before war's end a few bishops had established seminaries for the education of priests and catechism programmes for the laity. Early reforms were local and piecemeal, doomed for the most part to die with the bishops who began them. But after 1598 pastoral reform gathered new steam. Although the renewal of Catholic religious life would not crest at the parish level until the late seventeenth or even early eighteenth century, the cause of reform was well advanced by 1650, though projects and results varied from diocese to diocese.

A model for French reforming bishops was François de Sales, bishop of Geneva-Annecy (1602–22), a native of Savoy with close personal ties to France through his family, education, and correspondence. Geneva-Annecy was a French-speaking diocese on the kingdom's eastern frontier, lying mostly within the independent duchy of Savoy. With the duke's support, François continued his predecessor's efforts to shore up Catholicism in his diocese of mixed Protestant, Waldensian, and Catholic populations. He held synods, reformed the clergy, visited the diocese's parishes and monasteries regularly, and improved education for parish clergy and laity. Believing that more Protestants and lukewarm Catholics would be brought to the true faith through persuasion than conquest, François de Sales also instituted diocesan preaching missions, offered spiritual direction to members of the nobility, and staged magnificent Eucharistic processions to display the strength and truth of the Catholic faith.

François de Sales's preaching and publication also helped to shape Catholic devotional life after the wars of religion. Crowds at his Paris sermons of 1602 and 1618–19, and his Dijon sermons of 1604, admired François's optimistic message of Christian love and reconciliation — so different from the bombastic, divisive sermons of the League preachers of the 1590s. The tone of his devotional books likewise contrasted with the dogmatic ferocity of contemporary religious works. Published in many editions, François de Sales's books won a wide readership over the course of the seventeenth century. The most popular was *Introduction to the Devout Life* (1609), an engaging and readable guide to spiritual life for laypeople. François encouraged renewed commitment to God through frequent attendance at the mass and sacraments, regular prayer and examination of conscience, spiritual direction by sympathetic priests, and devout conversation with like-minded friends. For the book's guide to meditation

François borrowed freely from Ignatius Loyola's *Spiritual Exercises*, the mainstay of Jesuit training and spirituality since the 1530s. Though following François's advice to the letter would attach his readers securely to the Catholic Church, the previous century's Catholic–Protestant debates in many ways directly fashioned *Introduction to the Devout Life*. Assuring readers that 'we cannot go to the Father except through Christ', that grace was essential for salvation, and that laymen and laywomen could be as devout as professed religious, François de Sales also claimed that preaching, publishing, and spiritual direction were integral parts of the bishop's duty to lead souls to God.[3] Absent in the book, as in his sermons, are lengthy discussions of dogma and direct criticism of Protestantism—a noteworthy feature at this moment of theological controversy that pitted the great Catholic and Calvinist orators against one another in well-attended public disputations.

Not every bishop followed François de Sales's example. Some continued to collect benefices, live in Paris, and cultivate political careers. Others had good pastoral intentions and perhaps even plans, but toiled in the lee of the religious wars under circumstances that made reform nearly impossible: destroyed churches, absent clergy, no worship services, and failure to collect the *dîme* and other revenues essential for the local church's financial survival. This was the situation facing Pierre de Valnerod when he was named bishop of Nîmes in 1598. Though a client of the Montmorency family who owed his appointment to their patronage and might have neglected pastoral duties as many contemporaries did, Valnerod nevertheless set about restoring Catholicism and episcopal authority in what was until at least the mid-seventeenth century a region of overwhelmingly Protestant majority. He used his formidable political skills to re-establish Catholicism in Nîmes' churches, neighbourhoods, and public life. Under the protection afforded by the Edict of Nantes, he made a priority of restoring the mass, which in 1598 was said in only a few places in the city. Valnerod also relied on the new religious orders, especially the Jesuits and the Capuchins, to strengthen the Catholic presence in the diocese. Though the majority Protestant city council declined to support reconstruction of the destroyed cathedral,

---

[3] François de Sales, *Introduction to the Devout Life*, trans. and ed. J. Ryan (Garden City, NY, 1972), pp. 81, 37.

Valnerod arranged financing from episcopal coffers, the cathedral chapter, and assessments on the city's Catholic residents. Other urban and rural churches were restored through donations from noble and bourgeois benefactors. Valnerod also visited the diocese's rural parishes, including remote villages where he celebrated mass 'in the place where there used to be a church' and enquired about long-absent pastors. Although episcopal visits provided bishops with information about the state of the diocese's clergy, laity, and property, in regions of Huguenot strength like Nîmes they also amounted to a rite of reclaiming episcopal authority and of asserting Catholic authority over local religious life.

With its majority Huguenot population, Nîmes was the frontier of Catholicism. But the way Valnerod and his successors proceeded there conformed to the characteristic pattern of Catholic reform between the Edict of Nantes and its revocation: collaboration among the bishops, religious orders, and the lay elite, with royal officials in a supporting role. In Nîmes the bishop directed reform efforts for the most part, but elsewhere religious orders or prominent lay people might take the initiative. Lyon and Brittany furnish useful examples of leadership from lay elites and the religious orders.

The lay elite of Lyon and its surrounding regions played a leading role in reforming that archdiocese. The Catholic Reformation began early in Lyon: in the late 1560s and 1570s wealthy merchants and lawyers joined with the cathedral clergy to undermine local attraction to Protestantism by hiring charismatic Jesuits to preach from the parishes' pulpits, sponsoring the new religious orders, and establishing Penitent confraternities. These patrons of Catholic reform were succeeded in the following century by lay activists who turned their attention to the rural regions of the archdiocese. Cooperating with church officials and rural notables they encouraged reform of the parish clergy, established schools and charities, and initiated moral reforms (banning festive associations, closing cemeteries to nonreligious uses, regulating public and private behaviour). New devotional confraternities, especially the local chapter of the Company of the Holy Sacrament (est. 1630), became powerful tools of *dévot* activism. These confraternities display the complicated social dynamics behind local Catholic reform: led by lay elites with ties to elites in other parts of the kingdom, the new confraternities attracted members among the notables, officers, and artisans, but they also received powerful support from the religious orders. In Toulouse, for example, the Jesuits and Capuchins cultivated lay elites through their sponsorship of confraternities in order to overcome episcopal and magistrates' opposition to reform. A similar pattern of elite leadership on behalf of Catholic reform may be observed in other regions of the kingdom—for example Limoges and the Limousin, where after the religious wars noble and bourgeois enthusiasm for the League evolved into vigorous support for the Jesuits, new confraternities, and new monastic houses for men and women.

In Brittany pastoral reform was initiated by members of religious orders engaged in 'interior missions', so-called for their resemblance to Christian missions to the Americas, Asia, and Africa. Brittany presented formidable challenges to Tridentine reform. Only definitively united to the French crown in 1532, the province comprised seven dioceses, a variety of local cultures, and two major languages (French and Breton). The first missionary of the era was Michel Le Nobletz, a Jesuit-educated native of the region, an itinerant but persistent preacher of Catholic doctrine. His hand-picked successor was Julien Maunoir (1606–83), like Le Nobletz a French-speaking Breton. But as a young Jesuit in Quimper, Maunoir had studied the Breton language, dreaming of becoming a missionary to the Bretons just like his Jesuit brothers who were evangelizing the peoples of New France. Le Nobletz had been a loner, but Maunoir set up an elaborate organization for his missions. Working collaboratively with the parish clergy and local notables, Maunoir scheduled, staged, and arranged funding for nearly 400 missions during his forty-three year long career. Each mission consisted of four or five weeks of preaching, catechism class, special retreats for curés and lay elites, theatrical productions, group singing, confessions, confirmations, outdoor masses, and public processions in which entire towns and villages participated. At the start of the mission Maunoir promised a plenary indulgence to each person who completed a stated course of religious acts. Maunoir himself was a charismatic preacher and gifted pedagogue. 'No one explained better than he the mysteries of our religion', wrote his late seventeenth-century biographer.[4] Maunoir was such a compelling preacher that he was said to have brought the most reprobate of

---

[4] Quoted in Alain Croix, *Cultures et religion en Bretagne aux 16e et 17e siècles* (Rennes, 1995), p. 277.

sinners to tears of sorrow and fear. Each day thousands flocked to confession and communion. Though Maunoir had a longer career and more effective organization than most, other domestic missionaries, including Vincent de Paul's Lazarists, also used ceremony, music, and preaching to attract people they considered only minimally Christian to a deeper attachment to the Catholic Church, its doctrines and practices. Key to Maunoir's success was the support he received—and the collaboration he sought—with diocesan officials, Jesuits, local clergy, and lay elites, including his dedicated women patrons.

Maunoir and other contemporary reformers saw a great need for their evangelizing projects. As Vincent de Paul wrote to the bishop of Périgueux in 1650: 'We know by experience that the fruits of missions are very great, corresponding to the extreme needs of country people; but as their minds are generally rather rough and little educated, they readily forget what they have learnt and their good resolutions, unless they have good pastors who maintain the high standards they have reached.'[5] Missionaries and reformers wanted to improve the spiritual and moral behaviour of the popular classes, which quite often entailed proscribing feasts, cabarets, and other cherished customs both sacred and profane. Parents of newborns were instructed to limit numbers of god-parents to two adults who would supervise their child's Catholic education, a potentially serious disruption to long-standing kin and patron-client networks. Also among proscribed customs were the bonfires of the feast of St John, described as 'the shameful debris of paganism' in the constitutions of the diocese of Geneva-Annecy.[6]

Plainly this kind of religious and social disciplining blends into cultural transformation. Some historians have termed this process 'Christianization' or 'acculturation', seeing in it an effort on the part of lay and clerical elites to impose their own moral code and their own model of Christianity on their social inferiors. To ask whether this spiritual and moral campaign was successful is to ask about the effectiveness of Catholic reform more generally. What did the advocates of Tridentine reform accomplish? Was the Catholic Church less corrupt and more pastorally inclined than it had been before the

[5] Quoted in Jean Delumeau, *Catholicism between Luther and Voltaire*, trans. J. Moiser (London, 1977), p. 194.

[6] Quoted in Jean Delumeau, *Un chemin d'histoire* (Paris, 1981), p. 124.

religious wars? Were mid-seventeenth-century Catholics better educated, more pious, and morally upright than their predecessors had
been?

To pose the questions this way borrows the language and standards
of the reformers. But it is possible to sketch the outlines of Catholic
religious life in this period in a way that responds to those concerns
without assuming that the reformers were correct in their dismal
evaluation of popular religiosity. Catholic religious life and the
Church had changed since the early sixteenth century. While the
Church's basic structure remained what it had been in 1500, reformers successfully focused attention on pastoral and sacramental
ideals: the pastoral bishop; the competent, educated curé; the pious,
informed laity; and above all the clerically directed parish as the
centre of sacramental and devotional life. These were ideals, not
necessarily reality, but they were standards of behaviour and belief
against which local religious life would begin to be judged. Popular
Catholicism was every bit as vital as it had been on the eve of the
religious wars, though it began to change as clerics and lay *dévots*
tried to implant the ideals of the Catholic Reformation. The diversity
and local specificity of saints, shrines, and pilgrimages diminished. By
the mid-seventeenth century there were fewer saints and cults, and
those that remained were more securely attached to the Tridentine
Church: Christ and his passion, the Eucharist, the Virgin Mary, the
holy family. The black virgin of Le Puy (Auvergne), whose image
began to be coupled with the Eucharist, and the pilgrimage of Sainte-
Anne-d'Auray (Brittany), an ancient shrine that received a 'miracu-
lously' discovered image of St Anne (Jesus's grandmother) in 1625, are
good examples of the tridentization of pilgrim shrines. Pastors,
increasingly expected to be knowledgeable about doctrine in addition
to competent at rites, directed the parish's *fabrique* (vestry) and confraternities. Confraternities which had been so numerous and varied
in the early sixteenth century had largely disappeared by the early
seventeenth century, replaced by fewer new confraternities more
firmly under clerical control. Local chapters of confraternities of the
Rosary, the Blessed Sacrament, and the Marian congregations
counted members in the tens of thousands. Though they had lay
officers, these associations were directed by members of religious
orders working in cooperation with pastors or bishops. The ultra-
Catholic Penitents and Company of the Holy Sacrament continued

the earlier confraternities' tradition of uneasy relations with the ecclesiastical hierarchy, though bishops and pastors gained from them valuable support for reforming projects.

By 1650 the collective life of French Catholics was probably more securely rooted in the parish, the Eucharist, and the sacraments than it had been a century earlier. In the previous century Christian humanists and Protestants had questioned the authority by which doctrine, beliefs, and rites were to be judged. For the advocates and patrons of Catholic reform, the Church, not scripture, was the authority over all things religious. The Church also mediated the relationship between God and the faithful. Anchoring religious life in the parish and the sacraments was the Catholic answer to questions about salvation and the Church raised by the Protestant movement.

Related changes can also be detected in individual piety. Bequests and books perhaps best measure the transformed Catholic spirituality of the period. The statistical indicators historians have recently developed to gauge individual commitment to devotions associated with Catholic reform—for example, the frequency with which testators left money in their wills for confraternities, anniversary masses, churches, convents, and altars—had begun to rise, as Philip Hoffman has shown for the archdiocese of Lyon.

A century of rising literacy rates and religious controversy left its mark on book production and ownership. Numbers of editions issued by French publishers increased dramatically beginning in the mid-sixteenth century. Catholic authors published voluminously on the religious controversies of the day, defending Catholic positions on ecclesiology, salvation, purgatory, the clergy, the sacraments, and especially the Eucharist. Paraphrases, excerpts, and even a few French translations of the Bible appeared, as well as catechisms intended for both teachers and lay readers. Enormous numbers of saints' lives were published as well—everything from scholarly editions, and vernacular translations of those editions, to short illustrated pamphlets recounting the exploits and miracles of holy people in the mode of romance novels. The latter formed part of the *bibliothèque bleue*, collections of mostly illustrated chapbooks named after their cheap blue paper covers, and sold in city, town, and villages by itinerant peddlers. One publisher of the *bibliothèque bleue*, Nicolas Oudot of Troyes, provided lives of saints like Catherine, Augustine, Claude, and Roch, *A Life of the Three Marys*, and *The Life, Death, Passion, and*

Resurrection of Christ—alongside pamphlets about prophecy, cookery, medical remedies, almanacs, and heroic tales from history and myth. Available to even the illiterate or marginally literate—still a majority of the French population before 1700—were illustrated broadsheets combining images of saints, the Virgin Mary, or Christ with prayers and miracle stories.

A new kind of religious book gained in popularity among more educated readers: the manual of piety or spirituality, written in French, addressed to lay people. Books like François de Sales's *Introduction to the Devout Life* (1609) and *Treatise of the Love of God* (1614) were the heirs of Erasmus's *Handbook of a Christian Soldier* (1503). To read these books and others like them was to cultivate the 'learned piety' advocated a century earlier by both Erasmus and devout Protestants, albeit a piety securely rooted in the authority of the Catholic Church.

The new religious orders

The seventeenth century was the golden age of religious orders in France. Newly founded orders and newly reformed branches of older orders made an essential contribution to Catholic renewal. Working together with members of the lay elite, who financed and facilitated local authorities' approval of their projects, the religious orders reclaimed for Catholicism the public spaces of cities and provinces contested during the religious wars, and worked to build a distinctive Catholic identity among the local nobility, robe nobility, and bourgeoisie who were the political and cultural leaders of the kingdom. New congregations for secular priests aimed to cultivate a better educated and more pious parish clergy. Members of the new orders contributed to Catholic theology, scholarship, and popular religious literature. And finally, through rural preaching missions that climaxed with the hearing of hundreds, sometimes thousands, of confessions, they stimulated a new piety and emotional identification with the Catholic faith among country folk.

The Jesuits were arguably the most prominent and influential religious order of the era. The Society of Jesus traced its beginnings to Paris, to efforts made in the late 1530s by Ignatius Loyola, then a

Basque theology student, and a few companions to 'help souls' in a time of religious controversy. From that time on the Jesuits saw France as a prime battleground for the Catholic faith, and provided the kingdom with many preachers, confessors, spiritual directors, and teachers. Suspected of treason in the early 1590s because of their pro-Spanish ties, the Society was expelled from the kingdom in 1594. But Henry IV, who had Jesuit confessors and advisers, readmitted them in 1603. By that time the Society had established more than twenty colleges where the sons of France's lay elite received a good humanist and Catholic education. By 1650 the number had reached 95. Until most dioceses established seminaries, Jesuits also prepared local candidates for ordination in their colleges. They started the Marian congregations, confraternities where the colleges' alumni could attend mass together and build their own patron–client networks. For wives and daughters of alumni there were women's auxiliaries to the Marian congregations. Jesuits also provided teachers for seminaries, preachers for Lenten sermon series, and in religiously mixed regions, formidable opponents to Huguenot controversialists. They served theology and religious publishing as well. The Bollandists, a community of Jesuits in the Low Countries, provided probably the greatest scholarly service by initiating production of the *Acta Sanctorum*, a monumental documentary collection of the lives of the saints (still in progress to this day). French scholarship did not shine quite as brightly, though French Jesuits made important contributions to scripture studies and apologetics, and developed a ministry devoted to publishing catechisms, liturgical books, and a wealth of vernacular religious and spiritual books. Some of the Jesuit lecturers in Paris attracted not only college and university students, but also members of the educated public both Catholic and Protestant.

Reformed branches of older religious orders took on many of the same roles the Jesuits did, albeit on a smaller scale. The Capuchins, a branch of the Franciscans practising strict observance of the order's rule, served the cause of Catholic reform by preaching, teaching catechism, establishing confraternities, organizing revivalist missions in the countryside, and orchestrating rites like the Forty Hours Devotion, a magnificent public display of the Eucharist accompanied by processions, public prayer, sermons, and illumination of churches, cathedrals, and religious monuments. Several different reforms of the Cistercians effectively renewed an order that had fallen onto hard times by the end of the sixteenth century. And beginning in 1618 a reformed branch of the monks of St Benedict, the Congrégation de Saint-Maur, established communities devoted to austere observance of St Benedict's rule coupled with a commitment to scholarship. During the seventeenth century the Maurists of the abbey of Saint-Germain-des-Prés in Paris embarked on ambitious documentary and historical projects, most importantly editions of patristic texts, biblical commentaries and editions, and *Gallia Christiana*, a documentary history of Christianity in France. The Maurists' brightest star of this era was Jean Mabillon (1632–1707), a Jesuit-educated pioneer in historical scholarship, documentary editing, and diplomatics.

Many of the new religious orders established in this period devoted themselves to domestic missions, catechesis, and the education of secular priests. Among these were the Congrégation de la Doctrine Chrétienne (the Doctrinaires), founded by César de Bus, and the Congrégation de Jésus et Marie, whose members were called Eudists after their founder Jean Eudes. But in the first half of the seventeenth century two founders of religious orders were particularly influential in Catholic institutional and spiritual life: Pierre de Bérulle, founder of the Oratory, and Vincent de Paul, founder of the Congrégation des Prêtres de la Mission (also called the Lazarists), the Filles de la Charité, and other 'congregations', or non-cloistered religious communities, for both men and women. Bérulle (1575–1629), the son of a prominent Parisian robe family who had studied with the Jesuits, was, like his friend François de Sales, both an active church administrator and a writer on theology and spirituality. He was later named a cardinal and acted as a royal envoy in several important diplomatic affairs. In his influential mystical treatise, *Discourse on the State and Grandeur of Jesus* (1623), Bérulle argued for a vigorous Catholic piety centred on Christ, the Eucharist as Christ's real presence on earth, and the Church as the guardian of Christ's legacy as the 'incarnate word of God'. Together with a few other devotional writers, Bérulle was one of the founders of what by the later seventeenth century came to be known as 'the French school of spirituality', writers of works on spirituality, asceticism, and mysticism who had a profound impact on elite Catholic piety. The Oratory, an organization devoted to the education, formation, and support of diocesan priests, was in some ways the institutional expression of Bérulle's conviction that it was through the Church, the heir of Christ's redemptive mission on earth, that human beings developed a relationship with God and attained eternal salvation.

Vincent de Paul (1581–1660) sought in his many activities — launching rural preaching missions; organizing women's communities dedicated to poor relief, education, and catechesis; establishing orphanages, hospitals, and workhouses — to unite spiritual aid and poor relief in one great project of evangelization through which both charity workers and those they helped would grow in love for God and the Catholic Church. Lay support was the foundation on which all Vincent de Paul's work rested. Nothing would have been accomplished without the funds and efforts of Catholic nobles and bourgeois: great noble patrons like Philippe-Emmanuel de Gondi and his wife Françoise-Marguerite de Silly, but also the countless bourgeoises and noble ladies who responded to the call to serve the poor. Devout women close to Vincent de Paul encouraged Queen Anne of Austria to lend her support to his charitable projects. The queen showed her great confidence in Vincent de Paul's judgement by appointing him her spiritual director and naming him to the *conseil de conscience* created after Louis XIII's death to advise her on ecclesiastical appointments; Vincent de Paul used the latter position to lobby for higher standards for episcopal office.

The contribution of lay *dévots*

It was not only Vincent de Paul who depended on the contributions of pious laymen and laywomen. The Catholic renewal was far more broadly dependent upon the patronage of the wealthy men and women who contributed the vast sums needed to build new monasteries and churches; found orphanages, hospitals, and schools; and sponsor rescue missions to provinces in the throes of war. Pious aristocrats used their political connections to secure the royal and ecclesiastical permissions needed for the new foundations, and, along with magistrates, merchants, and their wives, gave their time and energy to administering new charitable services to the poor.

The last, climactic struggles of the wars of religion combined with the first preaching and writing of the Catholic Reformation to give rise to a new ultra-Catholic sensibility. Moved by calls for penitence and a return to godliness on the part of preachers convinced that the wars were a sign of God's wrath, pious laymen and laywomen reformed their dress and behaviour on narrowly ascetic lines, adopted rigorous programmes of meditation and prayer, and sought to imitate Christ by humble service to the sick and poor. Called '*dévots*' by both their admirers and those who found their piety excessive and even hypocritical, they formed a receptive audience for François de Sales's repeated admonition to serve the poor as a way of serving Christ. 'Make yourself a servant of the poor', he wrote in *Introduction to the Devout Life*, advising his devout readers to tend the ill with their own hands, to feed them and even wash their soiled linens.[7]

Individually and in new confraternal societies, the *dévots* undertook a broad range of charitable activities. They comforted the sick and dying in hospitals, visited prisons, and attempted to rescue young girls from prostitution. Very early in the seventeenth century, the informal circle of clerics and lay *dévots* that gathered in the home of Parisian bourgeoise Barbe Acarie encouraged local abbesses in their efforts at reform and secured the necessary funding and permissions to bring the Discalced Carmelites of Saint Teresa of Avila's reform to France. The same group was subsequently responsible for founding the Ursuline teaching order in Paris and Bérulle's Oratory. A more formal collaboration between devout laymen and clergy occurred with the foundation in 1630 of the Company of the Holy Sacrament. The company's members, sworn to secrecy, combated duels, promoted the confinement and assistance of the poor, found jobs for repentant prostitutes, provided dowries for indigent girls, and pressured authorities for the strict enforcement of legal restrictions on Protestants, among other goals. Within a short time, sister companies had been founded in upwards of fifty towns.

For many historians, the Company of the Holy Sacrament typifies the worst traits of the *dévots*, and of the Catholic Reformation more generally. They see it as an elitist and coercive organization, intent on the repression of popular culture and the imposition of a rigid discipline on society's unfortunates. Citing the company's efforts to build institutions for the confinement of unrepentant prostitutes, beggars,

---

[7] François de Sales, *Introduction to the Devout Life*, pp. 165–6.

and other undesirables as evidence of this urge to discipline society, they also condemn it for undermining domestic and international peace by subjecting all policy decisions to a rigid test of Catholic orthodoxy. Although there is some justice to these criticisms, it is important to separate the eventual results of the company's policies from its members' motives, which were spiritual and not political. Members of the company sincerely believed that they were doing good works with redemptive value for themselves and others. Even attempts to enclose prostitutes and beggars in new institutions where, by working, they might learn honestly to provide for themselves were driven by the desire to rescue lost souls and not by the simple urge to get undesirables off the streets. At the same time, it is true that the social projects of the *dévots* had unintended consequences. Worsening economic conditions and the crisis of the Fronde vastly increased the number of indigents requiring aid, and the overcrowded institutions *dévots* founded became as a consequence more punitive and bleak. The *dévots'* political ambition of bringing France into the Thirty Years War on the Catholic side ultimately failed, but there is no question that their anti-Protestant agitation placed an added stress on the already tense religious situation within France.

The *dévotes*: gender and religious change

Though they received too little credit both then and since, women's work and money were crucially important in the work of Catholic renewal. The seventeenth century is justifiably known as the golden age of new religious orders for women in France. The role that a few celebrated men—most prominently François de Sales and Vincent de Paul—played in this achievement should not blind us to the even more enormous contribution of the large numbers of women who planned, built, and ran these institutions. Nor should we overlook the contribution of the lay *dévotes* who, living in informal communities without religious vows or special forms of dress, ran schools that offered local girls both religious and secular instruction. And if the Company of the Holy Sacrament refused to found a women's auxiliary, the Dames de la Charité organized by Louise de Marillac and Vincent de Paul served something of the same function. The ladies

engaged personally in good works but also, and even more importantly, they used their personal fortunes and aid solicited from their
friends to fund hospitals for foundlings and the aged, supply food
and shelter to war refugees, and support other pious causes.

The first years of the seventeenth century marked an important
renewal of religious life for French women. The same currents of
ascetic spirituality that prompted Barbe Acarie to help found a
French order of Discalced Carmelites modelled on St Teresa of Avila's
reforms inspired a new generation of abbesses to require of their
nuns a stricter observance of their religious vows. Perhaps the most
celebrated case is that of Jacqueline-Angélique Arnauld, who was just
18 when she began the reform of Port-Royal, where her parents had
had her made abbess in 1602 at the tender age of 11. Determined to
return Port-Royal to strict observance of the Cistercian rule, Mère
Angélique cultivated in her nuns an austere and penitential faith. She
later helped other convents renew themselves as well. Lax convents
were never reformed without a struggle, and often even dedicated
abbesses had to settle for only partial success, allowing nuns who
refused to change their ways to live out their comfortable lives alongside others who accepted the more strenuous religious life. The very
difficulty of reforming old institutions helped encourage the foundation of new. The Carmelite order spread rapidly, establishing fifty
convents in just thirty years, but other new and reformed orders grew
up as well—among them the Ursulines, Visitandines, and Congrégation de Notre-Dame, but also reformed branches of the Benedictine,
Dominican, and Franciscan families. Indeed, the magnitude of the
religious revival is startling. In Paris alone, more than forty-five new
religious houses were founded for women by 1650, compared with
about twenty new houses for men. A similar phenomenon occurred
in other French cities, though the numbers were of course smaller, in
proportion with the cities' populations. Bordeaux, which had only
one convent within its walls in 1600, counted eight religious houses
for women by 1650.

Most of the earliest foundations were contemplative convents,
whose nuns remained inside their cloisters to pray for the living and
the dead, but there was also a move afoot to create new houses for
women who felt an apostolic mission to teach young girls or care for
the sick and ageing. The congregation of Ursulines that Angela
Merici founded in Brescia with the aim of teaching poor city girls the

tenets of the faith spread to southern France by the last years of the sixteenth century. As in Italy, the first French Ursulines were not cloistered nuns but rather brought their teaching into the urban community. When an Ursuline house was founded in Paris in 1610 by members of Barbe Acarie's circle, this changed. The founders adopted the principle of bringing the pupils into the school so that the nuns could remain in their cloister instead of going out into the community to teach. They adopted this principle in support of the reforms promulgated by the Council of Trent, which insisted that all religious women should live in enclosed convents, neither going out nor allowing outsiders in. The Council of Trent's decrees had not yet been adopted in France, and the *dévots* who founded the Parisian Ursulines wished to show their support for them by incorporating their principles in the new foundation. But the founders of Paris's Ursuline convent also truly believed that religious enclosure was both desirable and consistent with the Ursulines' teaching mission. Some historians have viewed enforcement of the rules of strict enclosure as a misogynistic attempt on the part of male clerics to lock women behind convent walls. In doing so, they have tended to overlook the religious justification for monastic enclosure, which lay in the belief that separation from the world was the surest path to the ultimate goal of mystical union with Christ. It was not the men but rather the women in Barbe Acarie's circle who most vigorously advocated cloistering the Ursulines. They admired the ascetic practices of the Carmelites, whose foundation they had helped to sponsor, and believed that the benefits of spiritual retreat could be effectively combined with a teaching mission to create an order of nuns in which the active and the contemplative lives might be combined.

The same is true of the Visitation Sainte Marie, founded by Jeanne Frémiot de Chantal and François de Sales. The first convent of the Visitation was founded in 1610 outside the borders of France in Annecy. The founders wished to create a religious congregation that was less rigorous in its practices than other new orders, whose mortifications were often so punishing to the health that only young and hearty women could endure them. They also wanted a congregation that would not be strictly enclosed but whose members might, under certain conditions, go out into the community to comfort and care for the sick. When a house of Visitandines was founded in Lyon in 1615, however, the local bishop insisted that the sisters be cloistered in keeping with the decrees handed down at Trent. François de Sales and Jeanne de Chantal accepted the change because they wanted the Visitandines to spread into France but also because they did not consider visits to the sick to be essential to the congregation's mission of providing a saintly retreat for women unable to enter more rigorous new orders. In their compromise with the bishop, moreover, they also maintained another important principle. The Visitandine convents were to provide a place where pious laywomen could escape their usual family burdens to spend time in recollection and prayer. The novelty of this purpose—allowing laywomen to make spiritual retreats—has been little appreciated, and yet it was to serve an important role in the religious education and deepening piety of seventeenth-century women. Other congregations imitated the Visitandines and extended the same sort of religious retreat to women from the middling and even the lower reaches of society.

If the Ursulines and Visitandines found ways to incorporate a mission to their sex within the rules of religious enclosure, other pious women remained convinced of the importance of taking this mission out into the community. By the 1620s there were scattered communities of lay *dévotes* who, without taking religious vows, ran schools for both day and boarding pupils in order to catechize them, teach them to read and write, and train them in domestic skills that might later help them to earn a living. Some of these communities later acquired more formal institutional structures. French bishops' insistence on adhering to the rules of religious enclosure faded, and these informal communities became the sort of open congregation of women leading a religious life 'in the world' that the early Ursulines and Visitandines had set out to be. By the 1640s, the Filles de la Croix and Filles de la Providence were running schools for girls in both rural and urban parishes. The Filles de Saint Joseph ran orphanages, and the Filles de la Charité provided a range of services that extended from running a foundling home to bringing food and medical supplies to the parish poor. All of these congregations received important assistance from the Dames de la Charité, who supplied them with funds but also helped administer the Filles de la Croix and Filles de la Providence, demonstrating once again the close involvement of pious laywomen in the new charitable enterprises of the Catholic revival.

The women who established the religious orders and congregations of the Catholic Reformation displayed remarkable energy and initiative. Barbe Acarie, for example, not only played a crucial role in securing the financial support and official permissions necessary to bring the Discalced Carmelites to France, but she personally oversaw the construction of their first Paris convent and played a determinant role in selecting the women who were to become their first novices. When it was time to select novices for the Ursulines' new convent, Barbe Acarie was again invited to examine the candidates who presented themselves. This was an extraordinary mark of respect to show a laywoman, a married woman at that. Normally only a priest had the right to probe an individual's conscience. Clearly Acarie's reputed spiritual gifts conveyed an informal authority that allowed her to overstep the bounds of accepted female behaviour.

Nor was she alone in achieving this sort of informal spiritual authority. We find it most often within convents, where celebrated abbesses but sometimes also simple nuns gained such a reputation for sanctity that not only their sisters in religion but also laymen and laywomen came to seek their spiritual advice. A few isolated mystics outside convents also gained a following on account of their visions and prophecies. At the same time, it is important to recognize that these pious women were allowed their exceptional role precisely because they had no official standing in the Church. Their opinions and advice were attributed to personal graces, the spiritual rewards of their saintly lives. Such women, moreover, were always closely supervised by male clerics. Their authority remained private and, as such, did not contradict women's public powerlessness or threaten gender hierarchies.

Indeed, male clerics used the lives and examples of these exceptional women to reinforce traditional gender roles. André Duval's 1629 biography of Barbe Acarie, for example, emphasized her wifely obedience in telling how, even in the midst of important negotiations with builders at work on the Carmelites' new house, she was prepared to drop everything to rush home to serve her husband his midday meal. Duval also narrates numerous incidents that show how Barbe Acarie instructed her three daughters in perfect obedience and taught them to repress any semblance of will. These were considered necessary virtues for women, whether they were destined for marriage or religious life. Pious biographies such as Duval's book on Barbe Acarie became an important genre of didactic literature aimed at elite Catholic women in the mid-seventeenth century. Devout women were expected to shun novels as immoral encouragement to dissipation, but for those addicted to fiction's pleasures, Jean-Pierre Camus, bishop of Belley, adapted the lessons of pious biography to fictional form, publishing a whole stream of edifying novels in the 1620s. There is a strong moralistic streak in all of this literature. We usually associate Calvinism with a puritanical attitude towards behaviour, but reformed Catholicism was also characterized by the teaching of a newly restrictive morality.

Religious minorities: Huguenots and Jews[8]

For the roughly one million French men and women who worshipped in the approximately 700 Reformed churches that came through the fire of the religious wars, there was no forgetting their minority status. As they had been during the sixteenth century, Huguenots were unevenly scattered across the kingdom, with around 80 per cent of the total population concentrated in the south and south-west. In some regions of Aquitaine and the Midi Protestants were numerically in a position of near equality with Catholics; in the cities of Nîmes, Montpellier, and La Rochelle they constituted a majority of the population. Huguenots generally comprised a small and powerless minority in the north, including cities like Rouen where there had been sizable Reformed communities in the mid-sixteenth century. During the seventeenth century the overall Huguenot population declined: by the time Louis XIV revoked the Edict of Nantes in 1685 it had fallen to about 75 per cent of what it had been around 1600. Numbers dropped most decidedly during the 1610s and 1620s, the difficult decades following Henry IV's death when Protestants abjured or emigrated in the face of erosion of royal guarantees of their freedom of worship and civil rights and renewed religious war. Given the increasing pressures members of the Reformed Church faced to abjure or emigrate, the numbers of the kingdom's Huguenots remained remarkably stable.

The Edict of Nantes provided the legal framework for the religious, social, and political life of French Protestants for most of the

---

[8] Philip Benedict is the author of the section on the Jews.

seventeenth century. The edict allowed members of the Reformed Church of France the right to worship together in legally approved locations, mainly those where they had been meeting since 1596. In addition, the edict recognized to a limited degree the right of Huguenot lords to worship in their own domain (*culte de fief*), an acknowledgement of traditional seigneurial authority over local religious life. The *culte de fief* was restricted to the primary residences of Huguenot lords holding seigneurial lands, who wished to hold services 'for themselves, their families, subjects, and others who wish to come'. Reformed worship was severely restricted in most cities and towns, and proscribed entirely in the capital, forcing many of the faithful to travel long distances to attend services. Synods, consistories, and academies were authorized to continue operations; publishing, public religious discussion, and proselytizing were severely curtailed. The edict also affirmed Huguenots' rights to hold office, exercise professions, practise trades, and attend universities.

The religious settlement Henry IV formulated in the Edict of Nantes implicitly acknowledged a majority–minority relationship between the two Christian confessions, and established conditions for peaceful coexistence between them. The settlement displeased extremists in both camps, but particularly the most intransigent Catholics, who continued to criticize Reformed doctrine, ecclesiology, and civil rights throughout the reigns of Henry, Louis XIII, and Louis XIV. However, the strict boundaries between the confessions that activists in both Reformed and Catholic camps wished for were sometimes overcome when Catholics and Protestants lived together in local communities. Some individuals, families, and local communities refused to live in harmony with those of the other confession. But peaceful religious coexistence had its best chance for success in the everyday life of families, businesses, and communities. Mixed marriages were common, especially in religiously mixed regions, despite entreaties of both clergies against them. Many Catholic families and nearly all Protestant ones had a relative who attended the other Church. Patron–client networks among nobles, merchants, officials, and artisans also crossed religious frontiers. Forced to contend with religiously mixed communities, Catholic parishes and Reformed congregations usually, though grudgingly, accepted godparents and spouses from the other Church. Each Church recognized as valid baptisms and marriages performed in the other. And eventually each formulated a 'protestation of faith', a rite through which those who wished to join from the other Church would be received.

The size and vitality of Reformed congregations varied greatly in the years immediately following the Edict of Nantes, due both to the geography of Protestant population and to the relative size and strength of neighbouring Catholic communities. The tiny, beleaguered Reformed community of the Auvergnat town of Le Puy resisted the efforts of fellow citizens, including many former League supporters, to prevent them from holding religious services despite the edict's authorization. Only the support of the royal commissioners, who visited the town in 1601 to supervise execution of the edict, allowed Le Puy's Protestants to keep the building and land they had purchased for a temple and cemetery. Following announcement of the commissioners' decision a gang of young people followed the Reformed ministers around town, shouting that they were 'ravenous wolves', probably a reference to the Gospel passage warning about false prophets (Matt. 7: 15).[9] Similar difficulties might present themselves to Catholics in majority Protestant communities. Minority Catholics in Languedoc and Dauphiné trying to reclaim churches could also face local authorities hostile to the re-establishment of Catholicism, though bishops, Jesuits, and Capuchins effectively devoted their power and resources to the Catholic cause in those regions. In communities of greater parity between the two confessions the situation was different. Continuing long-standing efforts to have Catholics and Protestants live together in civic peace during the religious wars, residents of the town of Montélimar (Dauphiné) established a workable compromise between Catholics and Protestants in the first years of the seventeenth century. For a while Catholics and Protestants shared use of the hospital's great hall on Sundays, and the consuls' bell rang the hour for services held by both faiths.

Similar kinds of compromises were worked out in religiously mixed communities around the kingdom. Cemeteries presented a particularly delicate problem. The Edict of Nantes ordered local communities to provide places of burial for residents of both faiths, a measure far more easily commanded than executed. Catholics and Huguenots held profoundly different views on funerals, burial rites,

---

[9] *Mémoires de Jean Burel: Journal d'un bourgeois du Puy à l'époque des guerres de religion* (Saint-Vidal, 1983), pp. 483–4.

and prayer for the dead. Catholics, believing that souls in purgatory could be aided towards salvation by the faithful's prayers, favoured an elaborate funeral mass and burial rite; while Protestants, consistent with the belief that human beings were saved through faith alone not human effort, preferred a simpler rite without pomp, intercessory prayer, or even ministerial participation. This official difference could be blurred in mixed communities, where in conformity with local custom Reformed burials were sometimes quite elaborate. But beyond that, conflicts over burial could arise because the local cemetery symbolized the community itself in ways beyond doctrine and politics. Huguenots claimed their right to be buried with ancestors and neighbours: 'our fathers had rights to [parish cemeteries] . . . that were public and common. Have we not inherited their rights just as much as this French air we breathe, the cities we frequent, and the homes we inhabit?'[10] The chance that a community's Protestant and Catholic inhabitants could agree to share the local cemetery was higher where the disparity in numbers between the groups was lower, and where royal commissioners intervened on the side of the minority. But by the 1630s, as royal support for the Edict of Nantes' religious settlement faded away, and as the great aristocratic families and provincial nobility increasingly deserted the Reformed cause, such compromises were gradually undermined, replaced by increasingly militant Catholic control over local religious life throughout most of the kingdom. Reformed communities were then precariously balanced between the Edict of Nantes' protection, which to be effective always had to be supported by royal authority, and provincial and royal decrees ending the state's financial support of Reformed churches, preventing destroyed temples from being rebuilt, dismantling and outlawing Protestant *places de sûreté*, and declaring Huguenots unfit for judicial office and teaching posts. Religious coexistence at the local level required royal support of the minority, as Protestants realized with painful clarity in the years following the peace of Alais, in which Louis XIII and Cardinal Richelieu stripped the Huguenots of their military capabilities after the siege of La Rochelle in 1629.

During the same seventy years when France struggled its way to a

---

[10] Quoted in Keith Luria, 'Separated by Death? Burials, Cemeteries, and Confessional Boundaries in Seventeenth-Century France', *French Historical Studies*, 24 (2001), 204.

grudging acceptance of two Christian confessions within the realm, a third religious group was also permitted once again to take up residence in the kingdom in small but significant numbers: the Jews. The first openly observant Jews to receive official permission to settle in the lands of the king of France were three families of Ashkenazim allowed in 1564 to live in Metz, a city that had just come under the protection of the French crown and was destined to become central to the military defence of the eastern border. Despite predictable protests from the city's inhabitants, the Jews proved so useful in provisioning the city's garrisons with grain and horses that successive governors allowed more to follow. By 1637, 351 individuals crammed into the city's little ghetto.

Even before 1564, a number of Spanish and Portuguese New Christians fleeing the Inquisition's persecution of suspected 'judaizers' (those who resumed Jewish ritual practices) had made their way into France. Royal letters patent of 1550 allowed the settlement of members of the 'Portuguese nation' anywhere in the kingdom. These so-called *conversos* or *marranos* were initially expected to live as Christians. Indeed, failure to do so represented a great risk: French courts imposed death sentences for the crime of judaizing well into the seventeenth century, and when one elderly Portuguese New Christian in Saint-Jean-de-Luz was seen taking the consecrated host from her mouth and hiding it in her handkerchief rather than swallowing it after receiving communion in 1619, the townsfolk did not even wait for the judicial authorities, but burned the woman to death in a barrel of pitch. The attraction of ancestral practices and of identification with the children of Israel for a fraction of New Christians is nonetheless well known, and it became particularly pronounced among those members of the Sephardic diaspora who traded with the great port of Amsterdam after its prosperous community of 'Hebrews of the Portuguese nation' returned to the open observance of Judaism early in the seventeenth century. By the 1620s enough freedom existed within certain French localities for resident groups of *conversos* to distance themselves from Christian practices and resume Jewish rituals. Whether the often peripatetic members of the little communities of New Christians that established themselves in France began to return to Jewish practices as early as the sixteenth century, and how rapid and extensive the subsequent movement in this direction was over the centuries that followed, will probably never be known with confidence. In any event, Bordeaux, Rouen, Paris, Nantes, and a number of small towns close to the Spanish border all came at different times to include significant clusters of these people who by the eighteenth century had clearly assumed a legal identity as Jews, and whose presence within the kingdom added another small measure of religious diversity to the kingdom's population. The little bit of room made for both the Jews of Metz and the New Christians of the south-west and the Atlantic ports signified the crown's willingness to allow considerations of economic and military utility to outweigh concern for the purity of a most Christian France.

The creation of a measure of religious pluralism within the kingdom should not be equated with the triumph of tolerance in the modern sense. Only a few exceptional figures argued for the general principle that members of all faiths be allowed to practice their religion. Permission for specific religious minorities to worship publicly within the kingdom was generally justified on the grounds that it was less harmful for the country to put up with this evil than to try to eliminate it. The view that France was a Catholic country whose welfare was tied to loyalty to the true faith had many defenders. Indeed, in 1638 Louis XIII placed the crown and its subjects under the special protection of the Virgin Mary in thanksgiving for a series of victories during the Thirty Years War. From this era forward, it would nonetheless be the case that the country was a multi-religious one that recurrently had to grapple with the vexed question of the status of its Protestant and Jewish minorities.

8

Redrawing the lines of authority

Mack P. Holt

The end of civil war in 1598 brought about by the Edict of Nantes guaranteed neither a sustained and lasting peace nor the certain restoration of the authority of the crown, much less the rise of an absolute monarchy. Although a more powerful French state with a much larger army and bureaucracy of civil servants did eventually emerge in the later seventeenth century, this process was by no means inevitable in 1598. What was most in the mind of Henry IV was recovery from the instability of the previous forty years, along with an abiding desire to strengthen royal institutions so that no future challenge to the crown like those of the Huguenots and the League during the religious wars could ever occur again. Moreover, there was never any vocalized plan or revealed strategy by either Henry or his son Louis XIII (or their respective ministers) to launch a programme of absolute monarchy. Thus the growth in state power that took place in the seventeenth century was not so much planned, as it was the consequence of historical and contingent events; it was anything but a foregone conclusion.

Having said that, however, it is possible to distinguish four major problem areas which Henry IV and his successors were forced to address: (1) the lingering religious tensions left over from the civil wars, as well as a long-term solution to the Huguenot 'state within a state'; (2) how to prevent powerful subjects—aristocratic, clerical, judicial, as well as civilian—from being in a position to challenge the crown as had been the case during the Wars of Religion; (3) the perennial problem of insufficient crown

revenues, especially during wartime, and the inability of French
kings to control the assessment and collection of tax revenues in
their own kingdom, thereby undermining the advantage of
France's huge population compared to other European states; and
(4) how to overcome the military deficiencies that prevented the
crown from inflicting a quick and decisive defeat to both the
Huguenots and the Catholic League in the religious wars, not to
mention how to renew efforts to wage war abroad as both Henry
IV and Louis XIII attempted to do in the early seventeenth century. This chapter will examine each of these four problems in
turn. The solutions to these problems offered first by Henry IV
and then by Louis XIII were varied and did not always work as
planned. Absolutism in this period was always more a prototype of
how government was supposed to work, rather than how it actually worked in practice. Nevertheless, if Henry IV and Louis XIII—
as well as their respective ministers, the duke of Sully and Cardinal
Richelieu—may not quite be the predestined architects of absolutism claimed in traditional historiography, there is no question that
by 1648 France had not only restored the authority of the monarchy, but had also helped to defeat Spain in the Thirty Years War
and replaced this rival as the most powerful dynastic state in
Europe.

The religious problem

When Henry IV abjured his Calvinist faith and converted to Catholicism in July 1593, the principal task ahead of him was to convince
French Catholics that his conversion was sincere and not just a cynical act of political opportunism. So, when the League bastion of Paris
surrendered to him in March 1594, Henry made explicit efforts to
demonstrate both his zeal and devotion to his new faith as well to the
French tradition of sacral monarchy. Being in the capital during Holy
Week, he made numerous public demonstrations of his devotion:
marching in religious processions on Palm Sunday, washing the feet
of the poor in numerous parish churches throughout the city on
Maundy Thursday, and publicly attending mass and receiving communion on Easter Sunday in Notre-Dame. The same scenario

occurred when other League cities surrendered to him throughout 1594 and 1595. In Dijon in May 1595, for example, after publicly receiving mass and praying for two hours at the tombs of the dukes of Burgundy on the day of his entry into the city, Henry remained several weeks in order to march in the Corpus Christi Day procession directly behind the consecrated Host. The popular reactions to these events in Paris, Dijon, and other League cities suggests that Henry's efforts were largely successful, as large crowds cheered him wherever he went, and men, women, and children everywhere sought a glimpse of him or even a chance to touch him. And though public behaviour was so often staged and controlled at many royal entries, the evidence suggests that on these occasions the popular response was both spontaneous and genuine.

Nevertheless, in his efforts to heal old wounds, restore the French economy, and generally return the kingdom of France to some kind of normalcy after near four decades of civil war, Henry IV was unable to rely exclusively on the power of royal ritual and ceremony nor on the traditional appeal of sacral monarchy to reconstruct a sense of national community. In fact, Henry sought to distance himself from some of these more traditional symbols and ceremonies precisely in order to prevent the still volatile religious tensions from flaring up once more into violence. Thus although Henry realized that his royal person was still the only acceptable focus for national unity in his kingdom, he was very aware that the legacy of the Wars of Religion meant that this focus would have to be somewhat different from what it was forty years earlier. While many French Catholics—and not just former Leaguers—were seeking to introduce and implement a renewed post-Tridentine Catholicism after 1598, as were many Catholics all over Europe, Henry found himself trying to disengage the monarchy from some of its more traditional Catholic moorings in order to better maintain the peace. And while the more ancient and classical (and thus more secular and less divisive) symbol of a Gallic Hercules might suffice to supplant some of the traditional Catholic ceremonies and rituals, Henry realized that he would have to rely on more than this if he were to succeed in restoring any sense of unity to the French nation. A short war against Spain to drive out the remaining troops of Philip II in France was a useful first step, but that was hardly enough to overcome the religious divisions of the previous forty years.

Ultimately, Henry was forced to deal with a peace edict that left the Huguenots armed and in military control of nearly two hundred towns throughout the kingdom (though concentrated mainly in the south). Although he was determined never to force his former co-religionists to convert to Catholicism, the clearly preferred solution was for them to be voluntarily reunited with his Catholic subjects under a single Gallican Church: thereby preserving the traditional mantra of 'one king, one faith, and one law'. Henry did keep to his word and never used force against the Huguenots, though he did provide a number of incentives—generally in the form of offices and pensions—to try to induce them to follow his own example and abjure their Protestant faith in favour of Catholicism. Whether this would have been a successful long-term strategy remains to be seen, but it is certainly true that his policies towards the Huguenots, although unpopular with many French Catholics who wished for a sterner solution to confessional division, prevented the renewal of civil war during his reign. That it was a Jesuit critic of these policies who assassinated Henry in May 1610 only underscores the precarious nature of any possible solution to the Huguenot problem.

Peace slowly reverted to war, however, as Henry's son Louis XIII found himself raising royal forces against a Huguenot rebel army in the south-west in the early 1620s. This return to civil war was not simply a reprisal of past religious tensions. For one thing it was largely a military affair, with few of the civilian atrocities associated with the religious violence of the sixteenth century. Moreover, most of the Huguenot communities were content to subsist under the peace terms established by the Edict of Nantes and were largely loyal to the crown, to which they owed their limited and restricted privileges. Significant Huguenot opposition to the crown was limited to a few Huguenot areas such as the independent Bourbon principality of Béarn, where Catholicism had never been completely restored after the Edict of Nantes. Thus in the summer of 1620 Louis XIII dispatched a royal army southward, not only to enforce Catholic rights in Béarn, but also to reunite the principality with the French kingdom. When the Protestant governor of Béarn, the duke of La Force, quickly recognized the danger of openly resisting the king, however, the royal army entered the city of Pau in October 1620 without a shot being fired and turned the local church over to Catholic clergy for the first time in fifty years.

Yet less than a month later, the most militant of the Huguenots assembled in the stronghold of La Rochelle to reassess their future. Their fortunes clearly rested in the hands of the Protestant nobles and grandees who could still muster military support: men such as the duke of Rohan, his brother Soubise, La Force, and several others. These nobles soon organized armed resistance to the king and even set up their own system of justice and tax assessment in some selected Protestant towns. These latter acts raised the bar significantly for these militant Huguenots, explicitly calling into question their loyalty to the crown that had been more or less constant since the Edict of Nantes was issued in 1598. To be sure, most French Protestants did not support these militants, recognizing the danger of their actions; even the residents and local magistrates in the Huguenot stronghold of La Rochelle were not interested in associating with those involved in treason and crimes of *lèse-majesté*. These Huguenot rebels managed to muster enough troops and win over enough fortified towns, however, to force Louis XIII into action once again with royal military campaigns in the south-west in the summer and autumn of 1621 and 1622. These long campaigns resulted in the sieges of Montauban in 1621 and of Montpellier in 1622. And while both these Huguenot fortified towns were ultimately forced to submit to the king after lengthy and costly sieges, Louis XIII and his advisers were ultimately forced to recognize that it was the very provisions of the Edict of Nantes itself that allowed these rebel nobles to defy royal authority. The ability to maintain garrisons of troops in nearly two hundred towns in the Midi and south-west allowed Rohan, Soubise, and the other nobles to remain a constant threat to the crown. Louis himself certainly considered them to be treasonous rebels.

What to do about this armed defiance and resistance, however, was not immediately clear. While older members of the royal council advised maintaining Henry IV's policy of protecting the Huguenots and not forcing them to convert to Catholicism, one of the newest additions to Louis's council clearly believed otherwise. Armand du Plessis, Cardinal de Richelieu, was appointed to the king's council in April 1624 and quickly made his presence felt. Though he had come into royal service via the household of Marie de Medici, Louis XIII's mother, Richelieu had built his career in the Church. Initially appointed as bishop of Luçon by Henry IV, young Richelieu had studied at the Sorbonne, obtained a degree in theology, and eventually had become one of the most powerful figures within the Gallican Church in France. Thus once on the king's council, his desire to disarm the Huguenots for good, defeat the Huguenot nobles, and ultimately eliminate their garrisoned towns throughout France was a decision based as much on his religious convictions as on political necessity. 'As long as the Huguenots have a [military] foothold in France', he wrote in a memorandum for Louis XIII in 1625, 'the King will never be master at home and will never be able to undertake any glorious action abroad. . . . It is certain that as long as the Huguenot party subsists in France, the King will not be absolute in his kingdom. . . . There is no doubt that the first and principal objective His Majesty must have is to ruin this party.'[1]

Richelieu's influence on the king resulted in a final military show-down with the Huguenot nobles who still held out against the crown in the city of La Rochelle. A royal garrison was placed on the Île de Ré, just off the coast of La Rochelle, in 1626. The siege of this Atlantic port city began in earnest in the following summer, as 15,000 royal troops surrounded the Protestant citadel in an attempt to cut off all supplies and munitions and force surrender. When an English attempt to aid the Protestants by sea was repelled in November 1627, the Huguenots' fate was sealed. Famine and starvation decimated the population of the city before the Huguenot leaders reluctantly sur-rendered in October 1628. The Peace of Alais signed the following spring stripped the Huguenots of their political and military privil-eges. Even though they still retained their legal recognition granted to them by the Edict of Nantes, they were no longer allowed to keep their military garrisons in towns all across southern France. With this last conquest of Protestant political and military opposition to the crown now complete, the Huguenot problem had been resolved far differently than Henry IV had imagined back in 1598. From legal recognition and a seeming victory in the Edict of Nantes, the last religious war had now removed the Huguenots from French polity altogether. The Protestant minority nevertheless managed to survive through adaptation and learning to live in a Catholic state. They only had the king to protect them, however, as they were now stripped of any military ability to protect themselves. But survive they did,

---

[1] Richard Bonney (ed.), *Society and Government in France under Richelieu and Mazarin, 1624–1661* (London, 1988), pp. 5, 7–8.

despite the sensibilities of many educated French Catholics who chose to believe that the Huguenots had quickly dissipated into insignificance or even irrelevance after 1629.

The second principal religious problem that Henry IV and Louis XIII had to face was the group of militantly devoted Catholics, who came to be called *dévots*. Some of these individuals were leftovers from the Catholic League of the 1580s and 1590s who were dissatisfied with the legal recognition granted to the Huguenots in the Edict of Nantes. They were only too happy to support any effort to renew the war against the Huguenots. Others were imbued with the reforming spirit of Catholic reform that had emerged after the Council of Trent and felt that their principal focus should be on the spiritual renewal of the Catholic laity. And still others used the tag of *dévot* to house a political agenda which was anti-Huguenot at home, pro-Habsburg abroad, and aimed to buttress the position at court of Marie de Medici, the Queen Mother, during the reign of Louis XIII. Complicating this entire picture was the fact that Cardinal Richelieu himself was a product of the *dévot* spirit of Catholic renewal, which further exacerbated tensions between him and several other members of the king's council on issues of both domestic and foreign policy. Because the spiritual side of Catholic renewal has already been told (see Chapter 7 above), the focus here will be on the political problems that certain *dévots* posed for the crown in the 1620s, 1630s, and 1640s.

The renewal of the wars against the Huguenots in the 1620s seemed like an occasion for a natural alliance between Catholic *dévots* and the king's efforts to restore political order in the south of France where the Huguenot rebellions originated. And to a certain extent, this proved to be the case. But after the Huguenots were defeated at La Rochelle in the autumn of 1628, two specific issues turned some of these *dévots* against Cardinal Richelieu. First, many of them urged the king to continue to wage war against the Huguenots in the south rather than make peace with them. One such voice was Michel de Marillac, keeper of the seals and member of the king's council, who urged Richelieu to undertake some harsh measures against the Huguenots in Dauphiné in August 1630. The cardinal's response made it clear that he had another agenda. 'All these proposals seem to me excellent,' he wrote to Marillac, 'but I am not sure whether they are opportune in the existing circumstances ... nor am I sure whether it is wise to take this step at a time when we are engaged in a war outside the realm.'[2] Marillac had been critical of Richelieu's emphasis on foreign policy within the council for sometime, as he and many other *dévots* were much more concerned about domestic issues and saw little gain to be had from opposing the Catholic Habsburgs abroad. To them, Richelieu seemed dangerously pre-occupied with temporal affairs, while they felt his support for spiritual renewal and reform seemed lukewarm at best. And because the *dévots* had the backing of Marie de Medici, the queen mother, to give it some legitimacy, policy-making on the council had become very fractious. These tensions came to a head a few months later, however, when Louis XIII made a public display of his unhappiness with Marillac and the queen mother by dismissing them from the council in a pubic display of humiliation. Known as the Day of Dupes because just one day earlier Richelieu had felt certain that the king supported Marillac and Marie de Medici, this event on 10 November 1630 proved to be a turning point for Richelieu, the *dévots*, and for French policy generally. Marie de Medici was banished from court, and she eventually fled to the Spanish Netherlands. Marillac was stripped of the royal seals, arrested, and confined at Châteaudun, where the 70 year-old died two years later in disgrace. Cardinal Richelieu's policies were vindicated and his career at court as a confidant of the king was immediately boosted.

Although the Day of Dupes was certainly a heavy defeat for the *dévots*, some of them continued to criticize the cardinal and his policies. Many of them opposed his decision to covertly support the Protestant coalition fighting the Habsburgs in the Thirty Years War. Most of them had long detested Richelieu's refusal to continue the struggle against the Huguenots at home, and they were further incensed when he made alliances with a number of German Lutheran princes as well as the king of Sweden, Gustavus Adolphus. In their eyes, the cardinal's willingness to tolerate heresy at home while he parleyed with Protestant princes openly abroad made him highly suspect as a champion of the Catholic cause. He was reviled as 'patriarch of atheists . . . the supreme pontiff of the Calvinists and the cardinal of La Rochelle'.[3] Once again Richelieu prevailed, however,

---

[2] Quoted in Victor-L. Tapié, *France in the Age of Richelieu and Louis XIII*, trans. David L. Lockie (London, 1974), p. 281.
[3] Quoted in *ibid.*, p. 152.

this time by using one of his clients to blunt their criticisms. François Le Clerc du Trembley, better known as Father Joseph, was a Capuchin who had entered Richelieu's service years before when the cardinal was first appointed to the king's council. His support for Catholic reform, as well as his hostility to the Huguenots at home and Protestants abroad, was unquestioned. He recognized, however, that the Habsburg emperor's war strategy in Germany was a significant threat to France. As somewhat of a specialist on German affairs, Richelieu relied on Father Joseph both as a diplomat who began negotiations to bring France into the Thirty Years War, as well as a symbol to the *dévots* that their strategy of allying with the Habsburgs against the German Lutheran princes was dead in the water. Once France officially entered the Thirty Years War in 1635, the *dévots* were virtually finished as a political party of opposition to the crown. The cardinal continued to offer support for their spiritual reforms, however, and openly courted both the Capuchin and the Oratorian orders in these efforts. He was a Catholic bishop and cardinal, after all, but his political loyalties were to the king and the kingdom. Eradicating all opposition to the crown, whether it came from Huguenots or from *dévot* Catholics, was vital for the establishment of royal authority, and this proved to be one of Cardinal Richelieu's central missions.

The problem of individual loyalty

Many traditional acounts of the reign of Henry IV, often based on contemporary reactions, credit the king's personal charisma for restoring order after the civil wars. There is no doubt that Henry was a charming fellow, particularly when contrasted with his immediate predecessor, the more reticent and self-reflecting Henry III, but surely this is too simple an explanation. In any case, charisma is not some kind of magnetic force radiating out from leaders to their followers, drawing the latter to them irresistibly, but rather more a perception or characteristic projected onto them by their supporters. Thus, while Henry did benefit considerably from his popularity with his subjects at every social level, restoring the authority of the crown and the unity of the nation required much more than personality. It became immediately clear, even before he issued the Edict of Nantes in 1598, that Henry was going to make more systematic use of the royal client-age system than his predecessors had done in order to govern. The use of patronage—or affinities, as some historians now refer to the widest of these networks—had always been a traditional means of tying together various members of the elite classes since the decline of feudalism in the late Middle Ages. The problem was that the system enabled various nobles, and the Guise family is a prime example, to build vast clientage networks of their own throughout the realm, which could rival or even surpass that of the king.

When Henry IV finally defeated the Catholic League after his abjuration and conversion to Catholicism in 1593, he won over the loyalty of many of those who had opposed him through very traditional means. Although one (albeit cynical) way of assessing this process is to say that he simply bought them off, another is to point out that Henry simply brought them into his own personal clientage network in order to guarantee their loyalty to him as their patron. Indeed, the pattern that he followed most regularly as one League town after another finally submitted to his authority from 1594 was to place his own clients in positions of authority there to guarantee their loyalty, or to incorporate a local official he trusted, or perhaps someone who had helped negotiate the submission of the town to the king into his clientage network with a significant reward. Those whom he did not trust were neither rewarded nor placed in positions of authority. The example of Burgundy provides a number of useful examples.

In Burgundy members of the Guise family had been royal governors since 1543. When the crisis of the League broke out at the end of the religious wars, the Guises were its aristocratic leaders and their many clients in Burgundy became the foundation of opposition to the crown in the provinces. Thus, an entire aristocratic patronage network—and it expanded far outside Burgundy, including many powerful clients in Normandy and Champagne—was mobilized to oppose the legal recognition of Henry IV as king of France. When the king's abjuration persuaded many Leaguers, including many of those in Dijon, the Burgundian capital, to recognize him as their sovereign, Henry naturally was more inclined to negotiate with those Leaguers who favoured his legal recognition than with those who continued to hold out and oppose him. When the city of Dijon finally recognized Henry as king in May 1595, with royal troops led by Henry himself surrounding the city walls, Henry was led to appoint (or in some cases support the local appointment) of those who aided the process of submission. Like most of the parlements during the wars of the League, Dijon's had divided and royalists loyal to Henry fled Dijon to Flavigny, while those loyal to the League remained in Dijon. When the parlement was reunited in 1595, however, none of Henry's clients were in either group. Rather than appoint one of the presidents of the royalist parlement to preside over the newly reunited chamber, Henry reappointed the moderate Leaguer Denis Brulart to remain as First President of the parlement of Dijon, because Brulart had helped to win over the majority of the Leaguer parlement to the king's cause in the spring of 1595. Likewise, the elected mayor, René Fleutelot, had helped to persuade the city council, which had been extremely partisan toward the League, to recognize Henry as king, and Henry strongly endorsed Fleutelot's re-election as mayor of Dijon in June 1595. Finally, another moderate Leaguer and a client of the Guises, Pierre Jeannin, who had been Third President of the parlement of Dijon, had played a crucial role behind the scenes in getting Henry to abjure his Protestant faith in the first place. Henry came to trust him in the negotiations with the League and ultimately rewarded Jeannin with a promotion to a presidency in the parlement of Paris. Jeannin was later appointed to the king's Privy Council, where he became one of Henry's most trusted advisers, alongside the Huguenot Duke of Sully, and he eventually was appointed to carry out a number of highly sensitive diplomatic missions for Henry IV later in the reign.

Thus Henry IV's policy towards former League towns was designed neither to destroy municipal privileges nor to reduce local autonomy, even in extremely recalcitrant cases such as Amiens, which with Spanish support held out until 1597. Even his interference in local elections throughout the kingdom after 1595 was intended less as a royalist weapon against local privileges than a means of guaranteeing more municipal officials who were loyal to the crown. Henry's principal goal was simply to place clients—either his own or those of others whom he trusted—in positions of authority throughout his kingdom, or to co-opt into his clientage networks those former opponents who had demonstrated their loyalty to him at the end of the civil wars. This was neither a novel nor particularly surprising strategy, and it shows that Henry was using traditional methods to secure his authority, as all his predecessors had tried to do.

One of Henry's innovations, however, was a major reform in the system of venality of office, a system that had been in operation in some form since the fourteenth century. One problem was that wealthy nobles and magnates could often take advantage of the commerce in venal offices by steering their own clients into positions of influence through the venal system. Over the course of the sixteenth century most of the king's financial and legal officials became venal office-holders, and the system expanded significantly during the religious wars as successive kings needed more and more revenue. In theory, an office was purchased for life from the crown; in return the office-holder received an income (*gage*) that derived from interest earned on the original sum paid for the office, as well as various other perquisites and fees that added to the office-holder's financial reward. But in the case of judicial offices, it was respect and prestige that were the main benefits of owning an office. Dispensing the king's justice provided opportunities for further advancement and reward that were not connected directly to the office itself. And in a very few cases, certain offices—secretaries of state and judges in the parlements—even conferred nobility, though these nobles of the robe were forever criticized as social upstarts by the military nobility. These offices were not automatically inheritable by an office-holder's heir, however. Indeed, if the holder of an office died within forty days of passing his office to an heir, the office automatically reverted to the crown for resale. After 1568 office-holders could pay a sum of one-third the value of their office in order to be exempt from the forty-day rule, but this was usually too large a sum for most to afford. More often, they would have to bargain with brokers called *partisans* or *traitants*, who were middlemen in the exchange between the crown and office-holders, though this also usually resulted in paying yet more fees as well as an increase in the cost of the office. But this was exactly where local magnates with influence could be the most effective in insuring that their clients continued to profit from the system.

This began to change with the introduction of the *paulette* in 1604, a tax that made venal offices inheritable. The *paulette* was an annual tax of one-sixtieth of the office's value (the initial capital outlay paid for the office) that exempted the office-holder from the forty-day rule; he could pass on the office to an heir, usually a son or son-in-law, at death. This not only meant that there were more clients of the crown who were no longer so beholden to local magnates, but it also produced some significant revenues for the crown (this aspect will be explored in more detail below). The most immediate effect was to make offices much more desirable and valuable, and the costs of offices began to escalate considerably as a result. The cost of a counsellorship in the parlement of Rouen, for example, was valued at 7,000 *livres tournois* in 1593. After the introduction of the *paulette* in 1604, however, the value increased to 15,000 *livres* and continued to rise thereafter. It escalated to 40,000 *livres* in 1622, 66,000 *livres* in 1626, and up to as much as 80,000 *livres* by 1637. To better place these prices in context, a counsellorship in the parlement of Rouen would have cost the equivalent of 8,750 times the daily wage of a construction worker (a mason, plasterer, carpenter, or joiner) in 1593. By 1622 this rose to 40,000 times the daily wage of a construction worker, and by 1637 it escalated to 85,000 times the daily wage of a construction worker.[4] Moreover, the numbers of new offices created by the crown also rose dramatically. By the death of Henry IV in 1610, for just one vivid example, every financial office in the realm had three office-holders, each of whom served one year out of every three. In the long run this expansion of the system of venality of offices did manage to diminish the influence of local magnates somewhat to the benefit of the crown, though it also created significant political problems. Not only did traditional military nobles complain about the system, but even office-holders themselves soon came to see the increase in the number of offices as diluting their own authority. For the short run, however, Henry IV and his successors enjoyed the political as well as the financial benefits of the venal system and they used it to their advantage; the longer term problems would not come home to roost until 1648.

In many ways Louis XIII and his first minister Cardinal Richelieu built upon the efforts of Henry IV. They expanded their personal clientage networks and used them to try to centralize royal authority in the provinces. Cardinal Richelieu in particular has long had a reputation of placing his creatures into every level of government. In addition to his own family connections through the Church, upon which he built his own political career, Richelieu had loyal clients in Paris and throughout the kingdom. In Provence, for example, the

---

[4] These figures come from Roland Mousnier, *La Vénalité des offices sous Henri IV et Louis XIII* (Paris, 2nd edn., 1971), pp. 359–67.

cardinal had clients in the four municipalities of Aix-en-Provence, Arles, Toulon, and Marseille, as well as in the archbishoprics of Aix and Arles (he appointed his own brother as archbishop of Aix). This network consisted of a small group of interconnected nobles and their own clients, making it relatively easy for the cardinal to counteract hostile royal governors, such as Charles of Lorraine, duke of Guise, and his successor, the Marshall of Vitry, and ultimately to control the entire region from Paris. This strategy of surrounding recalcitrant nobles with administrative networks loyal to the cardinal was also used effectively in other provinces, such as in neighbouring Languedoc. There Richelieu managed to undermine the entrenched authority of the royal governor, Henri II, duke of Montmorency, by constructing his own clientage network to challenge the governor's authority. This policy proved so successful, in fact, that Richelieu ultimately managed to weaken the authority of royal governors throughout the kingdom by making them virtually redundant in certain provinces. It was an innovation that was continued by his ministerial successors in the reign of Louis XIV: Mazarin, Fouquet, Colbert, Le Tellier, and Louvois.

Richelieu's principal innovation in securing the loyalty of French subjects to the crown in the early seventeenth century, however, was in his novel use of intendants. Intendants were royal commissioners who had traditionally been deployed for at least a century as agents of the crown to deal with special commissions or particular emergencies as the need arose. These officials usually fell into three broad categories: intendants of justice, intendants of finance, and intendants of police. They had never previously been used in any systematic way as royal agents, much less as quasi-permanent officials based in the provinces to serve as the king's enforcers. And, indeed, Richelieu himself first used them immediately after the Day of Dupes in 1630 in the traditional way, to deal with the emergency security measures following the dismissal of Michel de Marillac as Keeper of the Seals. Moreover, between 1630 and 1633 the cardinal found them to be a useful solution to dealing with rebellion of all sorts. And in 1634–5 Richelieu empowered another group of intendants to deal with both justice and finance in an effort to reform the *taille*, the principal tax on property in France.

Events between 1635 and 1642, however, transformed the institution of the intendant. Not the least of these was war, as in 1636 a Spanish

army invaded France from Flanders and from Franche-Comté.
France was thus brought into the Thirty Years War fighting against
the Habsburgs, with its own tax revenue and military implications
(see below). By 1642 the practice of basing intendants throughout the
kingdom on a permanent basis had become established. Initially, one
intendant was assigned to each province or généralité (the twenty-two
administrative districts into which France was divided), but this
number was soon increased as more than one intendant was needed
in most of the larger districts. And to insure that these officials were
loyal to the crown rather than beholden to local elites, Richelieu
insisted on a pretty firm three-year maximum stay in any one locality.
There were a few notable exceptions—François de Villemontée, who
was particularly successful at dealing with revolts, was an intendant in
Poitou almost continuously from 1631 to 1648—but intendants were
commissioners, not office-holders, and in no sense were their jobs
considered lifetime appointments. The intendants did enable Louis
XIII's first minister to construct a more centralized and more bureaucratic administration in the provinces, and they helped transform
a system of personal loyalty based on patron–client relations to one
of loyalty to the state. When there had been no more than 120 intendants of all types appointed in the seventy years before 1630, in the
eighteen years thereafter up to 150 intendants were appointed by
Richelieu or his successor, Cardinal Mazarin. These new royal agents
naturally attracted the hostility of many royal office-holders whose
duties they seemed to usurp, the parlementaires in particular. And
when the government collapsed and bankruptcy was declared in 1648
at the outbreak of the Fronde, it was no surprise when the parlement
of Paris demanded that all intendants be recalled. Most of them, in
fact, were recalled, but there was no guarantee that in 1648 the
regency government headed by Anne of Austria and Cardinal Mazarin could defeat the Fronde, much less restore the institution of the
intendants. Thus, it was hardly inevitable that Louis XIV would
eventually succeed in doing exactly that.

The revenue problem

A third principal problem faced by French kings at the end of the Wars of Religion was how to reform the fiscal system to make it more efficient and productive for the crown. The French crown had never really had the ability to raise significant amount of cash revenue on short notice, which was one reason the civil wars lasted so long. The crown simply lacked the resources to defeat either the Huguenots or the Leaguers in a quick decisive war. Assessment and collection of the principal direct tax, the property tax called the *taille*, was grossly inefficient. For a start, the kingdom was split between two very different systems of tax assessment and collection. In most of the centre of the kingdom—including Paris and the Île-de-France—taxes were theoretically under the jurisdiction of royal tax officials called *élus*. Even in these areas, however (known as *pays d'élections*), there was not as much efficiency and uniformity as there could be. In some areas, rather than the royal *élus*, tax farmers or other professional tax collectors were paid on a commission basis to collect the *taille*. And nearly everywhere only a fraction of the amounts assessed was actually ever collected.

It was in the peripheral provinces along the French frontier, however, where the most serious impediments to a reformed tax system existed. The provinces of Burgundy, Brittany, Languedoc, Provence, Béarn, Guyenne, and Dauphiné were among those most recently incorporated into the French realm (most of these since the end of the Hundred Years War in 1453). These regions managed to retain many local privileges and liberties as part of their bargain with the crown upon their incorporation, not the least of which was to assess and collect their own taxation. Called *pays d'états* because these provinces retained their own provincial estates to assess and collect taxation, these regions not surprisingly turned over much less revenue to the crown from the *taille* than in the *pays d'élections*. For example, during the period 1598–1630 the total crown revenues from direct taxation were in the region of 20,000,000 to 30,000,000 *livres* per annum. The portion of that amount that came from the *pays d'états*, however, was rarely over 3,000,000 *livres* per annum. Thus, these regions with their own provincial estates made up between one-third

and one-fourth of the taxable population of France, yet they provided barely one-tenth of the crown's revenue from direct taxation.
That Henry IV and his superintendent of finances, the duke of Sully,
should see this as an anomaly can be no surprise. Both to keep the
peace at home as well as to make war abroad, the king needed a more
efficient stream of direct taxation.

The first salvo at the *pays d'états* was fired by Sully in 1603 in the
province of Guyenne in the south-west. A royal edict creating *élections* in Guyenne (along with the royal tax officials, the *élus*) was
issued in January 1603 and ratified by the parlement of Bordeaux the
following year. The provincial estates as well as many other local
notables in Guyenne protested, claiming that their traditional privileges were being abrogated by the crown. Sully stood firm, however,
and the assessments made by the provincial estates were ignored, as
royal *élus* began assessing and collecting the *taille* in the province.
Although the *élus* were abandoned and the provincial estates of Guyenne restored to their previous authority by Marie de Medici after
Henry's assassination in 1610, Louis XIII eventually reintroduced the
élus in 1621–2. And just a few years later in his reign an ever broader
and more systematic attempt to reform the tax system in the *pays
d'états* was undertaken.

Organized by Michel de Marillac, the Keeper of the Seals, and the
marquis d'Effiat, Louis's superintendent of finances and a client of
Richelieu, these efforts resulted in the creation of new *élections* in the
provinces of Languedoc, Provence, Burgundy, and Dauphiné between
1628 and 1630. Opposition in these areas quickly turned violent, however, as open revolts broke out in the cities of Dijon in Burgundy and
Aix in Provence in 1630. And although the revolts failed to prevent the
creation of the *élections*, they did make it clear that the king might
have to be flexible if he were to succeed in increasing the tax revenue
stream from the *pays d'états*. To be sure, in those areas where there
was little or no opposition, the crown was able to install its own tax
collection officials to supercede the provincial estates. The Estates of
Dauphiné would not meet again until 1788, and there were similar
successes elsewhere, as in Périgord and the Poitou. In the provinces
where the opposition was significant, however, Richelieu chose other
means to increase revenues. In the short run, he allowed certain provinces to remain exempt from the *élections*, that is, to buy back their
right to assess and collect their own taxes. The Estates of Languedoc,

for example, offered to pay the crown 2.9 million *livres* for this privilege, the Estates of Burgundy paid 1.6 million *livres*, and the Estates of Provence paid 1.5 million *livres*. Even in these provinces, however, Richelieu was not content to maintain a totally laissez-faire policy towards tax collection, and he initiated a series of traditional manoeuvres—bribery—as well as more recent innovations—the intendants—to insure that these provinces that still had their provincial estates would contribute their fair share of direct taxation to the crown. By 1648, in fact, the crown's ability to generate revenue from direct taxation in these provinces was virtually as secure as it was in the rest of France.

The point to be stressed here is that Cardinal Richelieu did not mount a systematic campaign to destroy provincial tax institutions in order to centralize the state government. Uniformity and centralization, while a modern ideal that is doubtless justified in the name of state efficiency and efficacy, was not really part of his plan. Richelieu was much more a pragmatist than an ideological proponent of some theory of absolutism. He wanted more secure and more immediate streams of revenue for his domestic and foreign policies, and reforming the tax assessment and collection procedures in the *pays d'états* certainly fit that bill. If he could find a way to insure that the crown had some oversight of taxation in the provinces, he was quite content to allow the provincial subjects of the king to maintain whatever local privileges and liberties they claimed to enjoy. The exception that proves the rule is the province of Brittany.

Although the Estates of Brittany enjoyed the same privileges and independence as the other provincial estates in matters of direct taxation, Richelieu chose never to interfere in their affairs even once. But then why would he? The cardinal was appointed royal governor in Brittany in 1630, and was its de facto royal protector. The same year the Estates of Brittany voted a *don gratuit* (literally, a free gift) of 900,000 *livres* to the crown and 100,000 *livres* to Richelieu himself. Moreover, because the cardinal had a dream of establishing a powerful royal navy and a royal trading company to rival the Dutch, Spanish, and English overseas, he needed the ports of Brittany to serve as its base. Many in the provincial estates as well as some local nobles supported Richelieu, since they could see the economic advantages and royal privileges attached to his scheme. Thus, the Estates of Brittany continued to meet right up to the Revolution.

By replacing the provincial estates in some of the *pays d'états*, and by manipulating the estates better in those where they survived, the crown managed to tap into the resources of many under-taxed parts of the kingdom. This was vital once France entered into the Thirty Years War in 1635. Figure 1 in Chapter 3 above shows a remarkable growth in crown revenues after 1635, virtually doubling between 1635 and 1645. While not all of this dramatic increase was attributable to direct taxation, much of it was, and it shows how skilful Richelieu was in manipulating an archaic and outmoded system of tax collection. The result certainly was not a new and centralized system, but it was a structure that was significantly more efficient in raising revenue for the crown. Without these efforts, France would have been hard pressed to raise an army of unheard of proportions in the 1640s, much less make much of a difference in the Thirty Years War. By 1648, however, when the outbreak of the Fronde threatened to undermine all the efforts of the previous fifty years, the problem of tax revenues had been temporarily resolved through a series of ad hoc policies that were more pragmatic than absolutist.

The other principal source of crown revenue that increased dramatically in the 1630s was income from the sale of offices. The system of venality seemed a natural source of income for Cardinal Richelieu to exploit once France entered the Thirty Years War in 1635. One way to increase revenues was simply to create entirely new companies of officers. New courts of aids were created in Lyon in 1636 and in Caen and Vienne in 1638; new bureaux of finances were established in Montauban in 1635 and in Alençon in 1640. Even more frequent was the practice of simply adding more officers to already existing companies. In 1635 alone twenty-three different companies had their numbers swelled by the creation of new officers. While this had the effect of stirring up great antagonism among existing office-holders, whose prestige and authority was now diluted by the newly created officers, the result for the crown was significantly increased income. Sometimes the existing office-holders paid the king to revoke the new creations, or often they purchased the new offices among themselves to prevent outsiders from joining their company. Either way, neither Richelieu nor Louis XIII much cared as the result was significant new revenues for the royal treasury. As one contemporary noted very frankly, these new creations have been made 'rather to draw help from the monies they yield to employ in the expenses of war than from any necessity to increase the number of offices'.[5]

Other ways the crown managed to squeeze more income from the venal system included exacting forced loans from venal office-holders. This could be done in a variety of ways, but one of the most efficient was to require office-holders to pay their *droit annuel* (*paulette*) in advance, requiring nine years' worth of dues to be paid in just three years. Another ploy was for the crown simply to stop paying office-holders their *gages*, the interest earned on the sum paid for the office. But defaulting on the *gages*, like the forced loans with the *paulette*, were nothing new to the world of venality. Since every office-holder wanted to hold on to his original investment, whose value had increased dramatically since the introduction of the *paulette* in 1604, officers had little option but to live with the deficiencies in the system. And the venal system, combined with new tax revenues from the *pays d'états*, increased the royal treasury significantly. The crown's total revenues in 1604 had been 98.6 million *livres tournois*. By 1624 when Richelieu first came onto the king's council, revenues totalled 203 million. By 1634 this had climbed to 333.5 million *livres tournois*, reaching 588 million by 1639. Even more dramatic was the relative proportion of revenues accruing from the venal system over this period. Whereas only 7.2 per cent of total crown revenues in 1604 had originated from the *parties casuelles*, where revenues from the venal system were deposited, income from the venal system made up 38.9 per cent of total crown revenues by 1634.[6] Even though revenues from the venal sale of offices declined somewhat in the 1640s, all of these financial measures got France through the Thirty Years War and resulted in a very significant military and political victory in 1648. The built-up anger and resentment of royal office-holders, however, could not be contained forever. That same year the regent Anne of Austria, mother of the young Louis XIV, would discover that this victory came at a price.

---

[5] Quoted in Mousnier, *La Venalité des offices*, p. 131, and in William Doyle, *Venality: The Sale of Offices in Eighteenth-Century France* (Oxford, 1996), p. 11.

[6] All these figures are from Richard Bonney, *The King's Debts: Finance and Politics in France, 1589–1661* (Oxford, 1981), pp. 312–13.

The military problem

A fourth problem that faced French monarchs in the first half of the seventeenth century was its relative weakness as a military state. France was openly invaded by a German Protestant army in 1576 and again in 1587, while a Spanish army invaded and occupied a number of French towns in 1590, 1592, and again in 1596–7. All of these invasions proved impossible to stop, and only the last of them was successfully repelled. Moreover, the crown was unable to defeat in any systematic way either the French Huguenot forces between 1562 and 1593 or the forces of the Catholic League between 1588 and 1593. With the largest tax base of any state in Western Europe—roughly 18 million people in 1600—it was more than a little concern for French kings that their ability to keep the peace as well as to make war was more restricted than it could be. Thus, a real concern for both Henry IV and Louis XIII was how to increase both the size and the supporting infrastructure of the French army. To be sure, developing a more secure tax revenue stream was critical, as the previous discussion made clear; but there was more to increasing the size of the army than simply raising tax revenues.

When Henry IV was assassinated in May 1610, he was on the verge of mounting a military campaign against the Spanish Habsburgs. His immediate goal was to raise an army of 50,000 men, a figure that was probably very close to the all-time high the French crown had in the field during the sixteenth century. And while the assassination forced the postponement of this particular military venture, it does provide a sense of proportion about how large an army France might be able to sustain. The size of the French army escalated in the 1630s and 1640s, however, as the delayed confrontation with the Habsburgs finally came to pass in the Thirty Years War. When Richelieu tried to mobilize an army against Spain in 1635, for example, he was operating in a system in which the size of the French army had increased dramatically since the beginning of the Habsburg–Valois Wars. When Charles VIII invaded Italy in 1494, he never had an army larger than 16,000–20,000 men. Francis I suffered his defeat at Pavia in 1525, however, with an army of 24,000–26,000 men. And at the battle of Saint Quentin in 1557 the French army had increased to a high of

40,000–50,000 men including mercenaries. This total was rarely surpassed during the Wars of Religion, and even when it was, it was the
result of private troops raised by individual nobles supplementing
royal forces. At the Jülich–Cleves crisis in 1610 Henry IV had an army
of 50,000 men, which seemed to be the upper limit that the crown
could keep in the field at any one time. Thus when Cardinal Richelieu marshalled 60,000–70,000 men to repel the Spanish invasion and
occupation of Languedoc in 1637, this was a significant achievement.
And this total may have increased up to as much as 80,000 men in the
field by 1642.[7] Although historians have rightly taken a more realistic
view of the size of French armies in light of some of the more exaggerated claims for numbers in the records of the army itself, there is
no question that this represented 'a quantum leap forward', as one
historian has recently described it.[8] It is certainly true that these
increased numbers did not lead to many immediate French military
victories, nor did they result in any overhaul of the military administration, so the question remains why France could not put even larger
armies into the field. The short answer is that despite the increased
revenues in the 1630s, the treasury was unable to sustain maintaining
any larger forces for extended periods of time. In short, until the
crown could come up with both permanent and regular funding
from ordinary revenues for an army larger than 70,000–80,000
troops, this was about the limit of what Richelieu could achieve.
Nevertheless, he managed to increase this limit roughly 50 per cent
from the sixteenth-century highs of 50,000.

But for what purposes was this expanded army used? Traditional
accounts have long maintained that it was a larger army that allowed
Louis XIII and Louis XIV to better control their unruly subjects,
thereby enabling absolutism to replace the weakness of the Valois
kings during the religious wars. While this argument has a grain of
truth to it in the context of the civil wars of the sixteenth century, it
does not stand up in the light of what happened after 1598. The fact is
that Louis XIII and Louis XIV—and by extension Cardinals Richelieu
and Mazarin—rarely used royal forces against civilians. During
peacetime most troops in the French army, somewhere in the region

[7] All these figures come from David Parrott, *Richelieu's Army: War, Government and
Society in France, 1624–1661* (Cambridge, 2001), pp. 182–3, 202, and 220.
[8] John A. Lynn, *Giant of the Grand Siècle: The French Army, 1610–1715* (Cambridge,
1997), p. 56. Lynn's estimates on pp. 55–6 are consistently higher than Parrott's.

of 10,000 men until 1635, were stationed in garrisons along the French frontier for protection against foreign invasion and were explicitly not deployed to police the kingdom. The army raised against the Huguenots in the 1620s was conceived of in the context of war, laying siege to Montauban, Montpellier, and La Rochelle, as well as defeating the army of the Protestant rebels led by the Duke of Rohan. Moreover, the uprisings of 1635–59, largely tax revolts, were themselves by definition wartime rebellions. The troops used against them were not part of any standing army, but wartime troops diverted to put down these rebellions. Even in the reign of Louis XIV, who did create a significant and revolutionary standing army of up to 200,000 men in peacetime, there was little effort by the Sun King to use his standing army to beat his subjects into submission. So, how does the growth of the royal army reflect the rise of a more absolutist state?

One answer lies in the many ways that a larger army increased royal power by allowing the king to remain free from his dependence on the private forces of major nobles. Prior to the 1630s, largely due to the fiscal limitations forced upon him, the king was required to call upon his greatest magnates to raise forces, which he then might be able to use for his own purposes. But as was quickly discovered during the civil wars of the sixteenth century, great magnates could also raise forces to oppose the king. The opposition of the Protestant Henry of Navarre and the Catholic Henri of Guise were just the most visible examples of how precarious noble support could be. Thus, the kings of France in the seventeenth century desired to be beholden to no one and to rely on their own forces. The growth of the royal army allowed them to do that. By the same token, the growth of the army eventually allowed kings to replace or co-opt potentially dangerous urban militias. Once again, during the 1590s many towns across France were ruled by bourgeois militias loyal to the Catholic League and in defiant opposition to the crown, further undermining the authority of the king. Although urban militias could be inexpensively raised and mobilized in wartime, they could also be very obstructionist. Thus by allowing the king to rely less on the use of urban militias both in peacetime and in wartime, his authority was less threatened by them.

Ultimately, the growth of the army in the wartime era of 1635–59 allowed the king to wield greater leverage over the aristocracy, not by expanding the army to appease noble dissidents, but by offering the lure of greater commissions and offices in the royal army as a means of winning support for royal policy among the aristocratic elite. The collaboration between the king and his nobles, as one historian has described the foundation of royal absolutism, was not so much a capitulation of the nobility to the power of the king as it was an attempt to co-opt the nobles' authority in the provinces for the royal programme of military expansion in exchange for honours and perquisites. In this sense, both the king and the aristocracy benefited from absolutism. Ultimately, however, the link between the growth of the royal army in the seventeenth century and the kind of state formation usually associated with a programme of royal absolutism was not in the way that kings used the army to threaten or subject violence upon their civilian populations, which rarely happened anyway, but in the ways that military expansion either intimidated or actually won over potential opposition to the side of the crown through mutual benefit. In the long run, military expansion allowed the king of France not only to strengthen his hand at home, but also to wage war abroad on an unprecedented scale as well as to establish an empire overseas.

The Fronde

Everything that Henry IV, Louis XIII, and Cardinal Richelieu had accomplished in terms of redrawing the lines of royal authority was instantly threatened by the deaths in 1642 of Cardinal Richelieu followed one year later by the death of Louis XIII himself. His successor was a young boy of 5, and during the new king's minority the government was left in the hands of two unpopular foreigners: Louis's queen, Anne of Austria, and the new first minister who replaced Cardinal Richelieu, the Italian Cardinal Giulio Mazarin. The regents seemed to ignore the traditional ruling elites both at court and in the parlements once they took over the reins of power, and the fact that both were foreigners only increased their unpopularity. The outbreak of the Fronde in 1648—a revolt by judges in the royal parlements, followed by a revolt of several royal princes against the policies of Anne of Austria and Cardinal Mazarin—challenged and threatened all the reforms that had been initiated since 1598. Facing bankruptcy by the end of 1647 Anne and Mazarin had forced through the parlement of Paris the creation of yet another round of new offices. Forced to register these new creations in January 1648 against their will in a *Lit de justice*, whereby the young king made a personal appearance in the court requiring registration, the judges, venal office-holders all, began to contemplate how to salvage their lost prestige as well as the income from the investment in their offices. Their anger over the new creations was exacerbated by the fact that the crown had defaulted on the *gages* of most office-holders for the previous six years.

The crisis reached a boiling point on 29 April when Mazarin announced the renewal of the *paulette* for another nine years. Most office-holders were required to pay another forced loan to the crown in order to renew the inheritability of their offices, while some officers, like the masters of requests, were denied access to the *paulette* altogether. *Gages*, already well in arrears, were to be suspended for another four years. Provoked into action by this announcement, the following month the parlement of Paris called a special meeting of representatives from all office-holding companies. They met in Paris over the next six weeks and ultimately came to challenge royal authority with a series of demands: a call for an end to the creation of further new offices, the restoration of the regular payment of *gages*, and the abolition of the intendants, who as non-office-holders had usurped so many of their duties in the provinces. Unwilling to agree to the office-holders' demands, but equally unable to oppose them, the queen mother and Cardinal Mazarin were eventually forced to flee the capital with the young king in tow once they saw that the sympathies of the people of Paris lay with the magistrates rather than with the regency government. And later, when some of the princes of the blood took the field with their own troops and threatened to call in more reinforcements from abroad, the threat of civil war breaking out once again was real. It was only the declaration of majority by the young Louis XIV in 1651 shortly after his thirteenth birthday that brought the crisis to an end, but the memories of being chased out of Paris by his own subjects haunted the young king for the rest of his life.

There is no question that the Fronde ultimately proved to be a less serious threat to royal authority than the religious wars of the sixteenth century. Moreover, it occurred during the minority of the young Louis XIV, a period when revolts of this kind traditionally broke out. There was a less significant revolt led by Henri II of Bourbon, prince of Condé, during the minority of Louis XIII in 1614, and the much more serious rebellion of Huguenot nobles led by his grandfather, Louis of Bourbon, prince of Condé, in 1562 during the minority of Charles IX. That the Fronde would never grow into the kind of serious challenge to royal authority as was the case during the religious wars was not so evident at the time, however. And the more important point is that even if the judicial and aristocratic revolts that made up the Fronde had never happened, there was still nothing inevitable about the continuing growth of royal authority during the reign of Louis XIV that historians have traditionally called royal absolutism. While order and stability had certainly been restored by 1648 after the chaos and rebellion of the Wars of Religion of the sixteenth century, there was no plan or model outlined by anyone, including Cardinal Richelieu, for the construction of an absolutist state. And while the Huguenots had been defeated, there was not yet in 1648 what we might call more modern and permanent solutions to France's other major problems. Although the intendants and military reforms may have made the king somewhat less dependent on the aristocracy than in the past, the Fronde would prove very clearly that individual subjects could still remain as recalcitrant and rebellious as ever. Thus in 1648 France was certainly not on a predetermined path towards absolutism, as has often been claimed. The greater authority that Louis XIV would come to wield in the later seventeenth century was contingent entirely on his policies, and especially on how successful he and his ministers were in selling them to his subjects.

And what had become of the French nation since 1598? One noticeable transformation since the Edict of Nantes, and even partly as a result of this peace, was the decline in the king's reliance on the imagery of sacral monarchy. That nearly a million Protestants had been legally recognized as French subjects by the edict was bound to diminish the power of the explicitly Catholic and Gallican images and symbols used to represent the crown. Whereas Henry III had chosen to represent his public persona during the civil wars wearing the habit of a religious order—as a penitent in a religious procession—Henry IV and his royalist promoters opted for a more classically heroic guise: the Gallic Hercules. In this reconstruction of royal imagery, a classical motif replaced a Christian one, though it still maintained the traditional notion that kings were in some way gods themselves. There was not, of course, any announced or publicized decision to eschew the traditional Catholic image of the consecrated king in favour of a more secular and classical figure. Nevertheless, in 1661 when the 23-year-old Louis XIV decided to govern alone without a first minister after the death of Cardinal Mazarin, he went even further, displaying himself at a festival at court as Apollo, the Roman god associated with the sun. From sun-god to Sun-King—the monarch as both deity and king, with everyone and everything basking in his own light—was thus an easy association for his subjects to make. And although the community of the French nation was still loosely held together by various personal ties to the crown, Church, and other institutions, those ties were obviously evolving. As the reigns of Louis XIV's successors in the eighteenth-century would demonstrate, however, they could not evolve fast enough to keep pace with the even greater changing needs of the French nation.

Conclusion

Mack P. Holt

There is no question that the single greatest threat to the French monarchy prior to the Revolution of 1789 was the civil wars of the sixteenth century. This long crisis forms the central focus of this book, while also helping us better understand the changes and continuities in France between 1500 and 1648. Not only did the experiences and memories of the religious violence and civil wars last far into the seventeenth century, but many of the things we now associate with France in the seventeenth-century—absolute monarchy, the Catholic Reformation, increased taxation and the accompanying tax revolts, for example—are themselves legacies in one way or another of the efforts to repair and restore the kingdom of France after the destruction of the Wars of Religion. But just how much had France changed over the century and a half prior to the Fronde?

In the political sphere it is clear that France, like most dynastic states, was only as strong as the royal members of its ruling dynasty. It suffered dramatically when weak kings proved unable to cope with or even offer credible solutions to the many problems the kingdom faced: religious division, insufficient revenues, foreign warfare, and the occasional power grab of an overmighty subject or subjects being among the most frequent. The series of inexperienced and ineffectual kings—all sons of Henry II and Catherine de Medici—who governed France from 1559 to 1589 form the most obvious example of the deficiencies in the Valois royal line. That the first two Bourbon kings were able to restore order and monarchical authority in the kingdom speaks as much about their personal skills and acumen as about their policies. And while Francis I and Henry II might question whether Henry IV and Louis XIII were actually stronger and more authoritative monarchs than they were—in terms of political theory all French kings were absolute monarchs as far as the phrase was understood in early modern France—it is equally true that the seventeenth-century kings had attempted and at least partially succeeded in creating a more reliable means of enforcing their authority throughout the kingdom. The system of absolutism under Louis XIV after 1661, however we may define it, was certainly not a foregone conclusion in 1648, as the advent of the Fronde and the 282 popular uprisings (most of them tax revolts) between 1635 and 1660 made very clear. Absent an undisputed and legitimate adult king, almost any kind of disorder or instability was possible. Yet the creation of a more efficacious and uniform tax collection system, the training and garrisoning of a professional standing army, and the diminishing of the religious tensions of the sixteenth century all made it more likely that once an adult and legitimate king came of age, he would be able to govern the kingdom with a greater chance of stability and order than before.

French identity and the perception of what defined the French nation also changed between 1500 and 1648. The late medieval concept of sacral monarchy—the idea that a god-king was anointed from the Valois bloodline by the Creator to govern France by divine decree—came under attack during the religious wars. Ironically, it was not so much the Huguenots, who might have been expected to reject such a Catholic concept of the nation, who were attacking it, as for the most part they remained loyal to the traditional state. It was in fact the radical members of the Holy Catholic League who made the most serious assault on the concept of sacral monarchy. In their justification for regicide as well as their rejection of the traditional dynastic lineage, some of the radical Leaguers unwittingly laid the foundations for a decline in sacerdotal kingship. What Henry IV and Louis XIII were forced to do was come up with a more inclusive way of retaining the loyalties of Huguenots and Catholics alike after 1598. Catholic political ceremonies, rituals, and symbols still may have carried great weight with many French Catholics in the seventeenth century, but in terms of defining the French nation, they were not as empowering as they had been prior to the civil wars. Nevertheless, the educational thrust of the Catholic Reformation at the end of the religious wars laid a foundation of common experience that would lead in the late seventeenth and eighteenth centuries to a greater shared vision of the nation in terms of language, values, laws, and ideals. Thus even though the powerful symbol of sacral monarchy may have been on the wane in the seventeenth century—despite the efforts of some like Bossuet to resurrect it in the reign of Louis XIV— it is still true that religion continued to play a significant role in helping define what was an evolving sense of French identity and nationhood by 1648. In their efforts to reform parish life, many of the *dévots* and members of the new religious orders also helped to create a foundation of education and learning in the early seventeenth century that would eventually provide a means of uniting the country around more secular symbols in 1789.

It was the transformation of the religious make-up of the kingdom that was most noticeable by 1648, however. In 1500, for all practical purposes, France was a nation made up exclusively of Gallican Catholics. And throughout the first half of the sixteenth century and into the period of the civil wars, anyone who was not sufficiently orthodox in belief and practice was closely scrutinized and sometimes persecuted. By 1648 a small but significant cohort of Protestants (about 5 per cent of the population as a whole is a reasonable estimate) managed to survive and eventually thrive within a kingdom that was still publicly Catholic. In some of the rural villages of the south where significant numbers of Protestants and Catholics lived side by side in the same village community, recent research has shown that there was some limited and peaceful integration of the two confessions immediately after the Edict of Nantes. Yet in the larger cities such as Montpellier, it is equally clear that the confessional lines hardened between the two faiths, as each community sought to distance itself from the other within the larger urban landscape. What stands out even there, however, is that the religious violence of the sixteenth century had dissipated. Protestants were no longer sacking Catholic churches and cemeteries in ritual orgies of purification, and Catholics were no longer prosecuting Huguenots for heresy. The importance of religion had hardly diminished by 1648, as the Catholic reforms of the early seventeenth century made clear. And in many ways some of the most visible religious changes in France during the period were the result of Catholic reform efforts after 1598 rather than a legacy of the civil wars. The reform of the episcopacy, the profusion of new religious orders, the expanded roles for women to participate in both lay and ecclesiastical life, as well as the impact of the catechism on education all helped to reshape everyday life in the parishes.

What had not changed very much by 1648 was the social

domination of the nobility. Yet even though the traditional social hierarchy remained intact until the French Revolution, it is nevertheless true that the make-up of the elite classes had evolved considerably since 1500. First of all, the purchase of royal offices had become a new springboard to wealth and influence. It was no longer the exclusively feudal markers of land and military service that enabled a commoner to achieve significant wealth and influence. Fuelled by the ever-increasing needs of greater revenues by the crown, the sale of venal offices provided a new element to the elite classes that both competed with and occasionally even integrated itself into the traditional military noble families. Second, trade and commerce came to be another route to success. And while nobles were traditionally forbidden from engaging in such common enterprises, there is no question that many aristocratic families only survived by investing in commercial activities. Third, humanism and humanist schooling brought about a much sharper intellectual role for nobles to play in French society. No longer just warriors on the battlefield, they educated themselves to such an extent that they continued to dominate the world of letters and education. If the Jesuits are usually given credit for educational advances after 1598, what is less well known is that Jesuit schools were designed principally to educate the sons of nobles and aristocrats. French nobles learned all too well that the pen was as mighty as the sword.

Finally, France in 1648 was a nation that had just helped defeat the Spanish and Austrian Habsburgs in the Thirty Years War. That the Catholic state of France could join together with Lutheran Sweden, the Calvinist Dutch Republic, and Hussite Bohemia, not to mention various other Protestant states, to defeat the two strongest Catholic states in Europe indicates how far France had evolved since 1500. It also makes clear that the confessional politics that often dominated European affairs in the sixteenth century was slowing giving way to a more secular *realpolitik*. Although bound up in the crisis of the Fronde until Louis XIV declared his majority in 1651, France was nevertheless well placed to fill the void left by the decline of Habsburg hegemony of Europe in 1648. The creations of a significantly larger army and an expanded royal bureaucracy, along with new sources of revenue to finance them, are evidence enough that French influence on the international stage was bound to be more visible in 1648 than in 1500. Yet while Louis XIV would eventually gain some modest successes in expanding the French state within Europe in the second half of the seventeenth century, and he would achieve more than modest success in propagating the idea of absolute monarchy to his fellow kings, the ascendancy of France as a European state was hardly inevitable in 1648. It was the combined efforts of the king and his subjects that enabled France to become the model of political stability, the epitome of intellectual creativity, and the envy of military expediency throughout the continent of Europe in the second half of the seventeenth century. Much of this effort was forged from a mutual desire to avoid any repetition of the disorder and instability of the Wars of Religion. Even though Henry IV attempted to banish the memories of the civil wars and confessional division in Article 1 of the Edict of Nantes, it was precisely these memories that continued to haunt Henry's successors and motivated them to build a stronger and more durable state. Louis XIV even alluded to this legacy of the religious wars of the sixteenth century in the preamble to the Revocation of the Edict of Nantes in 1685, where he sought to banish the memory of the Huguenots forever:

We have determined that we can do nothing better in order wholly to obliterate the memory of the troubles, the confusion, and the evils which the progress of this false religion has caused in this kingdom, and which furnished occasion for the said edict [of Nantes] and to so many previous and subsequent edicts and declarations, than entirely to revoke the said Edict of Nantes.[1]

But it is all too clear that even absolute monarchs were unable to control historical consciousness so completely.

---

[1] Orest Ranum and Patricia Ranum (eds. and trans.), *The Century of Louis XIV* (New York, 1972), p. 360.

Further reading

General

There have been a number of recent general works in English on early modern French history, although none covers the exact chronological parameters of this volume. For the fifteenth-century background and the first half of the sixteenth century, there is nothing better than David Potter, *A History of France, 1460–1560: The Emergence of a Nation State* (London, 1995). For the sixteenth century, see Frederic J. Baumgartner, *France in the Sixteenth Century* (New York, 1995), Mack P. Holt, *The French Wars of Religion, 1562–1629* (Cambridge, 1995), J. Russell Major, *From Renaissance Monarchy to Absolute Monarchy: French Kings, Nobles, and Estates* (Baltimore, 1994), R. J. Knecht, *The Rise and Fall of Renaissance France, 1483–1610* (London, 1996), and the same author's *The French Civil Wars, 1562–1598* (London, 2000). Although much older, J. H. M. Salmon's *Society in Crisis: France in the Sixteenth Century* (New York, 1975) is still fresh and has much to offer. For the seventeenth century, in addition to the older work of Victor-L. Tapié, *France in the Age of Louis XIII and Richelieu*, trans., D. M. Lockie (London, 1974; orig. French edn. 1967), see Robin Briggs, *Early Modern France, 1560–1715* (Oxford, 1978) and James B. Collins, *The State in Early Modern France* (Cambridge, 1995). Finally, there are now two excellent collections of documents in English translation that can usefully supplement all of these general studies: David Potter (ed.), *The French Wars of Religion: Selected Documents* (New York, 1997) and Richard Bonney (ed.), *Society and Government in France under Richelieu and Mazarin, 1624–1661* (London, 1988).

The Kingdom of France in the sixteenth century

For some recent attempts to define the French nation in this period, see Collette Beaune, *The Birth of an Ideology: Myths and Symbols of Nation in Late Medieval France*, trans. Susan R. Huston (Berkeley, 1991); David Bell, 'Recent Works on Early Modern French National Identity', *Journal of Modern History*, 68 (Mar. 1996), 84–113; and several of the essays in Pierre Nora (ed.), *Realms of Memory: The Construction of the French Past*, 3 vols., trans. Arthur Goldhammer (New York, 1998). For political rituals, the best place to start is Marc Bloch, *The Royal Touch: Monarchy and Miracles in France and England*, trans. J. E. Anderson (New York, 1989). After that, one can read with profit Ralph E. Giesey, *The Royal Funeral Ceremony in Renaissance France* (Geneva, 1961) and Richard A. Jackson, *Vive le Roi! A History of the French Coronation from Charles V to Charles X* (Chapel Hill, NC, 1984). Two recent analyses of the role of language come from different disciplinary approches, although they share complementary conclusions: Paul Cohen, 'Courtly French, Learned Latin, and Peasant Patois: The Making of a National Language in Early Modern France', Ph.D. thesis (Princeton University, 2001) and Timothy Hampton, *Literature and Nation in the Sixteenth Century: Inventing the French Renaissance* (Ithaca, NY, 2001). For the Habsburg-Valois Wars, see the relevant chapters in David Potter, *A History of France, 1460–1560: The Emergence of a Nation State* (London, 1995), R. J. Knecht, *Renaissance Warrior and Patron: The Reign of Francis I* (Cambridge, 1994), and Frederic J. Baumgartner, *Henry II, King of France, 1547–1559* (Durham, NC, 1986).

Social groups and cultural practices

Over the last fifty years, there has developed an immense and sophisticated historical literature dealing with French society and culture. What follows is a small sampling of this literature, with emphasis on works of synthesis available in English. Most studies of French rural life have been influenced by Marc Bloch's classic *French Rural History: An Essay on Its Basic Characteristics*, trans. Janet Sondheimer (Berkeley and Los Angeles, 1966; first published 1932). Among more recent studies, Emmanuel Le Roy Ladurie, *The French Peasantry 1450–1660*, trans. Alan Sheridan (Berkeley and Los Angeles, 1987) provides an excellent overview; see also his classic work *The Peasants of Languedoc*, trans. John Day (Urbana, Ill., 1974) and his collected essays, *The Territory of the Historian*, trans. Ben Reynolds and Siân Reynolds (Chicago, 1979). A briefer survey of the subject, from a somewhat different perspective, is provided by Jonathan Dewald and Liana Vardi, 'The Peasantries of France, 1400–1800', in Tom Scott (ed.), *The Peasantries of Europe from the Fourteenth to the Eighteenth Centuries* (London, 1998). Among numerous studies dealing with village culture, Natalie Zemon Davis, *Society and Culture in Early Modern France* (Stanford, Calif., 1975) and Philip Hoffman, *Church and Community in the Diocese of Lyon, 1500–1789* (New Haven, 1984); both include important material on urban cultures as well. Important studies of sorcery include E. William Monter, *Witchcraft in France and Switzerland: The Borderlands during the Reformation* (Ithaca, NY and London, 1976) and Robin Briggs, *Communities of Belief: Cultural and Social Tensions in Early Modern France* (Oxford, 1989).

For urban population statistics and causes of change, Jan de Vries, *European Urbanization 1500–1800* (Cambridge, Mass., 1984). William Beik, *Urban Protest in Seventeenth-Century France: The Culture of Retribution* (Cambridge, 1997) analyses both urban violence and the larger background from which it emerged. Many fine studies have examined the character of life in individual cities in these years, among them are Philip Benedict, *Rouen during the Wars of Religion* (Cambridge, 1981), Robert Schneider, *Public Life in*

Toulouse, 1463–1789: From Municipal Republic to Cosmopolitan City (Ithaca, NY and London, 1989), Orest Ranum, *Paris in the Age of Absolutism: An Essay* (New York, 1968), and Natalie Zemon Davis, 'The Sacred and the Body Social in Sixteenth-Century Lyon', *Past and Present*, 90 (Feb. 1981).

Roland Mousnier, *The Institutions of France under the Absolute Monarchy, 1598–1789*, trans. Brian Pearce (Chicago, 1979) provides English-language access to the ideas of a pre-eminent historian of French officialdom during the early modern period. Jonathan Dewald, *The Formation of a Provincial Nobility: The Parlement of Rouen, 1499–1610* (Princeton, 1980) and Nancy Roelker, *One King, One Faith: The Parlement of Paris and the Religious Reformations of the Sixteenth Century* (Berkeley and Los Angeles, 1996) provide somewhat different perspectives. On the officials' culture, Donald Kelley's works are especially important, among them *Foundations of Modern Historical Scholarship: Language, Law, and History in the French Renaissance* (New York, 1970) and *The Beginning of Ideology: Consciousness and Society in the French Reformation* (Cambridge, 1981). On the universities, see L. W. B. Brockliss, *French Higher Education in the Seventeenth and Eighteenth Centuries: A Cultural History* (Oxford, 1987). The larger contexts of literacy, schooling, and popular culture are addressed in François Furet and Jacques Ozouf, *Reading and Writing in France from Calvin to Jules Ferry* (Cambridge, 1982) and in Roger Chartier, *The Cultural Uses of Print in Early Modern France*, trans. Lydia G. Cochrane (Princeton, 1987). A useful introduction to later French cultural development is provided by David Maland, *Culture and Society in Seventeenth-Century France* (New York, 1970); on women's place within this developing culture, Faith Beasley, *Revising Memory: Women's Fiction and Memoirs in Seventeenth-Century France* (New Brunswick and London, 1990). Though many of its interpretations have been superseded, Philippe Ariès, *Centuries of Childhood: A Social History of Family Life*, trans. Robert Baldick (New York, 1962) remains an important view of how ideals of education and moral development changed; see also Roger Chartier, (ed.), *A History of Private Life, iii. Passions of the Renaissance*, trans. Arthur Goldhammer (Cambridge, Mass., 1989), which expands and updates many of Ariès's ideas. Studies of the nobility include Jonathan Dewald, *Aristocratic Experience and the Origins of Modern Culture* (Berkeley and Los Angeles, 1993) and Mark Motley, *Becoming a French Aristocrat: The Education of the Court Nobility, 1580–1715* (Princeton, 1990). George Huppert, *Les Bourgeois Gentilshommes: An Essay on the Definition of Elites in Renaissance France* (Chicago, 1977) explores anti-noble sentiment in the sixteenth century.

Rural, urban, and global economies

To understand the early modern French economy and to evaluate its performance, one has to appreciate the European context. In particular, one has to know what was feasible for an early modern economy. Fortunately, this context is readily available in three excellent introductions to the economic history of early modern Europe: Carlo M. Cipolla, *Before the Industrial Revolution: European Society and Economy, 1000–1700* (New York, 1976), Harry A. Miskimin, *The Economy of Later Renaissance Europe, 1460–1600* (Cambridge, 1977), and Jan De Vries, *The Economy of Europe in an Age of Crisis, 1600–1750* (Cambridge, 1976). De Vries is particularly good on the rise of England and the Netherlands in the seventeenth century; further details about the success of the Netherlands can be gleaned from his and Ad van der Woude's masterful *The First Modern Economy: Success, Failure, and Perseverance of the Dutch Economy, 1500–1815* (Cambridge, 1997).

The whole subject of early modern economic history has generated considerable interest in recent years, and Meir Kohn's *Finance, Business, and Government before the Industrial Revolution* (Princeton, forthcoming) will shed a considerable light on trade and financial developments in particular. A number of other scholars are doing comparative research on productivity and living standards, notably Robert Allen, whose work has proved essential for this chapter. See in particular his 'Agricultural Output and Productivity in Europe, 1300–1800', *European Review of Economic History*, 4 (2000), 1–26, and his 'The Great Divergence: Wages and Prices in Europe from the Middle Ages to the First World War' (University of British Columbia Department of Economics Working Paper 98–12, 1998). The monetary history of early modern Europe is another field that has recently spawned a great excitement. It is a subject that demands a knowledge of complex economics and of contemporary political and intellectual debates, but there are scholars such as Thomas J. Sargent and François R. Velde who have all the requisite tools. Their book *The Big Problem of Small Change* (Princeton, forthcoming) will completely change our understanding of the crucial problem of coinage in early modern Europe, a problem that vexed people greatly from the Middle Ages into the nineteenth century.

As for the economic history of early modern France itself, some of the greatest historians of the French *Annales* school worked on it between the 1930s and 1970s. Samples of their work would include Marc Bloch's masterful *French Rural History: An Essay on Its Basic Characteristics*, trans. Janet Sondheimer (Berkeley, 1966), Emmanuel Le Roy Ladurie, *The French Peasantry, 1450–1660*, trans. Alan Sheridan (Berkeley, 1987), idem, *The Peasants of Languedoc*, trans. John Day (Urbana, Ill., 1974), and Fernand Braudel's *The Mediterranean and the Mediterranean World in the Age of Philip II*, trans. Siân Reynolds, 2 vols. (New York, 1972), which covers much more than France.

More recently, the subject has drawn renewed attention from historians and economists, who have called into question the conclusions of the *Annales* school. For an overview of this recent work, see George Grantham, 'The

French Cliometric Revolution: A Survey of Cliometric Contributions to French Economic History', *European Review of Economic History*, 1 (1997), 353–405 and Philip T. Hoffman and Jean-Laurent Rosenthal, 'New Work in French Economic History', *French Historical Studies*, 23 (2000), 439–53. Specific examples of the new work, by both economic and social historians, include Philip Benedict, *Cities and Social Change in Early Modern France* (London, 1989), idem, 'More than Market and Manufactory: The Cities of Early Modern France', *French Historical Studies*, 20 (Summer 1997), 511–38, idem, 'Faith, Fortune and Social Structure in Seventeenth- Century Montpellier', *Past and Present*, 152 (Aug. 1996), 46–78, an important test of the Weber thesis; Jonathan Dewald, *Pont-St-Pierre, 1398–1789: Lordship, Community, and Capitalism in Early Modern France* (Berkeley, 1987), James L. Goldsmith, 'The Agrarian History of Preindustrial France: Where Do We Go from Here?' *Journal of European Economic History*, 13 (Spring 1984), 175–99, George Grantham, 'The French Agricultural Productivity Paradox: Measuring the Unmeasurable', *Historical Methods*, 33 (2000), 36–46; Daniel Hickey, 'Innovation and Obstacles to Growth in the Agriculture of Early Modern France: The Example of Dauphiné', *French Historical Studies*, 15: 2 (Fall 1987), 208–40, Philip T. Hoffman, *Growth in a Traditional Society: The French Countryside, 1450–1815* (Princeton, 1996), and idem, 'Early Modern France', in Philip T. Hoffman amd Kathryn Norberg (eds.), *Fiscal Crises, Liberty, and Representative Government, 1450–1789* (Stanford, Calif., 1994), pp. 226–52.

The literature on France overseas devotes considerable attention to economic history. Once again, a knowledge of the European context is indispensable; it is readily available in works such as J. H. Parry, *The Age of Reconnaissance* (Berkeley, 1981). R. J. Knecht, *The Rise and Fall of Renaissance France* (London, 1996) contains the best brief account of France overseas in the early modern period, but what it says about the settlements in Florida and Brazil has to be supplemented by John T. McGrath, *The French in Early Florida: In the Eye of the Hurricane* (Gainesville, Fla., 2000) and idem, 'Polemic and History in French Brazil, 1555–1560', *Sixteenth Century Journal*, 27 (1996), 385–97. McGrath points out that even specialists on France overseas have ignored Spanish sources and relied far too heavily on polemical French accounts of what happened in France and Brazil. McGrath's warning applies to nearly all the literature in French and in English, but subject to this proviso one can glean much useful information on all the early French voyages to the North and South America from Samuel E. Morison's *The European Discovery of America*, 2 vols. (Oxford, 1971–4), which is particularly good on fishing and sailing. For French Canada, Morison's *Samuel de Champlain, Father of New France* (Boston, 1972) and William Eccles's *The Canadian Frontier, 1534–1760* (Albuquerque, NM, 1974) and *France in America* (New York, 1972) are good, but readers who know French should also consult Marcel Trudel's detailed

Histoire de la Nouvelle-France, vols. 1–3 (Montreal, 1963–83), for the years before 1660.

Gender and the family

A History of the Family, ii. *The Impact of Modernity*, ed. André Burguière (Cambridge, Mass., 1996) and *A History of Private Life*, iii. *Passions of the Renaissance* (Cambridge, Mass., 1989) offer good introductions to the early modern family. See also Jean-Louis Flandrin, *Families in Former Times: Kinship, Household and Sexuality* (Cambridge, 1979). On family relations and legal constraints, see Barbara B. Diefendorf, *Paris City Councillors: The Politics of Patrimony* (Princeton, 1983), Jonathan Dewald, *The Formation of a Provincial Nobility: The Magistrates of the Parlement of Rouen, 1499–1610* (Princeton, 1980), and Julie Hardwick, *The Practice of Patriarchy: Gender and the Politics of Household Authority in Early Modern France* (University Park, Penn. 1998). See also Barbara B. Diefendorf, 'Women and Property in Ancien Régime France: Theory and Practice in Dauphiné and Paris', in John Brewer and Susan Staves (eds.), *Early Modern Conceptions of Property* (London, 1995), pp. 170–93. Sarah Hanley, 'Engendering the State: Family Formation and State Building in Early Modern France', *French Historical Studies* (1989) emphasizes the restrictions on women's roles. More generally, on the history of women, see Olwen Hufton, *The Prospect Before Her: A History of Women in Western Europe, 1500–1800* (New York, 1996), Merry E. Wiesner, *Women and Gender in Early Modern Europe* (Cambridge, 1993), and the articles in *A History of Women*, iii. *Renaissance and Enlightenment Paradoxes*, ed. Natalie Zemon Davis and Arlette Farge (Cambridge, Mass., 1993). Davis offers an engaging look at a French peasant woman's life in *The Return of Martin Guerre* (Cambridge, Mass., 1983). Her article on 'Women and the Crafts in Sixteenth-Century Lyon', in Barbara A. Hanawalt (ed.), *Women and Work in Preindustirial Europe* (Bloomington, Ind., 1986) and James Collins, 'The Economic Role of Women in Seventeenth-Century France', *French Historical Studies* (1989) are essential on women's work and the domestic economy. Nancy Lyman Roelker opened discussion of the impact of the Reformation on women with 'The Role of Noblewomen in the French Reformation', *Archive for Reformation History* (1972); Natalie Zemon Davis broadened the question with the chapter on 'City Women and Religious Change', in her *Society and Culture in Early Modern France* (Stanford, Calif., 1975). Charmarie Blaisdell's 'Religion, Gender, and Class: Nuns and Authority in Early Modern France', in Michael Wolfe (ed.), *Changing Identities in Early Modern France* (Durham, NC, 1997) is unequalled on sixteenth-century convents. The same volume has useful articles by Denis Crouzet on possession and exorcism, Richard Golden on the geography of the witch hunts, and Alfred Soman on infanticide. Soman's other writings on infanticide and

French witch trials have been collected in *Sorcellerie et justice criminelle (16ᵉ–18ᵉ siècles)* (Hampshire, 1992). See also Robin Briggs, *Communities of Belief: Cultural and Social Tensions in Early Modern France* (Oxford, 1989) and *Witches and Neighbours: The Social and Cultural Context of European Witchcraft* (London, 1996). The argument presented here about demonic possession in French convents draws on as yet unpublished writings of Moshe Sluhovsky, but see his 'A Divine Apparition or Demonic Possession? Female Agency and Church Authority in Demonic Possession in Sixteenth-Century France', *Sixteenth Century Journal* (1996).

Religion and the sacred

The institutions, beliefs, and practices of religious life from the late fifteenth through the sixteenth centuries are best understood through local studies: A. N. Galpern, *The Religions of the People in Sixteenth-Century Champagne* (Cambridge, Mass., 1976), Natalie Zemon Davis, *Society and Culture in Early Modern France* (Stanford, Calif., 1975), Philip T. Hoffman, *Church and Community in the Diocese of Lyon, 1500–1789* (New Haven, 1984), Philip Benedict, *Rouen during the Wars of Religion* (Cambridge, 1980), and Barbara Diefendorf, *Beneath the Cross: Catholics and Huguenots in Sixteenth-Century Paris* (New York, 1991). David Nicholls has written an important series of articles, among which are 'Inertia and Reform in the Pre-Tridentine French Church: The Response to Protestantism in the Diocese of Rouen, 1520–1562', *Journal of Ecclesiastical History*, 32 (1981), 185–97 and 'The Nature of Popular Heresy in France, 1520–1542', *Historical Journal*, 26 (1983), 261–75. Of the great wealth of scholarship in French, see especially Marc Venard, *Réforme protestante, Réforme catholique dans la province d'Avignon au XVIᵉ siècle* (Paris, 1993) and Claire Dolan, *Entre tours et clochers: Les Gens d'Église à Aix-en-Provence au XVIᵉ siècle* (Sherbrooke/Aix-en-Provence, 1981). On ecclesiastical institutions, the higher clergy, and theologians, see Frederic J. Baumgartner, *Change and Continuity in the French Episcopate* (Durham, NC, 1986) and James K. Farge, *Orthodoxy and Reform in Early Reformation France: The Faculty of Theology of Paris, 1500–1543* (Leiden, 1985). Larissa Taylor, *Soldiers of Christ: Preaching in Late Medieval and Reformation France* (New York, 1992) situates preaching in a broad religious and social context. On confraternities, see Catherine Vincent, *Les Confréries médiévales dans le royaume de France XIIIᵉ–XVᵉ siècle* (Paris, 1994) and Marc Venard, *Le Catholicisme à l'épreuve dans la France du XVIᵉ siècle* (Paris, 2000). On the eucharist, see Mack P. Holt, 'Wine, Community and Reformation in Sixteenth-Century Burgundy', *Past and Present*, 138 (1993), 58–93 and Virginia Reinburg, 'Liturgy and the Laity in Late Medieval and Reformation France', *Sixteenth Century Journal*, 23 (1992), 526–47. On private devotion, see Geneviève Hasenohr, 'Religious Reading amongst the Laity in France in the Fifteenth Century', in P. Biller and A.

Hudson (eds.), *Heresy and Literacy, 1000–1530* (Cambridge, 1994), pp. 205–21 and Reinburg, 'Books of Hours', in *The Sixteenth-Century French Religious Book*, ed. A. Pettegree et al. (Aldershot, 2001), pp. 68–82. On women and religion, see Davis, *Society and Culture* (cited above), Nancy Lyman Roelker, 'The Appeal of Calvinism to French Noblewomen in the Sixteenth Century', *Journal of Interdisciplinary History*, 2 (1972), 391–418, and Charmarie Jenkins Blaisdell, 'Religion, Gender, and Class: Nuns and Authority in Early Modern France', in Michael Wolfe (ed.), *Changing Identities in Early Modern France* (Durham, NC, 1997), pp. 147–68. On the Waldensians, see Gabriel Audisio, *The Waldensian Dissent: Persecution and Survival, c.1170–c.1570*, trans. C. Davison (Cambridge, 1999) and works by Venard (cited above).

Classic works by Lucien Febvre and Margaret Mann Phillips are still the best introduction to the early decades of humanism, evangelism, and reform. See Phillips, *Erasmus and the Northern Renaissance* (London, 1949) and Febvre's articles translated into English in *A New Kind of History: From the Writings of Febvre*, ed. P. Burke, trans. K. Folca (London, 1973). But see also a more recent revision of the problem by David Nicholls, 'Looking for the Origins of the French Reformation', in C. Allmand (ed.), *Power, Culture, and Religion in France, c.1350–c.1550* (Woodbridge, Suffolk, 1989). An excellent survey of the Reformation is Mark Greengrass, *The French Reformation* (Oxford, 1987). For evangelical and Protestant books, see Francis Higman's collected articles (many of them in English) in *Lire et découvrir: La Circulation des idées au temps de la Réforme* (Geneva, 1998). Local histories of the Reformation include the studies by Davis, Benedict, Diefendorf, and Venard (cited above), plus Penny Roberts, *Troyes during the French Wars of Religion* (Manchester, 1996). These works also provide insight into the beliefs, practices, and institutions of Reformed communities. On this subject, see also important studies by Janine Garrisson, *Protestants du Midi 1559–1598* (Toulouse, 1980), Raymond A. Mentzer, 'The Persistence of "Superstition and Idolatry" among Rural French Calvinists', *Church History*, 65 (1996), 220–33, and idem, 'Notions of Sin and Penitence within the French Reformed Community', in K. Lualdi and A. Thayer (eds.), *Penitence in the Age of the Reformations* (Aldershot, 2000), pp. 84–100.

The wars of religion, 1562–1598

Good, brief, recent introductions to France's troubled history during the later sixteenth century include R. J. Knecht, *The French Wars of Religion 1559–1598* (London, 1989) and Mack P. Holt, *The French Wars of Religion, 1562–1629* (Cambridge, 1995). Knecht has also written an excellent biography of *Catherine de Medici* (London, 1998) that covers most of the period of the wars. Current historical thinking about the wars is particularly well reflected in the essays in Philip Benedict, Guido Marnef, Henk van Nierop, and Marc Venard (eds.), *Reformation, Revolt and Civil War in France and the Netherlands 1555–1585* (Amsterdam, 1999). The intertwined history of the Reformed churches and civil wars through 1576 is explored in three classic studies by Robert M. Kingdon: *Geneva and the Coming of the Wars of Religion in France, 1555–1563* (Geneva, 1957), *Geneva and the Consolidation of the French Protestant Movement, 1564–1572* (Geneva, 1967), and *Myths about the St. Bartholomew's Day Massacres, 1572–1576* (Cambridge, Mass., 1988). Scott M. Manetsch, *Theodore Beza and the Quest for Peace in France, 1572–1598* (Leiden, 2000) casts much new light on the Protestant cause after the St Bartholomew's Massacre. Military aspects of the wars are illuminated by James B. Wood, *The King's Army: Warfare, Soldiers and Society during the Wars of Religion in France, 1562–1576* (Cambridge, 1996), while Stuart Carroll, *Noble Power during the French Wars of Religion: The Guise Affinity and the Catholic Cause in Normandy* (Cambridge, 1998) skilfully charts the growing political force of aristocratic clientage. Many recent studies have enriched our understanding of the wars by examining the experience of individual localities. Philip Benedict, *Rouen during the Wars of Religion* (Cambridge, 1981), Barbara B. Diefendorf, *Beneath the Cross: Catholics and Huguenots in Sixteenth-Century Paris* (Oxford, 1991), and Penny Roberts, *A City in Conflict: Troyes during the French Wars of Religion* (Manchester, 1996) are among the most important of these studies. For the period of the Catholic League, Garrett Mattingly, *The Armada* (Boston, 1959), De Lamar Jensen, *Diplomacy and Dogmatism: Bernardino de Mendoza and the French Catholic League* (Cambridge, Mass., 1964), Frederic Baumgartner, *Radical Reactionaries: The Political Thought of the French Catholic League* (Geneva, 1976), and Barbara B. Diefendorf, 'The Catholic League: Social Crisis or Apocalypse Now?', *French Historical Studies*, 15 (1987), 332–44, are particularly important studies in English. All serious students of the Wars of Religion must also grapple with Denis Crouzet's massive *Les Guerriers de Dieu: La Violence au temps des troubles de religion, vers 1525-vers 1610* (Seyssel, 1990).

Catholic reform and religious coexistence

Two good surveys of religious history in this period are Jean Delumeau, *Catholicism between Luther and Voltaire*, trans. J. Moiser (London, 1977) and Élisabeth Labrousse and Robert Sauzet, 'La Lente mise en place de la réforme tridentine (1598–1661)', in J. Le Goff and R. Rémond (eds.), *Histoire de la France religieuse* 4 vols. (Paris, 1988), ii. 321–473. Local studies are the best guide to religious life in the Catholic world. Among the best are important works by Robert Sauzet, *Contre-Réforme et Réforme catholique en Bas-Languedoc: Le Diocèse de Nîmes de 1598 à 1694* (Louvain, 1979) and Alain Croix, *Cultures et religion en Bretagne aux 16ᵉ et 17ᵉ siècles* (Rennes, 1995). A regional study with a chronological view stretching from the early sixteenth into the seventeenth century is Philip T. Hoffman, *Church and Community in the Diocese of Lyon, 1500–1789* (New Haven, 1984). Keith P. Luria's *Territories of Grace: Cultural Change in the Seventeenth-Century Diocese of Grenoble* (Berkeley, 1991) continues the story of Catholic reform and cultural transformation into the second half of the seventeenth century. There are a number of excellent studies of aspects of Catholic reform. Highly recommended are Louis Châtellier, *The Europe of the Devout: The Catholic Reformation and the Formation of a New Society*, trans. J. Birrell (Cambridge, 1989) and Joseph Bergin's comparative study, 'The Counter-Reformation Church and its Bishops', *Past and Present*, 165 (1999), 30–73. Robin Briggs's *Communities of Belief: Cultural and Social Tensions in Early Modern France* (Oxford, 1989) provides a panorama of religious, cultural, and social history. *Vincent de Paul and Louise de Marillac: Rules, Conferences, and Writings*, ed. Frances Ryan, D.C., and John E. Rybolt, C.M. (New York, 1995) is a good introduction to the writings of these key reformers. There are a number of translations of Francis de Sales's writings, but *Francis de Sales, Jane de Chantal: Letters of Spiritual Direction*, ed. Wendy Wright and Joseph Power (New York, 1988) is a good place to start. See Elizabeth Rapley, *The Dévotes: Women and Church in Seventeenth-Century France* (Montreal and Kingston, 1990) on the new active congregations of uncloistered *filles-séculaires*. Studies of cloistered nuns are hard to come by in English, but Barbara B. Diefendorf, 'Contradictions of the Century of Saints: Aristocratic Patronage and the Convents of Counter-Reformation Paris', *French Historical Studies*, 24: 3 (2001), 471–500, discusses the role of lay patronage in the new convents of the Catholic Reformation. On male orders, see A. Lynn Martin, *The Jesuit Mind: The Mentality of an Elite in Early Modern France* (Ithaca, NY and London, 1988) and P. J. S. Whitmore, *The Order of Minims in Seventeenth-Century France* (The Hague, 1967). On the question of religious vocation, see Barbara B. Diefendorf, 'Give Us Back Our Children: Patriarchal Authority and Parental Consent to Religious Vocations in Early Counter-Reformation France', *Journal of Modern History*, 68: 2 (1996), 1–43.

For the history of the Huguenots between the Edict of Nantes and its revocation by Louis XIV, see Élisabeth Labrousse, 'Calvinism in France, 1598–1685', in M. Prestwich (ed.), *International Calvinism, 1541–1715*, (Oxford, 1985), pp. 285–314. Equally essential are Raymond A. Mentzer, *Blood and Belief: Family Survival and Confessional Identity among the Provincial Huguenot Nobility* (West Lafayette, Ind., 1994) and Philip Benedict, *The Huguenot Population of France, 1600–1685: The Demographic Fate and Customs of a Religious Minority* (Philadelphia, 1991). On Protestant–Catholic coexistence, see Gregory Hanlon, *Confession and Community in Seventeenth-Century France: Catholic and Protestant Coexistence in Aquitaine* (Philadelphia, 1993), Keith P. Luria, 'Rituals of Conversion: Catholics and Protestants in Seventeenth-Century Poitou', in B. Diefendor and C. Hesse (eds.), *Culture and Identity in*

244

Early Modern Europe, (Ann Arbor, 1993), pp. 65–82 and idem, 'Separated by Death? Burials, Cemeteries, and Confessional Boundaries in Seventeenth-Century France', French Historical Studies, 24 (2001), 185–222. The longer history of religious coexistence is recounted in Philip Benedict, 'Un roi, une loi, deux fois: Parameters for the History of Catholic-Reformed Co-existence in France, 1555–1685', in O. Grell and B. Scribner (eds.), Tolerance and Intolerance in the European Reformation (Cambridge, 1996), pp. 65–93. A starting point for the history of the Jews is Béatrice Philippe, Etre juif dans la société française du moyen-âge à nos jours (Lausanne, 1979).

Redrawing the lines of authority

For the reign of Henry IV, see Mark Greengrass, France in the Age of Henri IV: The Struggle for Stability (London, 2nd edn. 1995), David Buisseret, Henry IV (London, 1984), Michael Wolfe, The Conversion of Henry IV: Politics, Power, and Religious Belief in Early Modern France (Cambridge, Mass., 1993), Annette Finley-Croswhite, Henry IV and the Towns: The Pursuit of Legitimacy in French Urban Society, 1589–1610 (Cambridge, 1999), and the still useful study of Roland Mousnier, The Assassination of Henry IV, trans. Joan Spencer (New York, 1973). For the reign of Louis XIII and the career of Cardinal Richelieu, see Joseph Bergin, The Rise of Richelieu (New Haven, 1991), the same author's Cardinal Richelieu: Power and the Pursuit of Wealth (New Haven, 1985), Richard Bonney, Political Change in France under Richelieu and Mazarin, 1624–1661 (Oxford, 1978), Joseph Bergin and Laurence Brockliss (eds.), Richelieu and His Age (Oxford, 1992), R. J. Knecht, Richelieu: Profiles in Power (London, 2000), Orest Ranum, Richelieu and the Councillors of Louis XIII: A Study of the Secretaries of State and Superintendents of Finance in the Ministry of Richelieu, 1635–16 (Oxford, 1963), and A. Lloyd Moote, Louis XIII: The Just (Berkeley, 1989). For the renewal of war against the Huguenots in the 1620s, see David Parker, La Rochelle and the French Monarchy: Conflict and Order in Seventeenth-Century France (London, 1980). Patron–client relations and the problem of individual loyalty are the focus of Sharon Kettering, Patrons, Broker, and Clients in Seventeenth-Century France (New York, 1986). A very different view of clientage is offered by Roland Mousnier, La Vénalité des offices sous Henri IV et Louis XIII (Paris, 2nd edn. 1971). For the tax revenue problem, see James B. Collins, The Fiscal Limits of Absolutism: Direct Taxation in Early Seventeenth-Century France (Berkeley, 1988) and Richard Bonney, The King's Debts: Finances and Politics in France, 1589–1661 (Oxford, 1981). For the army there are now the magnificent studies of John A. Lynn, Giant of the Grand Siècle: The French Army, 1610–1715 (Cambridge, 1997) and David Parrott, Richelieu's Army: War, Government, and Society in France, 1624–1642 (Cambridge, 2001). And for the Fronde, see Orest Ranum, The Fronde: A French Revolution, 1648–1652 (New York, 1993).

Chronology

1559	Treaty of Cateau-Cambrésis, ending the Habsburg-Valois Wars; death of Henry II in a jousting accident; execution of Anne du Bourg.
1559–60	Reign of Francis II
1560–74	Reign of Charles IX; Catherine de Medici served as regent until Charles came of age in 1563
1560	Conspiracy of Amboise; death of Francis II in December
1561	Colloquy of Poissy
1562	Edict of Toleration in January; violence at Vassy in March begins first civil war
1562–65	French fortifications established in Florida and South Carolina
1563	Edict of Amboise ends first civil war; Charles IX reaches his age of majority
1564–66	Royal tour of the kingdom by the court
1567	Second civil war begins when Huguenots seize several fortified towns
1568	Edict of Longjumeau ends second civil war in March, quickly followed by the beginning of the third civil war in September
1569	Battles of Jarnac and Moncontour result in heavy Huguenot defeats, as well as the death of Condé
1570	Edict of St Germain ends the third civil war
1572	St Bartholomew's Massacres in Paris and the provinces starts the fourth civil war
1573	Siege of La Rochelle; Peace of La Rochelle ends the fourth civil war; Henry, duke of Anjou is elected king of Poland
1574	Death of Charles IX in May
1574–89	Reign of Henry III.
1575	Escape from court of the Duke of Alençon in September begins the fifth civil war; German mercenaries led by the Duke of Casimir join Protestant army
1576	Henry of Navarre escapes from court in February; Peace of Monsieur (Edict of Beaulieu) ends the fifth civil war in May; Alençon becomes Duke of Anjou; the Estates-General meets at Blois in November
1577	Sixth civil war begins in March and ends in September with the Peace of Bergerac
1578–80	Peasant revolts in Provence, the Vivarais, and Dauphiné
1580	Seventh civil war erupts briefly, ending with the Peace of Fleix in November
1581–83	Duke of Anjou visits England and the Netherlands

1584   Death of Anjou in June makes the Protestant Henry of Navarre the heir to the throne and begins the eighth civil war; Treaty of Joinville signed in December between Spain and the Catholic League

1585   Treaty of Nemours signed by Henry III and the League in July

1587   Duke of Casimir leads another invasion of German mercenaries into France to support the Huguenots

1588   Day of the Barricades in May; Edict of Union in July; Estates-General meets in Blois in December; assassinations of the duke and cardinal of Guise lead to numerous towns supporting the League

1589   Death of Catherine de Medici in January; assassination of Henry III in August; Catholic League begins its reign of terror in Paris

1589–1610 Reign of Henry IV, though he is not crowned until 1594

1590   Siege of Paris by the army of Henry IV

1591   The Sixteen in Paris executes Barnabé Brisson in November

1592   Siege of Rouen by the army of Henry IV

1593   Estates-General of the League meets in Paris in the spring; Henry IV abjures Protestantism in July

1593–94   Peasant revolts begin in Burgundy, Limousin, Périgord, and Agenais

1594   Coronation of Henry IV at Chartres in February; Paris submits to the king in March, as other towns soon follow suit; expulsion of the Jesuits from France

1595   Henry IV receives papal absolution in August from Pope Clement VIII; the Duke of Mayenne submits to the king in September; Henry IV declares war against Spain

1596   Spanish army seizes Cambrai and Calais

1597   Spanish army seizes Amiens in the spring, which is then liberated by Henry IV in September after a three-month siege

1598   Duke of Mercoeur submits to the king in January; the Edict of Nantes ends the eighth civil war in April; Henry IV signs peace treaty with Philip II of Spain in May

1604   Introduction of the *paulette*

1606   The *brevets* of the Edict of Nantes are renewed

1607   French colony established in Canada by Samuel de Champlain

1608   Publication of François de Sales, *Introduction to the Devout Life*

1610   Assassination of Henry IV in May by François Ravaillac; regency government of the young Louis XIII is headed by Marie de Medici; foundation of an Ursuline house in Paris by Barbe Acarie; foundation of the Visitation Sainte Marie by Jeanne de Chantal and François de Sales

1610–43   Reign of Louis XIII

1611   Sully resigns from the privy council; Huguenot assembly at Saumur

1614   Revolt against the regency government led by the prince of Condé; Louis XIII reaches his age of majority; the Estates-General meets in Paris in October

1617   Assassination of Concini

1618   Protestants revolt in Bohemia against the Habsburg Emperor

1620   Royal military campaign in Béarn; Edict of Restitution restores Béarn to the crown of France in October; Huguenot assembly in La Rochelle opens in November; Jacqueline-Angélique Arnauld, at the age of 18, began the reform of the abbey of Port-Royal

1621   Military campaign against the Huguenots begins in the spring; fall of St Jean d'Angély in June; the siege of Montauban is lifted in November

1622   Renewal of military campaign against the Huguenots in the spring; Soubise is routed by royal troops at the Île de Riez in April; Montpellier submits to the king in October after a short siege

1624   Cardinal Richelieu is admitted to the privy council

1625   Soubise seizes the islands of Ré and Oléron off the coast of La Rochelle in January; Louis XIII's sister Henrietta marries Charles I of England

1626   Edict of La Rochelle signed in February; a royal garrison is placed on he Île de Ré

1627   English fleet under the command of the duke of Buckingham attacks the Île de Ré in July; Buckingham is repelled by royal forces in November; the siege of La Rochelle by the royal army begins in August

1628   Fall of La Rochelle and submission to the king in October

1629   Submission of the duke of Rohan to the king in the spring; Peace of Alais signed in June ending the last civil war

1630   Foundation of the Company of the Holy Sacrament; Day of Dupes, 10 November

1635   Cardinal Richelieu founded the French Academy; France entered into the Thirty Years War

1642	Death of Cardinal Richelieu
1643	Death of Louis XIII; regency government installed until Louis XIV came of age, with his mother, Anne of Austria, as regent
1643–1715	Reign of Louis XIV
1648	Peace of Westphalia ended the Thirty Years War; outbreak of the Fronde in Paris
1651	Louis XIV declared his majority

Map section

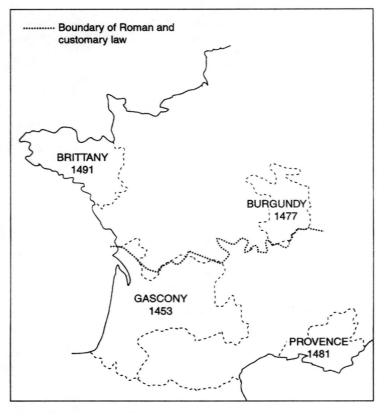

Map 1 Provinces recently incorporated into the French crown

Map 2 France during the Wars of Religion (source: Mack P. Holt, *The French Wars of Religion, 1562–1629* (Cambridge, 1995))

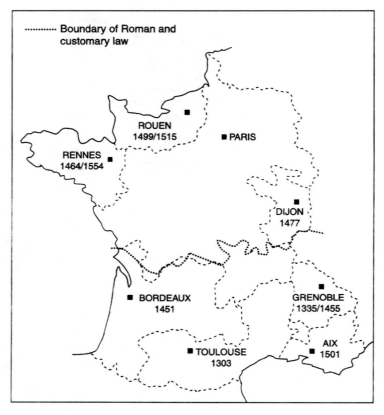

Map 3 Parlements in the sixteenth century (source: David Potter, *A History of France, 1460–1560* (London, 1995))

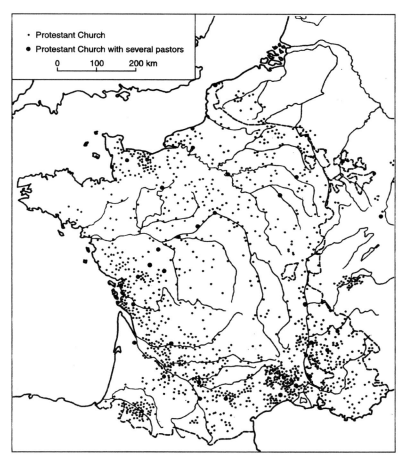

Map 4 Protestant churches in 1562 (source: Mack P. Holt, *The French Wars of Religion, 1562–1629* (Cambridge, 1995))

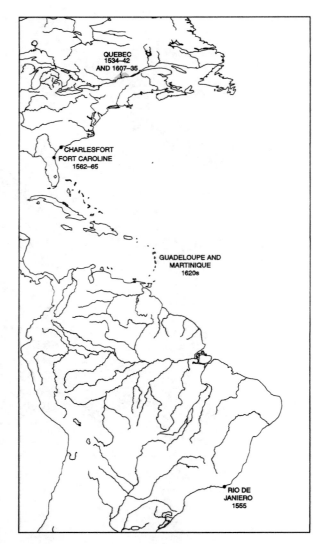

Map 5 French overseas exploration

Index